Sanatana
Dharma

Sanatana Dharma

Understanding the Knowledge and Ethics of Hinduism

RUPA

First published by
Rupa Publications India Pvt. Ltd 2023
7/16, Ansari Road, Daryaganj
New Delhi 110002

Sales Centres:

Allahabad Bengaluru Chennai
Hyderabad Jaipur Kathmandu
Kolkata Mumbai

Edition Copyright © Rupa Publications India Pvt. Ltd 2023

All rights reserved.
No part of this publication may be reproduced, transmitted,
or stored in a retrieval system, in any form or by any means,
electronic, mechanical, photocopying, recording or otherwise,
without the prior permission of the publisher.

P-ISBN: 978-93-90547-92-0
E-ISBN: 978-93-90918-61-4

First impression 2023

10 9 8 7 6 5 4 3 2 1

This book is sold subject to the condition that it shall not,
by way of trade or otherwise, be lent, resold, hired out, or otherwise
circulated, without the publisher's prior consent, in any form of binding
or cover other than that in which it is published.

सत्यमेव जयते नानृतम् ॥
उत्तिष्ठत जाग्रत प्राप्य वरान्निबोधत ॥

CONTENTS

Introduction 1

Part I
Basic Hindu Religious Ideas

1. The One Existence 25
2. The Many 40
3. Rebirth 56
4. Karma 68
5. Sacrifice 78
6. The Worlds—Visible and Invisible 87

Part II
General Hindu Religious Customs and Rites

1. The Samskaras 103
2. Shraddha 114
3. Shaucham 119
4. The Five Daily Sacrifices 123
5. Worship 130
6. The Four Ashramas 137
7. The Four Castes 148

Part III
Ethical Teachings

1. Ethical Science, What It Is 161
2. The Foundation of Ethics, As Given by Religion .. 164
3. Right and Wrong 170
4. The Standard of Ethics 179
5. Virtues and their Foundation 182
6. Bliss and Emotions 188
7. "Self-Regarding" Virtues 193

8.	Virtues and Vices in Human Relations Those in Relation to Superiors	208
9.	Virtues and Vices in Relation to Equals	222
10.	Virtues and Vices Towards Inferiors	234
11.	The Reaction of Virtues and Vices on Each Other	241
Index		247

ॐ
मंगलं दिशतु नो विनायको
मंगलं दिशतु न: सरस्वती।
मंगलं दिशतु न: समुद्रजा
मंगलं दिशतु नो महेश्वरी

INTRODUCTION

श्रीगणेशाय नम:। The Religion based on the Vedas, the Sanâtana Dharma, or Vaidika Dharma, is the oldest of living Religions, and stands unrivalled in the depth and splendour of its philosophy, while it yields to none in the purity of its ethical teachings and in the flexibility and varied adaptation of its rites and ceremonies. "It is like a river, which has shallows that a child may play in, and depths which the strongest diver cannot fathom." It is thus adapted to every human need, and there is nothing which any religion can supply to add to its rounded perfection. The more it is studied, the more does it illuminate the intellect and satisfy the heart. The youth who learns something of it is laying up for himself a sure increaser of happiness, a sure consolation in trouble, for the rest of his life.

धारणाद्धर्ममित्याहुर्धर्मो धारयति प्रजा:।[1]

"That which supports, that which holds together the peoples of the universe), that is Dharma."

Dharma is not merely a set of beliefs having no necessary connection with the daily life of humanity, but it is the very principles of a healthy and beneficent life. Therefore to know those principles and act upon them is to be, a true Âryan (or follower of Vaidika Dharma), and to tread the sure road to happiness, individual as well as general. The etymological meaning of "religion" is also the same, "that which binds together." "Vaidika" means "pertaining to the Veda or Perfect Knowledge. "Hence Vaidika Dharma means "the Religion of Perfect Knowledge."

---
[1]*Mahabharata*, Karna Parva. lxix, 59.

2 • SANATANA DHARMA

One of the most remarkable things in the Sanâtana Religion is the way in which it has laid down a complete scheme of knowledge, and has then crowned it with a Philosophy composed of six faces, but governed by one idea and leading to one goal. No such comprehensive and orderly view of human knowledge is elsewhere to be found. This has been sketched in the Elementary Text-Book, but now requires some further elucidation.

THE BASIS OF SANÂTANA DHARMA

The श्रुतिः: Shrutih, consisting of the Four Vedas is the final authority in the Âryan Religion, and these four Vedas form in their entirety THE VEDA, THE PERFECT KNOWLEDGE, revealed by Brahma, seen by the Rishis, and clothed in words by Them for the benefit of the Âryan peoples.

युगान्तेऽन्तर्हितान् वेदान सेतिहासान महर्षयः ।
लेभिरे तपसा पूर्वम् अनुज्ञाताः स्वयम्भुवा ॥[2]

"The Vedas, together with the Itihâsas, were withdrawn at the end of the Yugas. The Maharishis, permitted by Svayambhu (Brahma), recovered them by Tapas."

It appears that modifications were introduced on such recoveries, which took place at the beginning of each cycle, so as to suit the again revealed Vedas to the special conditions of the age. For we read in the *Devi Bhagavata*:

वेदमेकं स बहुधा कुरुते हितकाम्यया ।
अल्पायुषोऽल्पबुद्धींश्च विप्रान् ज्ञात्वा कलावथ ॥[3]

"Then, in the Kali age, He (Vishnu in the form of Vyása) divides the one Veda into many parts, desiring benefit (to men), and knowing that the Brâhmaṇas would be short-lived and of small intelligence," and hence unable to master the whole.

Thus the Rishis are ever watching over the Religion they gave, withdrawing and again giving revelation according to the needs and the capacities of each age. If so much has disappeared from the sacred

---
[2] Quoted by Shankaracharya, and attributed by him to Vyasa—*Shiriraka Bhashya*. I. iii. 29.
[3] *Loc. cit*. I. iii. 19.

books-as may be seen by com paring the number of shlokas said to be contained in some of them, with the extant shlokas-this disappearance has been brought about by the Riṣhis for men's benefit...

In Patañjali's *Mahâbhâṣhya* much higher figures, as regards the extent and content of the Vedas, are given than are found in the now extant books. He mentions 21 shâkhâs of the *Rigveda,* 100 of the *Yajurveda,* 1000 of the S*amaveda* and 9 of the *Atharvaveda.* The *Muktikopanishat* gives 21 shâkhâs of the *Rigveda,* 109 of the *Yajurveda;* 1000 of the *Samaveda,* and 50 of the *Atharvaveda.* Of these but few are now known.[4]

Each Veda has three generally recognised divisions:

1. The संहिता Samhita, or Collection, consisting of सूक्तानि Suktani, Suktas, hymns used at sacrifices and offerings, thé Mantras, on which the efficacy of the rite depends.

2. The ब्राम्हणानि Brahmaṇâni; Brāhmaṇas, described by Âpastamba as containing precepts for sacrifice, reproof, praise, stories and traditions; they explain the connection between the Sûktas and the ceremonies; they are treatises on ritual, but interspersed with the ritual directions are many illustrative stories, philosophical observations and profound ideas, especially in the *Tandya Mahabrahmaṇa* and the S*hatapatha Brahmana.* Treatises named आरण्यकानि Aranyakani, Aranyakas, or Books for the Forest, i.e., for study by recluses, are given at the end of the Brâhmaṇas.

3. The उपनिषद: Upanishadah, Upanishats, philosophical treatises of a profound character, embodying the ब्राम्हविद्या Brahmavidya, on which the Six Darshanas, or the great systems of philosophy are built up. They are many in number, 108 being the more important, and of these 10 or 12 are called Major, and the rest Minor. The Major have been commented on by the founders of the leading schools of Vedanta, or by their early disciples.

The Samhita, or Collections of the Mantras of the *Rigveda,* contains 1017 Sûktas, arranged in 10 मण्डलानि Mandalâni, Mandalas, literally

---

[4]Cf. on this point the *Charana-Vyuha.*

circles. The Sûktas are for the most part prayers to, and invocations of, the Devas, but we shall find later that the One Supreme Existence is also definitely taught in this ancient Âryan book. It is the book of the होता Hotâ, the priest who pours offerings into the fire, and, as its name implies, is the knowledge of Richas, or laudatory verses, to be recited aloud at the time of the sacrifice.

The Samhita of the *Yajurveda* consists of forty Adhyâyas, or chapters, containing 1886 shlokas, about half of which are also found in the R*igveda*. There are two main versions of it, the *Krishna*, the black, or *Taittiriya*, in which the Samhita and Brâhmaṇa are mixed up; and the *Shukla*, the white, or *Vâjasaneya*, in which the Samhita is separate from the Brâhmaṇa. There are other minor differences, The Samhità consists of the invocations and prayers offered in sacrifices in the preparation of the materials, the altar, the bricks, the stakes, etc., Details of the sacrifices often mentioned in histories—the Rajasuya; the Ashyamedha, etc.—may here be found as well as of domestic and other ceremonies. It is the book containing, as its name implies, the knowledge of sacrifices, and belongs especially to the अध्वर्युः Adhvaryuh (conductor), comprising his duties in a sacrifice.

The Samhita of the S*amaveda* contains 15 books divided into 32 chapters, again subdivided into 460 hymns. Most of these are also found in the *Rigveda* mantras, only 75 being different. The *Samaveda* is the knowledge of song, and its hymns were chanted by the उद्गाता Udgata, at sacrifices in which Soma was offered.[5]

The Samhita of the *Atharvaveda* is divided into 20 Kändas, and these again into 731 hymns. Its earthly compilation is ascribed to the descendants of Atharyana, the Angirasas and the Bhrigus, to whom it was revealed. It is sometimes called *Brahmaveda*, probably because it was the special Veda used by the ब्रम्हा Brahmâ, the chief priest at a sacrifice, who supervised the whole, and remedied any errors

---

[5]The samhita of the *Samaveda* comprises four different works, the आगनेयं, the ऊह:, the ऊहां and the आरण्यगानं. All these four include the whole of the *Samaveda* as set to music. But as the hymns with their musical notations became wholly unintelligible, even in early days, they were rearranged into a distinct compilation, called the Archika. On this compilation Sayaṇa wrote his Bhashya. The figures used on the top of the mantras in the printed text indicate the notes of the gamut.

that might have been committed by the Hotri, Adhvaryu and Udgâtri. The name, however, may refer to the fact that in the *Atharvaveda* is also expounded the knowledge of Brahman which bestows Moksha, liberation from rebirth, many of the more famous Upanishats forming part of it. Further, it throws much light on the daily life of the ancient middle class Âryan, the merchant and the agriculturist, as well as on that of the women of the same class, and thus has a special historical and sociological interest of its own.

There are two Brahmaṇas attached to the *Rigveda*; the *Aitareya,* consisting of 40 Adhyâyas, deals with the Soma sacrifices, the Agnihotra, and the ceremonies connected with the accession of a king. The *Aitareya Aranyaka* belongs to this Brâhmaṇa, in which the *Aitareya Upanishat* is included. The *Kaushitaki Brahmana,* sometimes called also S*hankhayana,* has 30 Adhyâyas and deals with the Soma sacrifices. The Âranyaka of the same name belongs to it, and includes the *Kaushitaki Upanishat.* There are attached to it also 8 minor Upanishats.

In the *Krishna Yajurveda* there are no separate Brâhmaṇas recognised by two schools, the prose portions mingled with the Samhità taking this place; but a third school separates these as the *Taittiriya Brahmana* in 3 Adhyâyas, with a *Taittriya Aranyaka* containing the *Taittiriya Upanishat.* The *Katha* and *Shvetaskvatara* Upanishats and 31 minor ones belong also to the *Krishna Yajurveda.* The S*hukla Yajurveda* has the *Shatapatha Brahmana* in 100 Adhyâyas, the Ar*anyaka* of which contains the *Brihadirnyakopanishat,* also called the *Vajasaneya*; the *Ishopaniṣhat* forms the last chapter of this Veda, together with 17 minor Upanishats.

The *Samaveda* has 3 generally known Brâhmaṇas; the *Talavakara,* which includes the *Kenopaniṣhat;* the *Panchavimsha* containing 25 books; the *Chhandogya Brahmana,* including the Upanishat of that name, and 14 minor ones.

The *Atharvaveda* has the *Gopatha Brahmana,* consisting of 2 books. Many Upanishats are attached to this Veda in different lists. The *Mandukya, Mundaka* and *Prashna* are among those classed as the 12 chief Upanishats, and there are 31 minor ones attached to it in the *Muktikopaniṣhat.*

The 12 chief Upaniṣhats are: the *Aitareya, Kaushitaki, Taittiriya, Katha, Shvetashvatara, Brihadaranyaka, Isha, Kena, Chhandogya, Mândukya, Mundaka* and *Prashna.* The student can find the complete list of the whole 108 in the *Muktikopanishat.*

On these Shrutis the whole fabric of Vaidika Dharma, the Religion of the Vedas, as it is truly named, is built. In modern days much criticism has been directed against the Vedas, because the occult knowledge, on the possession of which depends the understanding of their inner meaning, has disappeared. They contain in their entirety a system by the mastery of which all the energies of nature may be controlled, for it is the system by which these energies were vitalised in our universe at its beginning, and are still directed by Ishvara. A true Vedavit could rule nature, and all her energies would be at his service.

It is therefore not wise to conclude hastily that passages in the Vedas are rubbish, or "the babblings of a child-humanity," because they are not intelligible to the modern student, devoid of Yoga and of inner knowledge. The student should suspend his judgment whenever he feels inclined to see absurdity, remembering that some of the keenest intellects produced by humanity have seen wisdom where he sees none, and he should wait until riper years and increased purity of life have opened his eyes.

The Vedas are summed up in the Gâyatrî, the Gâyatrî in the Pranava, and the Praṇava is the expression of the Absolute. This statement is repeatedly made in the Vedas themselves, and occurs again and again in Sanskrit literature. The real meaning or significance of this mysterious fact can only be discovered by prolonged study and meditation.

Next in order to the Shruti in authority comes the स्मृतिः Smritih, which explains and develops Dharma, laying down the laws which regulate Âryan national, social, family and individual obligations. They are the text-books of law, and are very numerous[6], but four of them are regarded as the chief, and these are sometimes related to the four Yugas, Manu being said to be the authority for the Satya Yuga, Yajñavalkya for the Tretâ, Shankha and Likhita for the Dvâpara, and Parashara for the Kali.

---

[6]See the Introduction to Mandilik's translation of the *Vyavahara Mayukha and Yajnaralkya Smriti.*

कृते तु मानवा: प्रोक्तास त्रेतायां याज्ञवल्क्यजा:।
द्वापरे शंखलिखिता: कलौ पाराशरा: स्मृता:॥

"[The laws] of Manu are declared for the Krita Yuga, those of Yajñavalkya for the Treta; those of Shaskha and Likhita are remembered for the Dvâpara, those of Parâshara are remembered for the Kali."

Thus we see that, as in the case of the Vedas, the Rishis with the necessary authority made alterations and adaptations to suit the needs of the time. It was this flexibility, characteristic of the Sanâtana Dharma, that preserved it through so many ages, when other ancient religions perished. The above saying, however, is in no way followed today.

Of the authority of the Shruti and Smriti, Manu says:

श्रुतिस्तु वेदो विज्ञेयो धर्मशास्त्रं तु वै स्मृति: ।
ते सर्वार्थेष्वमीमांस्ये ताभ्यां धर्मो हि निर्बभौ ॥[7]

"The Veda is known as Shruti, the Dharma shâstras as Smriti: these should not be doubted (but carefully consulted and considered) in all matters, for from them Dharma arose."

Of these Smritis, the two of Manu and Yajñavalkya are universally accepted at the present time as of chief authority all over India, and Yajñavalkya is chiefly consulted in all matters of Hindu law. The other Smritis are drawn upon when it is necessary to supplement these.

Manu, the original lawgiver of the Âryan race, is said in the *Narada Smriti* to have composed a Dharmashastra in 100,000 shlokas, arranged in 1080 chapters: this was reduced by Nárada to 12,000 shlokas, by Markandeya to 8000, and by Sumati, Bhrigu's son, to 4000. The Laws now exist in 12 books, containing only 2685 shlokas. Manu expounds the origin of the universe, and then desires Bhrigu to recite the Institutes as taught by himself. Bhrigu, accordingly, sketches the work, and then expounds in detail the duties of the student (chap. ii.), the householder (chap. iii.), and of one who is a Snataka (chap. iv.); he then deals with food, impurity and purification, and with women (chap. v.), and finishes the orderly life by describing the two last stages of the forest-dweller and the Sannyasî (chap. vi.). The duties of a king are then laid down (chap. vii.), and the administration of civil and criminal law (chap.

---

[7]*Loc. cit.* ii. 10.

viii.). This is followed by the "eternal laws for a husband and his wife," the laws of inheritance, the punishments for some crimes, and some additional precepts as to royal duties (chap. ix.). The rules for the four castes, chiefly in times of distress, (chap. x.), and then laws on penances (chap. xi.). The 12th chapter deals with transmigration and declares that supreme bliss is to be gained by the knowledge of Atmâ, on whom "the universe rests."

The *Yajñavalkya Smriti* consists of 3 Adhyâyas or chapters, which contain 1010 shlokas. They deal respectively with Achâra (Conduct), Vyavahâra (Civil Law), and Prayashchitta (Penances). In the first Adhyâya the duties of the Castes and Ashramas are expounded, foods are dealt with, gifts, offerings, certain rites, and the duties of a king are explained. In the second, civil law and procedure and punishment for crimes are laid down. In the third, purifications are given, and these are followed by an explanation of duties in time of distress, and those of a forest dweller and an ascetic, and some physiological details; then follows a disquisition on the universal and the individual Soul, the paths of liberation and of bondage, yoga, the siddhis, and transmigration, together with a number of penances.

Next in succession to the Smriti come the पुराणानि Purânâni, the Purânas, which, with the इतिहासा:, Itihasah, the history, are sometimes said to form the पञ्चमो वेद: Panchamo Vedaḥ, the Fifth Veda. (Narada, in telling Sanatkumara what he has read[8], calls them the fifth, and Shankara says on this पञ्चमो वेद:) In the *Vishnu Bhagavata* occurs the phrase:

ऋग्यजु:सामाथार्वाख्यवेदाश्चत्वार उद्धृता: ।
इतिहासपुरागं च पञ्चमो वेद उच्यते ॥[9]

Vyasa "having recovered the four Vedas, named the *Rig, Yajur, Sâma,* and *Atharva,* completed the Itihasa and Purana, called the fifth Veda"
So also is it written:

प्रादु:करोति धर्मार्थी पुराणानि यथाविधि ।
द्वापरे द्वापरे विष्णुर्व्यासरूपेण सर्वदा ॥[10]

---

[8]*Chhandogyop.* VII. i. 2.
[9]*Loc. cit.* I. iv. 20.
[10]*Devi Bhag.* I. iii. 18.

INTRODUCTION • 9

"Always, in each Dvâpara age, Vishṇu, in the form of Vyâsa, reveals the Puranas, as is fitting, for the sake of Dharma."

Madhava says that "like the six Angas, the Purâṇas, etc. are adapted to give a knowledge of the Vedas, and are therefore worthy objects of study."

So also Yajñavalkya:

पुराणन्यायमीमांसाधर्मशास्त्राङ्गमिश्रिता: ।
वेदा: स्थानानि विद्यानां धर्मस्य च चतुर्दश ॥
इतिहासपुराणाभ्यां वेदं समुपबृंहयेत्। इति ।[11]

"The Vedas, along with the Purâṇas, the Nyâyas the Mimansâs, the Dharmashâstras and the Angas, are the fourteen sources of knowledge and Dharma. (The student should) expound, the Vedas with (the help of) the Itihâsas and Purâṇas."

Eighteen Puranas are reckoned the chief, and there are another eighteen, styled Upa-Purâṇas, or lesser Purâṇas. The 18 mukhya, or great, Purâṇas are: Brahma, Padma, Vishṇu, Shiva, Bhagavata, Vâraha, Márkandeya, Agni, Bhavishya, Brahmavaivarta Linga, Vârâha, Skanda, Vamana, Kurma, Matsya, Suparṇa or Garuda, and Brahmânda. The 18 Upa-Purâṇas are: Sanatkumara, Narasimha, Brihannaradiya, Shivarahasya, Durvâsas, Kapila, Vamana (in addition to the Purâṇa thus named) Bhargava, Varuṇa, Kalikâ, Sâmba, Nandi, Ṣurya, Parashara, Vasiṣhtha, Devi Bhagavata, Ganesha, and Hamsa.

There has arisen a dispute as to which of the two, the *Vishnu Bhagavata* or the *Devi Bhagavata*, is the Purana and which is the Upa-Purâṇa, and the point remains undecided: but it is certain that both are equally valuable and instructive. The *Devi Bhagavata* is specially fitted for those who are inclined to metaphysics and science, while the *Vishnu Bhagavata* is most acceptable to the devotional temperament.

The Purâṇas contain the history of remote times, when the conditions of existence were quite different from those which prevail in our days; they also describe regions of the universe not visible to the ordinary physical eye. Hence it is unfair to regard the conceptions of the Purâṇas as being of the same nature as those of modern Science. When

---

[11]*Loc. cit.* I. i. 3.

Yoga-siddhis are developed, the Paurâṇika pictures of the universe and its past history are seen to be infinitely more correct than those arrived at by the modern scientific use of our physical organs of perception, however much these may be aided by delicate scientific apparatus. Certain definite characteristics of a Purâṇa are given in the *Viṣhnu Purana* and in others:

सर्गश्च प्रतिसर्गश्च वंशो मन्वन्तराणि च ।
वंशानुचरितं चैव पुराणं पञ्चलक्षणम् ॥

"Creation, Secondary Creation[12], Genealogy, Manvantaras, and History, such are the five marks of a Purâna."

Vyása is the compiler of the Puranas from age to age, as we have seen, and for this age he is Kriṣhṇa Dvaipayana, the son of Parâshara.

The other part of the Fifth Veda is the Itihasa, the two great epics, the *Ramayana* and the *Mahabharata*. These are so well known that little need be said of them here.

The *Ramayana* has for author Valmiki, and is the history of the family of the Solar Race, descended from Ikṣhvâku, in which was born the Avatara of Vishnu, Ramachandra and his three brothers. The story of their birth, education, and marriages, the exile of Ramachandra, the carrying off and recovery of Sîtâ, his wife, the destruction of Ravana the Râkṣhasa, and the reign of Ramachandra, are detailed at length. The whole epic gives a vivid picture of the Indian life, as led towards the close of the Tretá Yuga, and is intended to provide, in the life of Ramachandra and his brothers, a model of fraternal affection and mutual service, leading to prosperity and general welfare, that may serve as a lesson and inspiration in true Âryan living, and a model of kingship for all Âryan rulers. It is, perhaps, almost needless to add, that the life of Sîtâ has always been, and is, regarded as the most perfect example of womanly fidelity, chastity and sweetness to be found in literature.

The *Mahabharata* was compiled by Vyâsa, early in the Kali Yuga, but different recensions of it have been made.

The story is far more complicated and more modern than that of the *Ramayana,* and relates the varying fortunes of a family of the

---

[12]Some interpret the word as meaning reabsorption, destruction.

Lunar Race, which, rent by jealousies and rivalries, are perished by internecine strife. Against this dark background stands out the figure of the Avatara, Shrî Krishna, dominating the whole, surrounded by the Pandava family, which triumphs by virtue of its righteous cause over the opposing Kurus; while, among the latter, shine forth the heroic Bhishma, Drona, and Karna, the splendid but doomed defenders of wrongful sovereignty. The story opens the Kali Yuga, in which good and evil contend with almost equal forces, and in which ethical problems and the complicated workings of Karma baffle and bewilder the mind; in the destruction of the best and wisest of the Kshatriya caste it seems to presage the coming invasions of India, and in the gloom of its closing Earthly scenes to forecast the darkness that was soon to settle down on Âryavarta. The main thread of the story is constantly broken by interludes, consisting of instructive lessons and stories, among which are the immortal discourses of Bhishma, on Dharma, and the most famous jewel of Âryan literature, the *Bhagavad-Gita.* The whole forms an encyclopædia of history, morals and religion, not surpassed, or even rivalled, by any other epic in the world.

THE SCIENCE AND PHILOSOPHY OF SANÂTANA DHARMA.

The Science of ancient India was contained in the षड्ङ्गानि Shad-anigâni, Six Limbs, or Branches, of the Vedas. Its Philosophy was contained in the षड्दर्शनानि Shad-Darshanâni, the Six Views, or Systems, also called the षडुपांगानि Shad-upangani, Six Subsidiary Limbs. They are all designed to lead man to the One science, the One wisdom, which saw One self as real and all else as unreal. The rishis, realising the unity of all knowledge, made no distinction between science, philosophy and religion. All alike were based on the Veda; the sciences were the Vedângas, the limbs of the Veda, the philosophies were the Vedopangas, other limbs of the Veda, all culminating in the Vedanta, the end of the Veda. And they were all summed up together as the Lesser Knowledge, the Knowledge of the One being along Supreme and indivisible; even the revealed Veda was included in the former, in virtue of its being revealed, whereas in the latter, the Atma knows Itself. Thus it is written:

द्वे विद्ये वेदितव्ये इति ह स्म यद्ब्रह्मविदो वदन्ति परा चैवाऽऽपरा च ।
तत्राऽऽपरा ऋग्वेदो यजुर्वेद: सामवेदोऽथर्ववेद: शिक्षा कल्पो व्याकरणं
निरुक्तं छन्दो ज्योतिज्ञमिति । अथ परा यया तदक्षरमधिगम्यते ।।[13]

"Two knowledges are to be known, thus say the knowers of Brahman—the Supreme and the lower. The lower: *Rigveda, Yajurveda, Samaveda, Atharvaveda*, the Method of Study, the Method of Ritual, Grammar, Dictionary [Philology] Prosody, Astrology. The supreme, whereby That Eternal is reached."

The six Angas are expounded in a vast mass of literature divided under six heads; it is composed of सूत्राणि Sütrâni, Sûtras, with commentaries. A Sûtra is an exceedingly terse aphorism, literally a "thread," and it is easy to understand that where knowledge was orally transmitted, this style of composition would be exceedingly valuable. It appears to be certain that the Sûtras were the summing up of teachings contained in a vast mass of literature, long lost. These brief condensed aphorisms obviously contain the distilled essence of profound and abstruse teachings. These being lost, the Sûtras needed to be again expanded and explained by the teacher, and hence grew up a huge array of commentaries, containing traditional explanations, with the comments of the immediate writer.

The six Angas, as just mentioned, were:

1. Shiksha, method of study: that is a knowledge of phonetics, in which pronunciation and accent were fully dealt within an extensive literature, the text of the Vedas being arranged in various forms or Pâṭhas, which guarded it from alteration-the Pada-pâṭha, giving each word its separate form, the Krama-pâṭha, connecting the words in pairs, and other more complicated methods.

2. Kalpah, method of ritual: to this belong the *Shrauta Sûtras*, explanatory of the ritual of sacrifices in the three fires; their supplement, the *Shulva Sûtras*, dealing with the measurements needed for laying out the sacrificial area, a subject that entailed full knowledge of geometry, which is consequently taught therein (the 47th proposition of Euclid is the first subject dealt with in the *Shulva Sutras*); the *Grihya Sutras*, relating to domestic life;

---
[13]*Mundakop.* 1 i. 4, 5.

and the *Dharma Sutras*, treating of customs and laws, etc.
3. Vyakaranam, grammar: of which Panini is the latest great representative, having summed up what went before him, and dominated all who followed him.
4. Niruktam, philology, etymology: Yaska represents this Anga, as Panini represents the Vyakaranam, and has left a great commentary based on an earlier work.
5. Chhandah, metre, dealing with prosody, a matter of vital importance in connexion with the Vedas, of which the latest and best representative is Pingala.
6. Jyotisham, astronomy, including astrology: dealing not only with the movements of the heavenly bodies, but with their influence on human affairs.

The six darshanas are best understood by being seen in relation to each other rather than in opposition, for they form, in their entirety, one great scheme of the philosophic truth. They are arranged in pairs:

न्यायः	Nyayah	वैशेषिकं	Vaisheshikam
सांख्यं:	Sankhyam	योग:	Yogah
मीमांसा:	Mimamsa	वेदान्त:	Vedantah

The *Prasthana Bheda* of Madhusudana Sarasvati after sumarising the six darshanas, lays stress on their unity. "In reality, all the munis who have put forward these theories agree in wishing to prove the existence of the One supreme Lord without a second... These munis cannot be in error, considering that they are omniscient; and these different views have only been propounded by them, in order to keep off all nihilistic theories, and because they were afraid that human beings, with their inclinations towards the objects of the world, could not be expected at once to know the true goal of man."[14]

As the shruti says:

गवामनेकवर्णानां क्षीरस्याप्येकर्णता ।
क्षीरवत्पश्यते ज्ञानं लिंगिनस्तु गवां यथा ॥[15]

---
[14] Quoted in Max Muller's *Six Systems*. Pp. 107, 108.
[15] *Brahmabindup.* 19.

"Cows are many-coloured; but the milk (of all) has but one colour. Look on knowledge as the milk, and on the teacher as the cows."

In each Darshana, there is a rishi as teacher, who gives its principles in the form of aphorisms, Sûtras, and a भाष्यं bhashyam, a commentary, regarded as authoritative.

On these Sûtras and commentaries the darshanas are based. The object of all is the same to rescue men from sufferings, and the way of rescue is the same—the removal of ignorance, which is बन्ध: bandhah, bondage, and consequent union with the Supreme. Thus, the nyaya calls ignorance मिथ्याज्ञानं mithyajnanam, false knowledge; the Sankhya calls it अविवेक: avivekah, non-discrimination between the real and the unreal; the Vedanta calls it अविद्या avidya, nescience. Each philosophy aims at its removal by ज्ञान jnanam, wisdom, whereupon आनन्द: anandah, bliss, is enjoyed. This ananda is the nature of the self, and therefore cannot accurately be said to be obtained. The self is bliss, and it is only necessary to remove the illusion which causes suffering in order that bliss may be enjoyed. The hence speaks of its object as अपवर्ग: apavargah, salvation or deliverance, and मोक्ष: mokshah, or मुक्ति: muktih, liberation, is the universally accepted goal.

The Rishi of Nyaya, the system of logic, is Gautama, and his Sûtras are divided into 5 books. The authoritative commentary is that of Vatsyayana. He lays down (by उद्देश: uddeshah) पदार्थो: padarthah, or topics, into which he divides knowledge, and then proceeds to define them, (by लक्षण lakshana) and finally to examine them (by परीक्षा pariksha). He begins with प्रमाणं pramanam, measure, or proof, or right perception, which comprises: प्रत्यक्षं pratyaksham, sense perception, अनुमानं anumanam, inference, उपमानं upamanam, comparison, or analogy, and शब्द: shabdah, the word of an expert, testimony. By these means, objects of knowledge, प्रमेयं prameyam, are established. He then, after discussing the four succeeding padarthas, defines syllogism, reasoning, conclusion, argument, and then deals with various kinds of fallacies and sophisms. When man by right reason has freed himself from false knowledge, then he attains liberation.

The Vaisheshika, the system of particulars, literally, has for its rishi Kanada, and for its bhashya-kara, prashastapada. Kanada laid down 6 padarthas, under which all nameable things could be classified-categories, in fact. These are: द्रव्यं dravyam, substance; गुण: gunah, quality; कर्म karma, action; सामान्यं, samanyim, what is common, *i.e.*, makes a genus; विशेष: visheshah, particularity, what makes an individual; and समवाय: samavayah, inseparability. अभाव: abhavah, privation, non-being, a seventh padartha, is required by later philosophers of this school. Kanada has 9 subdivisions under the head of substances—the 5 भूतानि bhatani or elements; काल: kalah, time; दिक् dik, space; आत्मा Atma, the self; and मन: manah, mind. The universal form of the self is God, the individual the जीवात्मा jivatma; of the bhatas, आकाश: akashah is eternal and infinite, whereas पृथिवी Prithivi, Earth, आप: apah, Water, तेज: tejah, fire, वायु: vayuh, air, are atomic; the atom, अणु: anuh, of each is eternal, but the aggregations that make our Earth, water, light, and air, are temporary; creation is due to the conjunction of the atoms, the ceasing of a universe to their disjunction.

The sankhya, the system of number, looks back to kapila as the giver of its Sûtras, but their extant form is not regarded as that in which they were originally delivered. There are two bhashyas considered to be authoritative, those of aniruddha and vijnana-bhikshu. There is also a third bhashya, by Vedanti Mahadeva. Another and older authority for the sankhya is the *Sankhya-karika* of Ishvara Krishna with the bhashya of Gaudapada, and the much later Tika called the *Sankhya Tat. Tattva-Kaumudi* of Vachaspati Mishra. There is a higher authority mentioned by Vijnana-bhikshu as the text book of the Sankhya, and as older than the present sutras, ascribed to Kapila himself, the *Tattva-Samasa-Sutras*, on which several commentaries have been written.

The sankhya is an account, primarily, of the "How" of creation; it is often called Anishvara, without a Supreme Lord, but there is in it no denial of Ishvara, and the repeated appeals to the shruti as the final authority, above perception and inference, are evidence to the contrary. But Kapila was engaged with the order of happening, not with the cause thereof. There are two primary roots of all we see around us, पुरूष: purushah, spirit, प्रकृति: prakritih, matter. Purusha is many, as appears by the differences in happiness and misery, birth and death, etc., but all are of like essential nature; purusha thus may be taken to represent a totality, the subject side of existence. Prakriti is the object side of existence, and produces 23 substances, 7 of which share the name of prakriti, and 16 are विकाराः vikarah, or विकृतयः viktitayah, modifications. Prakriti, as the opposite of purusha, is अव्यक्तम् avyaktam, the unmanifested, the producer of all, but itself unproduced. From this, in contact with purusha, are produced in order: महत् mahat or बुद्धिः buddhih, the pure reason; अहंकार ahamkarah, the "I" making principle, the individualising or separative power; the 5 तमन्मात्राणि tanmatrani, measures of that, the essential powers that later form the senses. Then come the 16 vikaras: 5 बुद्धीन्द्रियाणि buddhindryani, the perceptive organs, or senses; the 5 कर्मेन्द्रियाणि karmendriyani, the organs of action: मनः manah, the mind, which is the unifying centre of the Indriyas; the 5 महाभूतानि mahabhutani, great elements—ether, air, fire, water, earth. After this enumeration of the principles of the evolution of the universe, the sankhya alleges the त्रैगुण्यं traigunyam, or the triple nature of matter, its three gunas, or constituent factors: तमः tamah, रजः rajah, and सत्त्वं sattvam. When these are in equilibrium there is no activity, no evolution; when they are out of equilibrium evolution begins. This evolution संचारः sancharah, is next dealt with, and the succeeding dissolution, प्रतिसंचरः pratisancharah, and the meaning of अध्यात्मं adhyatmam, अधिभूतं adhibhutam, and अधिदैवतं adhidaivatam, as applied to buddhi, manas and the 10 indriyas. This is followed by an elaborate enumeration of activities, facts, and qualities, that must be studied in the books on the system, concluding with an explanation of the triple nature of bandha, moksha, pramana and दुःखं duhkham.

The Yoga, the system of effort, or of union, has, as the giver of its sutras, patanjali, and the Vyasa Bhashya is its commentary. It is sometimes called the Seshvara Sankhya, the Sankhya with an Ishvara, because it accepts the sankhya as philosophy, and in adding to it a system of effort which should set the purusha free, it inakes one of the means of freedom ईश्वरप्राणिधानं[16] Ishvara-pranidhanam, "self-surrender to the Lord." Patanjali then defines Ishvara, as a special purusha who has not been touched by pain, action, consequences of action, and desires, unlimited by time; तस्य वाचकः प्रणवः "His name is Om." The

---

[16]*Sutrani*, i. 93.

Sûtras are 198 in number, arranged in 4 padas, and have as aim the exposition of the means of stopping the constant movements of the चित्तं chittain, the thinking principle, and thus reaching समाधि: samadhih, the persectly steady and balanced condition, from which कैवल्यं kaivalyam, the isolation of the purusha, i.e., the separation from prakriti, can be gained. One book out of the four is devoted to the description of the विभूति: vibhutih, the powers, obtained in the course of Yoga, but it is remarked that these सिद्धय: siddhayah, are obstacles in the way of samadhi, and they are therefore not desirable.

The remaining pair of systems is entitled the Mimamsa, for both deal primarily with the leading principles to be adopted in interpreting the text of the Vedas. But the Purva Mimamsa generally bears the name, the Uttara Mimamsa being usually known as the Vedanta.

The Purva, or earlier, mimansa has Jaimini as the giver of its Sûtras, Shabara's Bhâṣhya being the authoritative commentary. It is concerned with the कर्मकाण्डं karmakandam of the Veda, that is with the sacrifices, offerings, and ceremonials generally; while the Uttara, or later, mimamsa is concerned with the ब्रह्मज्ञानं Brahma-jnanam of the Veda, the knowledge of Brahman. The Mîmâmsa Sûtras are divided into 12 books, dealing with the karmakanda in minute detail; they also contain a discussion of the Pramanas, which are regarded as five, Pratyaksham, Anumânam, Upamânam, Arthâpatti (presumption), and Shabda, Authority is, in the Mîmamsa, vested only in the Veda, which, Jaimini devotes himself to proving, is of superhuman origin.

The Uttara Mimamsa, or Vedanta is the darshana which may be said to dominate Indian thought in the present day, in its three forms. Its sutras are the Brahma-Sûtras, given by Vyasa, or Krishna-Dvaipayana, called also Badarayana. The Vedanta has three great schools: the अद्वैतं, advaitam, non-duality, the authoritative bhashya of which is by Shankara; the विशिष्टाद्वैतं, vishishtadvaitam, non-duality with a difference, with the bhashya of Ramanuja; the द्वैतं, dvaitam, duality, with the bhashya of Madhva. Further, the student of the Vedanta being expected to travel through three stages, प्रस्थानत्रयं prasthana-trayam, the study of the *Bhagavad-Gita,* the *Upanishats,* and the *Sûtras,* each of the great commentators, or his early disciples, has written on each of these three. The *Bhagavad-Gita* is the application of the philosophy to life, the explainer and the guide of conduct. The *Upanishat*s contain the philosophy in an intellectual form, and on them the intelligence is exercised. The *Sûtras* sum up the philosophy in terse aphorisms, intended to serve as the seeds for meditation, their deepest meanings being only attainable in samadhi. For this reason to man was admitted to the study of the Vedanta until he possessed the four qualifications: वैराग्य vairagyam, (freedom from selfish attachment to the things of the world), विवेक: vivekah, (a strong sense of the distinction between the permanent and the transient), षट्सम्पत्ति: shat-sampattih (the six mental and moral requirements, peacefulness, self-control, resignation, endurance, faith and collectedness) and मुमुक्षा mumuksha, (the longing for liberation), and was thus fit for its reception.

The Dvaita Vedanta insists on the separateness of the Jivatma and Paramatma.

It teaches that Vishnu is the Supreme Deity, and formed the universe out of prakriti, already existing; Vishnu is the efficient cause of the universe, and matter is the material cause thereof, and the goldsmith and the gold are the double cause of the bracelet. Both Vishnu and prakriti are beginningless and endless, as also is jiva, the individual soul; but prakriti and jiva are subordinate to, and dependent on, Vishnu. Vishnu is Sat, reality, jnanam, wisdom, and anantam, infinite. He enters prakriti—called also Jada-prakriti—as purusha, the animating universal soul, and there upon follows the evolution of the universe, as given in the sankhya: mahat, ahamkara, the tanmatras and the indriyas. Then follow the devatas and vidya in five aspects; these six, from mahat to avidya, are called the प्राकृतसर्ग: prakrita-sargah, the material manifestation. It is followed by the वैकृतसर्ग: vaikrita-sargah, the organised manifestation, in three divisions, the minerals and plants, the animals, and men. The manifestations of Vishnu, guiding and ruling the preceding nine, are called the tenth creation. Jiva is immaterial, different from Vishnu, and each jiva is different from every other. The jiva attains moksha, in which it enjoys भोग: bhogah, eternal bliss; this is fourfold and the jiva reaches one or other of the four conditions, according to its deserts. These conditions are: सारूप्यं sarupyam, similarity to the divine form;

सालोक्यं salokyam, vision of the divine presence; सान्निध्यं sannidhyam, nearness to God; सायुज्यं sayujyam, union with God. This union must not be considered as one of the identities of nature.

The Vishishtadvaita Vedanta is for those who, conscious of separation, and longing for union with the Supreme, feel the necessity for an object of worship and devotion, and find it in the conception of the Saguna Brahman, the conditioned Brahman, Ishvara, the Supreme Lord. Brahman is the highest reality, the One, but has attributes inseparable from Himself; from Brahman comes सकर्षण: sankarshanah, the separated soul, which produces प्रद्युम्मनं: pradyumnah, mind, which produces अनिरूद्ध: aniruddhah, the I. These separated souls are व्यक्त: vyaktah, manifested, during the period of activity, and when प्रलय: pralayah approaches they are drawn in, become अवयक्तं avyaktam, unmanifested; Brahman is then in the कारणावस्थां karanavastha, the causal state, in which remain avyakta both soul and matter. Brahman is the object of worship on whom the soul depends, the soul being not Brahman, but a part of Brahman, the separation is insisted on but union is sought.

The Advaita Vedanta is summed up in the words तत्त्वमसि, "thou art that." Brahman is nir guna, without attributes, and is real; all else is unreal; Jivatma and Paramatma are the same, there is no difference. The idea of difference arises from avidya, nescience, and when the atma transcends nescience, it knows its own nature and is free. The universe springs from Brahman, as hairs from a man's head; it is the work of maya. Cause and effect are one and the same, कार्यकारणाभेद:, not two different things, as an aggregate of threads is cloth, and there is no cloth apart from the threads that run lengthways and crossways. The unreality of the universe, having reality as it were behind it has a kind of reality, like a shadow which could not exist without a substance, and this justifies and makes necessary activity of all kinds. Hence also there is an अपरा विद्या Apara-vidya, the knowledge of the phenomenal, as well as a परा विद्या Para-vidya, the knowledge of the noumenon. Having established the fundamental truth of unity, the Vedanta explains the conditions which surround the Atma, enveloped in avidya: the उपाधि Upadhih, which makes its illusory separateness, their grouping as the स्थूल Sthûla, सूक्ष्म Sûkshma and कारण शरीराणि Karana Sharirani and the states of consciousness belonging to these. While the atma identifies itself with the Upadhis, it is bound; when it knows itself as itself, it is free. For those who are not yet ready for this effort after self-knowledge, ritual is not only desirable but necessary; but for those who have reached the point where only the Atma attracts, Jnanam is enough, Brahman is the goal.

It must not be supposed from this that the Jnani is an abstainer from action. On the contrary, he best understands action, and has the best reason for engaging in it.

तस्मादसक्त: सततं कार्य कर्म समाचर ।
असतो ह्याचरन्कर्म परमाप्नोति पूरुष: ॥
सक्ता: कर्मण्यविद्वांसो यथा कुर्वंति भारत ।
कुर्याद्विद्वांस्तथाऽसक्तश्चिचकीर्षुर्लोकसंग्रहम् ॥[17]

"Therefore, without attachment, constantly perform action which is duty, for in performing action without attachment, man verily reacheth the Supreme."

"As the ignorant act from attachment to action, O Bharata, so should the wise act without attachment, desiring the maintenance of mankind."

And so Shankara himself: "If I had not walked without remission in the path of works, others would not have followed in my steps, O Lord."[18] The Jnani recognises his duties to all around him, plants, animals, men, Gods, Ishvara, and performs them the better, because he acts with opened eyes, and without personal object to confuse his judgment. But he performs actions as free, and, being without desire, is not bound by them.

The six darshanas may now be seen as parts of a whole. In the nyaya and vaisheshika, a man learns to use his intellectual powers rightly to detect fallacies and to understand the material constitution of the universe. In the sankhya, he learns the course of evolution, and in the Yoga how to hasten his own growth. In the mimamsa he is trained to use invisible world for the helping of the visible, and in the three schools of the Vedanta he learns to climb from the idea of

---

[17]*Bhagavad-Gita*. iii. 19. 25.
[18]Quoted in Max Muller's *Six Systems*. P 217.

himself as separate from Brahman to the thought that he is a part of Brahman that can unite with Him, and finally that he is and ever has been Brahman veiled from himself by avidya.

Further, a coherent view of the whole vast school of Âryan teachings, as an ascending path of evolution for the Jivatma, may now be gained. The literal meaning of the Veda, with its ritual and daily obligations, developed the manas, the mind, of the Âryan, disciplined his Kama, his passions and desires, and evolved and directed his emotions. It is said in *Amrita-bindupania-shat:*

मनो हि द्विविधं प्रोक्तं शुद्धं चाशुद्धमेव च ।
अशुद्धं कामसंकल्पं शुद्धं कामविवर्जितम्[19]

"Manas is said to be of two kinds, pure and impure: moved by kama it is impure; free of kama, it is pure."

Manas, joined to kama, was gradually purified by a life led according to vaidika rules. Such a manas, become pure, was further developed in capacity by the study of the Angas, was trained and developed, and thus became capable of the strain of philosophic thought. To a mind thus trained to see and to understand the many, the Veda would unfold its deeper occult meanings, such as intellect could master and apply. The end of all this study was to make possible the evolution of pure reason, buddhi, which cannot unfold unless manas is developed, any more than manas can unfold without the development of the senses. It thus led up to the darshanas, which develop the pure reason, which sees the One in the many, and then realises its unity with all, which therefore hates and despises none, but loves all. To the buddhi, thus unfolded to see the One, the Veda would unveil its spiritual meaning, its true end, Vedanta, intelligible only to the pure compassionate reason. Then, and then only, is man ready to reach the goal, the Para-vidya is attained, Atma beholds itself.

Thus utterly rational, orderly, and complete is the Sanâtana Dharma, the Âryan religion.

---

[19] *Loc. cit.* I.

PART I

BASIC HINDU RELIGIOUS IDEAS

CHAPTER 1

THE ONE EXISTENCE

एकमेवाद्वितीयम्।[20]

"One only, without a second."

Thus all the Shrutis proclaim.

Infinite, absolute, eternal, changeless, the all, is that, without attributes, without qualities, beyond name and form, निर्गुणब्रह्म, Nirguna-Brahman.

नासदासीनो सदासीत्
आनीदवातं स्वधया तदेकं तस्माद्धान्यन्न पर: किञ्चनास।।[21]

"Then was not non-existence nor existence... That only breathed by its own nature: apart from that was naught."

It contains all, therefore can no particular thing be said of it. It is all, therefore can no one thing be ascribed to it. It is not Being only, for that would exclude non-being; but being arises in it, and non-being is also there.

यदाऽतमस्तन दिवा न रात्रिर्न सन्न चासच्छिव एव केवल:।[22]

"When no darkness (was), then (there was) not day nor night, nor being nor not being, (but) the blessed alone."

The same Upanishat says:—

द्वे प्रक्षरे ब्रह्मपरे त्वनन्ते विद्याऽविद्ये निहिते यत्र गूढे।[23]

"In the imperishable infinite Supreme Brahman knowledge and ignorance are hidden."

अस्तीति, "It is,"[24] such is all that can be said:

One mysterious sound alone denotes THAT which is beyond number

---

[20]*Chhandogyop*. VI. ii. I.
[21]*Rigveda*. X. cxxix, 1. 2.
[22]*Shretashratarop*. iv. 18.
[23]*Kathop*. II. vi. 12.
[24]*Ibid*. v. 1.

and beyond name: it is the Pranava. When Nachiketah presses Yama, Lord of Death, to reveal to him the Supreme secret, and when Yama has admitted that he is worthy, Nachiketah prays:

अन्यत्र धर्मादन्यत्राधर्मादन्यत्रास्मात्कृताकृतात्।
अन्यत्र भूताच भव्याच्च यत्तत्पश्यसि तद्वद।।[25]

"Other than dharma and adharma, other than action and inaction, other than past and present, that which thou seest, that declare."
And Yama answers:

सर्वे वेदा यत्पदमामनन्ती तपांसि सर्वाणि च यद्वदन्ति।
यदिच्छन्तो ब्रह्मचर्यं चरन्ति तत्ते पदं संग्रहेण ब्रवीमि,
ओं इत्येतत् एतदूह्लेवाक्षरं ब्रह्म एतद्ध्येवाक्षरं परम् ।।[26]

"That which all the Vedas declare, that which all austerities utter, that, desiring which, they lead the life of Brahmacharya, that word I tell thee briefly: it is AUM. That word is even Brahman; that word is even the Supreme."

This unity, which never appears but which is, is implied in the very existence of universes, and systems, and worlds, and individuals. It is not only recognised in all religion, but also in all philosophy and in all science as a fundamental *necessity*. Endless disputes and controversies have arisen about it, but none has denied It. Many names have been used to describe it, and it has been left unnamed; but all rest upon it. It has been called the all and the nothing, the fullness and the void, absolute motion and absolute rest, the real, the essence. All are true, yet none is fully true. And ever the words of the Sages remain as best conclusion: नेति नेति, "Not this, not this."

Words seem to put far off and to veil in mystery that which is in truth nearest and closest, nay, which is more than close, is our very self. One name, perhaps, speaks most clearly, the परमात्मा, Paramatma, the Supreme self.

अयमात्मा ब्रह्म[27]

---

[25]*Ibid.* I. ii. 14.
[26]*Ibid.* I. ii. 15-16.
[27]*Mandukya* p. 2.

"This Atma (is) Brahman."

Such is the truth declared over and over again, insisted on in various forms, lest it should not be grasped. As by knowing one clod of clay all clay is known, as by knowing one piece of gold, all gold is known, as by knowing one piece of iron all iron is known, no matter by what number of names men may call the objects made of clay, or gold, or iron; so to know one self is to know THE SELF, and knowing it, all is known.[28]

Moreover, as is said in the *Chhandogyopanishat*:

सर्वं खल्विदं ब्रह्म[29]

"All this verily (is) Brahman."

"This" is the technical word for the universe, and the universe is Brahman, because तज्जलानिति, "therefrom it is born, thereinto it is merged, thereby it is maintained."[30] All that we see around us comes forth from that fullness and is as the shadow of that substance. And yet, as the Upanishad declares, we need not go far to seek:

एप म आत्मान्तर्हृदय एतद् ब्रह्म[31]

"This my self within the heart, this (is) Brahman."

It is not necessary for a youth to try to grasp metaphysically this great truth, nor to grapple with the questions that spring up in the thoughtful mind when it is stated. It is enough that he should know that this truth is recognised in some shape or another by all thoughtful men, that it is the foundation of all right thought, and later may be known to himself by deeper study. Enough for the present—in the case of most, at least—if he try to feel the unity as a centre of peace and a bond of fellowship with all. It is the heart of the universe, equally in all and therefore in himself; and this may be felt before it is understood intellectually.

This knowledge is the Para-vidya, the supreme wisdom, and it is to be gained by purity, devotion, self-sacrifice and knowledge.

---

[28]*Chhandogyop.* VI. i. 4, 5, 6.
[29]*Ibid.* 111. xiv. 1.
[30]तज्जलात् is equal to तत्र जायते, लीयते, अनिति।
[31]*Chhardogyop.* III. xiv. 4.

नविरतो दुश्चरितानाशान्तो नासमाहित:।
नाशान्तमानसी वापि प्रज्ञानेनेनमाप्नुयात्।।³²

"(He who) has not renounced evil ways, nor (is) subdued, nor concentrated, nor (of) subdued mind, even by knowledge he may not obtain it."

नाऽयमात्मा बलहीनेन लभ्यो।
न च प्रमादात्तपसो वाप्यलिङ्गगात्।
एतैरुपायैर्यतते यस्तु विद्वां
स्तस्यैष आत्मा विशते ब्रह्मधाम।।³³

"Nor is the Atma obtained by the strengthless, nor by the careless, nor without marks of austerity: the wise, who strives by these means, of him the Atma enters the abode of Brahman."

Here is the supreme peace, the nirvana of Brahman,

लभन्ते ब्रह्मनिर्वाणमृषय: क्षीणकल्मषा: ।
छिन्न द्वैधा यतात्मान: सर्वभूतहिते रता: ।।³⁴

"The Rishis, their sins destroyed, their doubts removed, their selves controlled, intent upon the welfare of all beings, obtain the Brahma nirvana."

Of such a one says Shri Krishna, शांतिमृच्छति,³⁵ "he goeth to peace."

But now we read:

एतद्धै सत्यकाम परञ्चापरञ्च ब्रह्म यदोङ्कार:।³⁶

"Verily, O Satyakama, this Omkara (is) the supreme and the lower Brahman."

And again:

द्वे वाव ब्रह्मणो रूपे मूर्त्तञ्चैवामूर्त्तञ्च ।
मर्त्यञ्चामृतञ्च स्थितञ्च यच्च सच्च त्यच्च³⁷

"There are two states of Brahman, formfull and formless, changing

---

³²*Kathop.* I. ii. 24.
³³*Mundakop.* III. ii. 4.
³⁴*Bhagavad-Gita.* V. 25.
³⁵*Ibid.* 29.
³⁶*Prashnop.* V. 2.
³⁷*Brihadaranyokop.* II. iii. I.

and unchanging, finite and in finite[38], existent and beyond (existence)."

This, second, lower, formfull, changing, finite, existent Brahman is not "another," but is Brahman conditioned—and therefore limited, manifesting—and therefore सगुण saguna, with attributes.

The *Rigveda*, in the hymn before quoted, gives this appearing:

तपसस्तन्माहमा जायतैकम्।[39]

"By the great power of Tapas uprose THE ONE."

Again, the wise are asked:

वि यस्तस्तम्भ पडिमा रजां-
स्यजस्य रूपे किमपि स्विदेकम्।।[40]

"What was that one, who, in the form of the unborn, hath established these six regions?"

THE ONE: that is His name, for that where in he arises is numberless, beyond number, and being the all is neither one nor many,

Manu describes that uprising in stately shlokas:

आसीदिदं तमोभूतमप्रज्ञातमलक्षणम् ।
अप्रतर्क्यमविज्ञेयं प्रसुप्तमिव सर्वत: ॥
तत: स्वयंभूर्भगवानव्यक्तो व्यञ्जयन्निदम् ।
महाभूतादि वृत्तौजा: प्रादुरासीत्तमोनुद: ॥
योऽसावतीन्द्रियग्राह्य: सूक्ष्मो ऽव्यक्त: सनातन: ।
सर्वभूतमयोऽचिन्त्य: स एव स्वयमुभौ ॥

... ...

यत्तत्कारणमव्यक्तं नित्यं सदसदात्मकम् ।
तद्विसृष्ट: स पुरुषो लोके ब्रह्मोते कीर्त्यते।।[41]

"This was in the form of darkness, unknown, without marks (or homogeneous), unattainable by reasoning, unknowable, wholly, as it were, in sleep.

"Then the self-existent, the Lord, unmanifest, (but) making manifest.

---

[38]Shankara gives thus the meaning of स्थितञ्ज यच्च.
[39]*Loc. cit.* X. cxxix. 3.
[40]*Ibid.* I. clxiv. 6.
[41]*Manusmriti.* i. 5, 6, 7, 11.

This—the great elements and the rest—appeared with mighty power, dispeller of darkness.

"He who can be grasped by that which is beyond the senses, subtle, unmanifest, ancient, containing all beings, inconceivable, even He Himself shone forth."

◆

"That unmanifest cause, everlasting, in nature sat and asat, that produced the purusha famed in the world as Brahma."

"This" is the universe, but here in darkness, i.e., in the unmanifested condition, as मूलप्रकृति: mula-prakritih, the root of matter, unknowable. This becomes manifest only when Svayambhû shines forth. The emergence is simultaneous; for He cannot become manifest save by clothing Himself in this, and this cannot become manifest save as illumined, ensouled, by Him. This two-in-one, by nature Sat and Asat,[42] the Self and the Not Self, purusha and prakriti, everlasting but appearing and disappearing, is the cause of all things.

तमेव भान्तमनुभाति सर्वं तस्य भासा सर्वमिदं विभाति।[43]

"When He hath shone forth, all shines forth after (Him); (by) the shining forth of Him all this shines forth."

We have seen that He is the Saguna Brahman, and He is declared to be in His own nature, सत्, चित्, आनन्द, sat, chit, ananda, pure being, pure intelligence, pure bliss. He is called अक्षर Akshara, the indestructible one, on whom the other—prakriti—is woven;[44] He is the आत्माऽन्तर्याम्यमृत:, Atma-ntryamy-amritah, the self, the inner ruler, immortal, who dwells in the earth, the waters, the fire, the atmosphere, the wind, the heavens, in all that is, in the Devas, in the elements, in the bodies of all beings, the all-prevading.

अदृष्टो द्रष्टाऽश्रुत: श्रोताऽमतो मन्ताऽविज्ञातो विज्ञाता नान्योऽतोऽस्ति द्रष्टा नान्योऽतोऽस्ति श्रोता नान्योऽतोऽस्ति मन्ता नान्योऽतोऽस्ति

---

[42]सदसच्चाहमर्जुन "Sat and Asat am I, O Arjuna!" *Bhagavad-Gita.* ix. 19.
[43]*Kathop.* II. v 15.
[44]*Brihadaranyokop.* III. vii. 8.

THE ONE EXISTENCE • 31

विज्ञातैप त आत्मान्तर्याम्य मृतोऽतोऽन्यदाते॥[45]

"Unseen He sees, unheard He hears, unthought of He thinks, unknown He knows. None other than He is the Seer, none other than He is the Hearer, none other than He is the thinker, none other than He is the knower. He is the self, the inner ruler, immortal. That which is other perishes."

He is the आत्मा, सवभृताशयाधिथत:,[46] "the self, seated in the heart of all beings." This is the clearest idea to grasp. The conditioned Brahman is the self-conscious universal ego as against-the non ego, spirit as against matter, the "I" everywhere, always, and in all things, identical in nature with the Nirguna Brahman, but manifested, with qualities, and always united to Mulaprakriti.

In the language of symbols, so largely employed by the Sanâtana Dharma, Ishvara is represented by a triangle pointing upwards, the triangle symbolising His triple nature, Sat, Chit, Ananda.

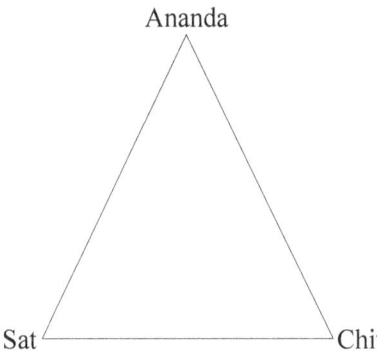

We see this, especially when interlaced with a second downward-pointing triangle which will presently be explained—in many temples.

This idea of the eternal subject, the spirit, the self, the "I," being firmly grasped, the student must next seek to grasp the eternal object, matter, mulaprakriti, the Not-Self, the Not-I.

We have already seen in *Manusmriti* that, in the unmanifested state,

---
[45]*Ibid.* 23.
[46]*Bhagavad-Gita.* X. 20.

this is homogeneous and unknowable; it is therefore often compared with the ether, formless but the root of all forms, intangible but the root of all resistances. Its inherent nature is divisibility, as that of the eternal subject is inseparateness; it is multiplicity, as He is unity. While He is the father, the life-giver, she is the mother, the nourisher. Matter is the womb in which the germ is placed.

मम योनिर्महद् ब्रह्म तस्मिन् गर्भं दधाम्यहम्।[47]

"My womb is the Mahat-Brahma; in that I place the germ" — explained by Shankara as त्रियुणात्मिका प्रकृति, the prakriti of three Gunas.

We must pause for a moment on the three gunas, for an understanding of them is necessary to any clear conception of the working of nature. The gunas are not qualities, nor attributes of matter, though both terms are often used in translation; they are the very materiality of matter, that which causes it to be matter. Matter cannot be thought of without these, and wherever there is matter, there are these, inseparable, existing in the ultimate particle as much as in the huge system. When these are in equilibrium, balancing each other, there is Pralaya, sleep, inactivity, and to matter in this state the term प्रधानं pradhanam is usually applied. These gunas are named: तम: tamah, or tamas; रज: rajah, or rajas; सत्त्वम्: sattvam, or sattva. Tamas—often translated darkness or foulness, the effect of tamasic predominance being taken as the guna itself—is resistance, stability, what is called in science the inertia of matter. All matter is fundamentally and always resistant; it resists. Its capacity for taking form is due to this constituent. Rajas is motion, the capacity of every particle to change its place, and the necessity of so changing it unless prevented; in scientific phrase this is motion, inherent in matter. Sattva is rhythm, the limiting of movement to an equal distance in an equal time on each side of a fixed point, the power and necessity of what is, in scientific phrase, vibration. Hence every particle of matter has resistance, motion, and rhythm. When the equlibrium of the three is disturbed by the breath of Ishvara, these three gunas at once manifest: tamas appearing as inertia, resistance; rajas throwing every particle of the resistant mass into active movement, thus producing what is called

---

[47]*Bhagavad-Gita.* xiv. 3, and Shankara's Commentary.

chaos; and sattva imposing rhythm on the movement of each particle, each thus becoming a vibrating, i.e. a regularly moving particle, capable of entering into relations with the surrounding particles. All the qualities found in matter arise from the interaction of these three gunas, their endless permutations and combinations producing the endless variety of at tributes found in the universe. The predominance of tamas in a body made up of countless particles gives rigidity, immovability, such as is seen in stones and other things that do not move of themselves. The predominance of rajas in a body gives unregulated hasty movements, restlessness, excess of activity. The predominance of sattva gives harmony, controlled rhythmical movements, order, beauty. But in the most immovable stone, the minute particles are in a state of unceasing vibration, from the presence of rajas and sattva; in the most restless animal there is stability of material and vibration of particles from the presence of tamas and sattva; and in the most harmonious and controlled man there is stability of material and movement from the presence of tamas and rajas.

As the triple nature of Ishvara, sat-chit-ananda, was symbolically represented by a triangle pointing upwards, like a flame, so is the triple nature of Mulaprakriti symbolised as a triangle, but now it points downwards, like a drop of water.

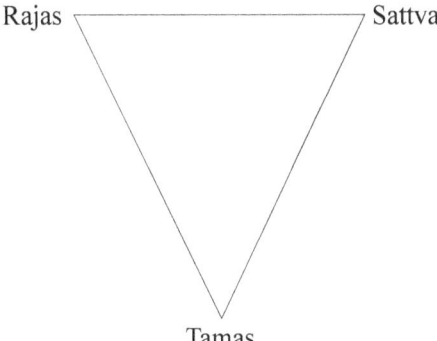

From these two triangles is formed the symbol of Ishvara and His universe, often seen in temples, the two interlaced, and a point in the centre, the symbol of the One, the whole giving the great septenary, the supreme Brahman and the universe.

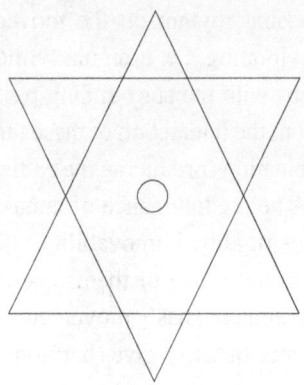

Thus we have before us the second member of the duality which, as we saw above in *Manusmrti*, is the cause of all things.

The divine power, or शक्ति: shaktih, the will of Ishvara, His light sent forth and making "this" manifest, as says the smriti, is called maya. Maya is inseparable from Ishvara; "their unity is like that of the moon and the moonlight, or that of the fire and its power to burn," says Nilakantha, commenting on *Devi Bhagavata.* VI. xv. 49.

Thus we read:

तस्य चेच्छास्म्यहं दैत्य सृजामि सकलं जगत् ।
स मां पश्यति विश्वात्मा तस्याहं प्रकृति: शिवा ।।[48]

"The Will am I, O Daitya, of Him [the supreme purusha]; I send forth the whole universe. He beholds me, He the universal self, I His benign nature."

Nilakantha, commenting on above, quotes one of the Shiva Sutras:

इच्छाशक्ति: उमा कुमारी

"Will-power (is) Uma, the Virgin."

While inseparable from the Lord, when turned towards Him she is called महाविद्या Mahavidya, supreme knowledge. She is also called, when turned away from Him, अविद्या, avidya, nescience, and emphatically

---

[48]*Devi Bhagavata.* V.xvi. 36.

महामाया, Mahamaya, the great illusion, as she permeates Mulaprakriti and becomes inseparable from it.

These are her two forms:

राम माया द्विधा भाति विद्याऽविद्येति ते सदा।[49]

"O Rama! Maya manifests as a duality; these (are) ever Vidya and Avidya."

This identification of the shakti of the Lord with Mulaprakriti often causes Maya to be called Mulaprakriti and prakriti. So Shri Krishna-having defined prakriti as generally understood:

भूमिरापो ऽनलो वायुः खं मनो बुद्धिरेव च ।
अहङ्कार इतीयं मे भिन्ना प्रकृतिरष्टधा।।
अपरेयम्...

"Earth, water, fire, air, ether, manas, and buddhi also, and ahamkara, these are the eight fold division of my prakriti. This the inferior—" goes on:

...अन्यां प्रकृतिं विद्धि मे पराम्।
जीवभूतां महाबाहो ययेदं धार्यते जगत्।।[50]

"Know my other prakriti, the higher, the life element, O mighty-armed, by which the universe is upheld."

This "other prakriti" is also spoken of by Him under the name of "मम दैवी प्रकृति" "My divine prakriti,"[51] His own Power, His योगमाया Yoga-maya, by which truly "the universe is upheld."

As says the shruti:

मायां तु प्रकृतिं विद्यान्मायिनं तु महेश्वरम्।[52]

"Let (the student) know maya as prakriti; the possessor of maya as the great Lord."

In the *Devi Bhagavata* some very beautiful descriptions are given of this matter side of nature, regarded as maya. Thus:

---

[49]*Adhyatma-Ramayana.* III. iii. 32.
[50]*Bhagavad-Gita.* vii. 4, 5.
[51]*Ibid.* ix.13.
[52]*Shvetashvatarop.* iv. 10.

एषा भगवती देवी सर्वेषां कारणं हि न:।
महाविद्या महामाया पूर्णा प्रकृतिरव्यया।
... ...
इच्छा परात्मन: कामं नित्यानित्यस्वरूपिणी॥
... ...
वेदगर्भा विशालाक्षी सर्वेषामादिरीश्वरी ॥
एषा संहृत्य सकलं विश्वं क्रीडति संक्षये ।
लिङ्गानि सर्वजीवानां स्वशरीरे निवेश्य च ॥
... ...
मूलप्रकृतिरेवैषा सदा पुरुषसंगता ।
ब्रम्हाण्डं दर्शयत्येषा कृत्वा वै परमात्मने ॥
तस्यैषा कारणं सर्वा माया सर्वेश्वरी शिवा ॥[53]

She (is) Bhagavati, the Goddess, the cause of us all, mahavidya, mahamaya, the fullness, the imperishable prakriti...

"The will of the supreme self verily (is She), in Her nature (uniting) the ever-lasting and the ever-passing...

"(Her) embryo the Veda, the long-eyed, the primal Goddess of all.

"At the Pralaya, having rolled up the universe, She sports, hiding within Her own body the types of all living beings...

"Mulaprakriti is she indeed, ever united with purusha. Having made the world-systems, she shows them to the supreme self...

"The cause of it (is) She, the all, maya, the benignant all-ruler."

This maya is inseparable from Ishvara, the Saguna Brahman, as said above:

सा च माया परे तत्त्वे संचिद्रूपे ऽस्ति सर्वदा ।
तदधीना प्रेरिता च तेन जीवेषु सर्वदा ॥
ततो मायाविशिष्टां तां संविदं परमेश्वरीम् ।
मायेश्वरीं भगवती सच्चिदानन्दरूपिणीम् ।
ध्यायेत्... ॥[54]

---

[53]*Loc. cit.* III. iii. 51-61.
[54]*Ibid.* VI. xxxi. 48, 49.

"She, maya, is ever in the supreme essence, whose nature is consciousness, subordinate to Him, and by Him ever sent forth among jivas.

"Therefore should be worshipped that consciousness, whose nature is sat, chit and ananda, Lord of maya, the Divine, with Maya, the Supreme Lady."

Being thus seen as the illusion-producing Power of the Lord, She is known as the cause of bondage and also as the path to liberation. As avidya she deludes; as Vidya she leads to Her Lord, and as She vanishes in Him the Atma knows itself as free.

भेदबुद्धिस्तु संसारे वर्तमाना प्रवर्तते ॥
आवद्येयं महाभाग विद्या च तान्नवर्तनम् ।
विद्याऽविद्ये च विज्ञेये सर्वदेव विचक्षणै: ॥
विनाऽऽतपं हि छायाया जायते च कथं सुखम् ।
अविद्यया विना तद्वत्कथं विद्यां च वेत्ति वै॥[55]

"This notion of separateness being present sends (the jiva) forth into Samsara. This is Avidya. O fortunate one! Vidya is the turning away from this. Vidya and Avidya should be always known by the wise. Without sunshine how (should the pleasure of shade be known? Without Avidya how should Vidya be known?"

प्रवृत्तिमार्गनिरता अविद्यावशवर्तिन: ।
निवृत्तिमार्गनिरता वेदान्तार्थविचारका: ॥[56]

"The travellers on the pravritti marga (the forth-going path) are under the power of avidya.

The travellers on the nivritti marga (the returning path) ponder the teaching of the Vedanta."

When the jiva goes forth, facing prakriti and looking at it, maya envelopes him as avidya. When he turns his back on prakriti, turns towards the Lord, then She turns with him and becomes vidya, and he is free. As Nilakantha says, quoting the S*haivagama*; अन्तमुखा शक्तिरेव विद्या[57] "The in ward-facing Shakti is vidya."

---

[55]*Devi Bhagavata.* I. xviii. 42, 43, 44.
[56]*Adhyatma-Ramayana.* III. iii. 32.
[57]*Commentary on Devi Bhag.* VI. xv. 47, 48.

Then he realises the mighty power of Maya, Her divine nature, and Her identity with the supreme, and hymns Ishvara and maya as one:

अनन्तकोटिब्रह्माण्डनायिके ते नमो नम: ॥
नम: कूटस्थरूपायै चिद्रूपायै नमो नम: ।
नमो वेदान्तवेद्यायै भुवनेश्वर्यै नमो नम: ॥
नेति नेतीति वाक्यैर्यां बोध्यते सकलागमै: ।
तां सर्वकारणं देवीं सर्वभावेन सन्नता:॥[58]

"Thou Sovereign of endless crores of world systems, we bow to thee !

"Hail! (Thou that art) in the form of the rock-seated (the changeless and motionless eternal), the form of consciousness, we bow to thee! Hail! (Thou that) mayest be known by the Vedanta, the ruler of the universe, we bow to thee!

"Thou whom all the sacred books only describe by the words 'Not thus, not thus."

"Goddess! the cause of all, with our whole nature we bow to thee !"

The supreme Ishvara, by His maya, creates preserves and destroys the innumerable world. systems that form the ocean of Samsara.

He produces the many.

तदक्षत बहु स्यां प्रजायेय।[59]

"That willed: may I be many, may I be born." Then, He is given many names:

एकं सद्विप्रा बहुधा वदन्ति।[60]

"To what is one, the wise give many names."

But whatever the names given, Ishavara is one, Thus has it ever been taught in the shruti and smriti, as we have seen, and this is repeated in the more popular teaching of which the *Vishnu Purana* may serve as example.

---

[58]*Devi Bhagavata*. VII. xxviii. 31, 32.
[59]*Chhandogyop*. VI. ii. 3
[60]*Rigveda*. I. cxiv. 46.

सृष्टिस्थित्यंतकरणाद् ब्रह्मविष्णुशिवात्मिकाम् ।
स संज्ञां याति भगवान एक एव जनार्दन: ।।[61]

"Thus the one only God, Janardana, takes the designation of Brahma, Vishnu and Shiva, accordingly as He creates, preserves or destroys... He is the cause of creation, preservation, and destruction." To sum up. The student must remember,

UNMANIFESTED
1. The absolute, the all, Paramatma, Nirguna Brahman.
MANIFESTED
2. The one, Ishvara, the self, the subject, sat, Saguna Brahman.
3. Mulaprakriti, the not-self, the object, asat.
4, Maya, the shakti, the power, the will, of Ishvara.
5. The Many, arising from Mulaprakriti by the maya of Ishvara.

As to the precise definition of the nature of these five, and of their mutual inter-relations, there is much discussion, and more less difference of opinion, in the six darshanas and their sub-divisions, as now taught. But the fact of these five, under whatever names, is recognised by all, and the student who studies deeply enough will come to the conclusion that the differences between the darshanas arise from each great teacher emphasising one aspect of the relations, and that all the six darshanas, rightly understood, form one organic whole.

---

[61]*Loc. cit.* I. ii. 62.

CHAPTER II

THE MANY

अव्यक्ताद्व्यक्तय: सर्वा: प्रभवंत्यहरागमे ।
रात्र्यागमे प्रलीयन्ते तत्रैवाव्यक्तसंज्ञके ॥
भूतग्राम: स एवायं भूत्वा भूत्वा प्रलीयते ।
रात्र्यागमेऽवश: पार्थ प्रभवत्यहरागमे ॥
परस्तस्मात्तुभावोऽन्योऽव्यक्तोऽव्यक्तात्सनातन: ।
य: स सर्वेषु भुतेषु नश्यत्सु न विनश्यति ॥
अव्यक्तोऽक्षर इत्युक्तस्तमाहु: परमां गातम् ।[62]

"From the unmanifested all the manifested stream forth at the coming of day; at the coming of night they dissolve, even in that called the unmanifested.

"This multitude of beings, going forth again and again, is dissolved at the coming of night; by law, O Partha, it streams forth at the coming of day.

"Therefore verily there existeth, higher than that unmanifested, another unmanifested, which, in the destroying of all beings, is not destroyed.

"Unmanifested, the indestructible, it is called; it is named the highest goal."

Here, in a few shlokas, the coming forth of the many is stated. At the beginning of the day of manifestation, all beings stream forth from the un manifested root of matter, Mulaprakriti, from " this" in darkness, as *Manusmriti* has it. When the day is over, and the night of Pralaya comes, then all these separated existences again dissolve into Mulaprakriti. Over and over again this occurs, for universes succeed universes, in endless succession. Behind this, then, there must be another unmanifested, Ishvara, the Saguna Brahman, other than Mulaprakriti, the indestructible Lord.

The wise man

---

[62]*Bhagavad-Gita.* iii. 18–21.

...भूतपृथग्भावमेकस्थमनुपश्यति ।
तत एव च विस्तारं...⁶³

"seeth the diversified existence of beings as rooted in One and proceeding from it."

We have now to study the nature of this procession from, or production of, the सर्ग, Sarga, the sending forth, or evolving. The Sanatana Dharma does not recognise an unscientific creation, a making of something out of nothing. The Supreme Ishvara evolves all beings out of Himself.

यथोर्णनाभिः सृजते गृह्णते च
यथा पृथिव्यामोषधयः सम्भवन्ति ।
यथा सतः पुरुषात्केशलोमानि
तथाऽक्षरात्सम्भवतीह विश्वम् ॥⁶⁴

"As the spider sends forth and retracts (its web), as in the Earth herbs grow, as from a living man the hairs of the head and body, so from the indestructible the universe becomes."

यथा सुदीप्तात्पावकाद्विस्फुलिङ्गाः
सहस्रशः प्रभवन्ते सरूपाः ।
तथाऽक्षराद्विविधाः सोम्य भावाः
प्रजायन्ते तत्र चैवापि यन्ति ।
        ...   ...
एतस्माजायते प्राणो मनः सर्वेन्द्रियाणि च।
खं वायुर्ज्योतिरापः पृथिवी विश्वस्य धारिणी ॥
        ...   ...
तस्माच्च देवा बहुधा सम्प्रसूताः।
साध्या मनुष्याः पशवो वयांसि ।⁶⁵

"As from a blazing fire in a thousand ways similar sparks spring forth, so from the indestructible, O beloved, various types of beings are born, and also return thither...

"From that are born breath, mind, and all the senses, ether, air,

---

⁶³*Ibid.* xiii. 30.
⁶⁴Mundakop. 1, i, 7.
⁶⁵*Ibid.* II. I, 1,3,7.

fire, water, and Earth, the support of all...

"From that in various ways are born the Gods, sadhyas, men, beasts, birds."

In *Manusmiriti* more details are given as to the order of evolution, and here again it is said that the immediate creator, Brahma, created all beings from Himself and from the elements previously produced from Himself, as we shall immediately see.

ब्रह्माण्डान, Brahmandani, literally eggs of Brahma, or as we should say, world-systems, are numberless, we are told.

अस्य ब्रह्माण्डस्य समन्तत: स्थितान्यतादृशान्यन-न्तकोटिब्रह्माण्डानि सावरणानि ज्वलन्ति। चतुर्मुख-पञ्चमुख-षण्मुख-सप्तमुखा-ष्टमुखादि-संख्याक्रमेण सह-सावधि मुखान्तैर्नारायणांशै रजोगुणप्रधानैरेकैकसृष्टि-कर्तृभिरधिष्ठितानि विष्णुमहेश्वराख्यैर्नारायणांशै: सत्त्व-तमोगुणप्रधानैरेकैकस्थितिसंहारकर्तृभिरधिष्ठितानि म-हाजलौघमत्स्यबुबुदानन्तसंघवद् भ्रमन्ति ।।[66]

"All around this Brahmanda, there blaze infinite crores of other similar Brahmandas, with their envelopes. Four-faced, five-faced, six-faced, seven-faced, eight-faced, successively, up to the number of a thousand-faced portions of Narayana, in whom the Rajoguna is predominant, creators each of one world-system, preside in them. Portions of Narayana, called Vishnu and Maheshvara, in whom the Sattva and Tamo Gunas predominate, also preside in them, performing the work of preservation and destruction in each. They wander about, these Brahmandas, like shoals of fishes and bubbles in a vast mass of water,"

संख्या चेद् रजसामस्ति विश्वानां न कदाचन।।
ब्रह्मविष्णुशिवादीनाम् तथा संख्या न विद्यते ।
प्रतिविश्वेषु सन्त्येव ब्रह्मविष्णुशिवादय:।[67]

"Grains of sand are perhaps numerable, but of universes (there is) not any (numbering).

"So there is no numbering of Brahmas, Vishnus, Shivas and the rest. In each of these universes there are Brahma, Vishnu, Shiva, and other (Devas)."

This we could have imagined, even had we not been told it, for

---

[66] *Atharvana* (or *Tripad-Vibhuti*) *Mayanaraayarop.* vi.
[67] *Devi Bhag.* IX, iii, 7. 8.

since, as we saw in the *Vishnu Purana*, the one only God, Janardana, takes the designation of Brahma, Vishnu and Shiva accordingly as He creates, preserves, or destroys, and creation, preservation and destruction must go on in every world-system, God must manifest in each in these three forms.

This is the Trimurti, the reflection as it were in space and time of that supreme triple unity, the source of beings-the Nirguna Brahman, the Saguna Brahman and Mulaprakriti, out of space and time, eternal.

The Trimurti is the manifestation, then, of Ishvara in a world system, or Brahmanda, and is therefore the supreme will, wisdom and activity in a concrete form.

Brahma is the creator, and His shakti is Sarasvati, the Goddess of Wisdom, without whom activity could not be wisely guided. He is pictured as with four heads, one looking towards each quarter, as the maker of the four quarters and their contents, and riding on the हंस:, hamsah, the swan. The name हंस:, a re-arrangement of स:अहं साऽहं, is an allusion to His relation with ahamkara, the divider, the maker of atoms.

Vishnu is the preserver and sustainer, the principle underlying and sustaining the universe in order, and preserving forms, holding them together by His attracting force. His shakti is Lakshmi, the Goddess of Happiness, of prosperity, of all desirable objects. He is pictured with four arms, as sustaining the four quarters, and rides on Garuda, the emblem of speed and of intelligence. He is the source of avataras, and in Them, or in His own person, is perhaps the most generally worshipped manifestation of Ishvara.

Indeed, as Narayana, He whose dwelling is in the waters, He is worshipped as Saguna Brahman, dwelling in matter.

Shiva, or Mahadeva, or Maheshvara, is the destroyer, He who frees Atma from imprisoning forms, who destroys avidya and so gives vidya, and who, finally rolling up the universe, brings the peace of liberation. His shakti is Uma, इच्छा, ichchha, will, called also ब्रह्मविद्या, Brahmavidya, who reveals Brahman.[68] He is pictured ever as an ascetic, it being He who is the object of worship for Yogis, who have renounced the world. He rides on the bull, the emblem of the mind (and sometimes

---

[68]See *Kenop.* iii, iv.

of physical nature), as having subdued it, and wears the tiger-skin, the emblem of the slain desire-nature. Hence is he, as the name Shiva implies, ananda, the peace and bliss of Atma, freed from desire and master of mind.

These supreme forms of Ishvara, separated by their functions, but one in essence, stand as the central life of the Brahmanda, and from and by them it proceeds, is maintained, and is indrawn. Their functions should not be confused, but their unity should never be forgotten.

Brahma, as the creative God, is spoken of as appearing first, born in the golden egg, which grows out of the seed of the One in the waters of matter.

सोऽभिध्याय शरीरात्स्वात्सिसृक्षुर्विविधा: प्रजा:।
अप एव ससर्जादौ तासु बीजमवासृजत्।।
तदण्डमभवद्धैमं सहस्रांशुसमप्रभम् ।
तस्मिञ्जज्ञे स्वयं ब्रह्मा सर्वलोकपितामह:।।[69]

"He, having meditated, desiring to produce various beings from His own body, first put forth the waters; in these He placed the seed."

"That became a golden egg, equal in radiance to the thousand-rayed (the Sun). In that was born Brahma Himself, the grandsire of all worlds."

Here the waters, matter, Mulaprakriti, receive the seed of life, and this becomes the Hiranyagarbha, the golden egg, in which the creator is born, in order to form His world-system. Hence a world-system is called a Brahmanda, a Brahma Egg, a very significant epithet, as world-systems are oval, like an egg, and seen from outside, present exactly an egg-like form, each planet following an egg-like orbit. Or this egg we read in the *Vishnu Purana* that within it Brahma and the world-system were contained, while it was invested externally by seven envelopes, water, fire, air, ether, the origin of the elements (Ahamkara), Mahat and Primal homogeneous matter, which surrounds the whole.[70]

Every world-system is thus surrounded by the great Kosmic elements, as described in the first chapter of *Manusmriti* by Manu

---

[69] *Manusmriti.* i. 8, 9.
[70] *Loc, cit.* I. ii.

himself (shl. 5 to 59). The account of the later creation is given over to Bhrigu, who explains briefly the repetition of the process within the world-egg. A similar and fuller account is given in the *Mahabharata*, and in the Vishnu and other Puranas.

It will be enough if the student grasps the general principles, and he can fill up later the complicated details from the many accounts given in the sacred books. He should remember that the process in the universe containing many Brahmandas, and in the separate Brahmandas, is similar.

A very fine and instructive description of the general principle of emanation—which will also be found illuminative when the student comes to the bodies in which the Jivatma dwells—is given in the *Devi Bhagavata*.

स पुनः कामकर्मादियुक्तया स्वीयमायया ।
पूर्वानुभूतसंस्कारात् कालकर्मविपाकतः ॥
अविवेकाच्च तत्त्वस्य सिसृक्षावान् प्रजायते ।
अबुद्धिपूर्वः सर्गोऽयं कथितस्ते नगाधिप ॥
एतद्धि यन्मया प्रोक्तं मम रूपमलौकिकम् ।
अव्याकृतं तदव्यक्तं मायाशबलमित्यपि ॥
प्रोच्यते सर्वशास्त्रेषु सर्वकारणकारणम् ।
तत्स्वानामादिभूतं च सच्चिदानन्दविग्रहम् ॥
सर्वकर्मघनीभूतमिच्छाज्ञानक्रियाश्रयम् ।
ह्रींकारमन्त्रवाच्यं तद् आदितत्त्वं तदुच्यते ॥
तस्मादाकाश उत्पन्नः शब्दतन्मात्ररूपकः ।
भवेत् स्पर्शात्मको वायुस्तेजोरूपात्मकं पुनः ॥
जलं रसात्मकं पश्चात् ततो गन्धात्मिका धरा ।

... ...

तेभ्योऽभवन्महत् सत्रं यल्लिङ्गं परिचक्षते ॥
सर्वात्मकं तत् संप्रोक्तं सूक्ष्मदेहोऽयमात्मनः ।
अव्यक्तं कारणो देहः स चोक्तः पूर्वमेव हि ॥
यस्मिञ्जगद् बीजरूपं स्थितं लिङ्गोद्भवो यतः ।
ततः स्थूलानि भूतानि पञ्चीकरणमार्गतः ॥

... ...

तत् कार्य घ विराड्देहः स्थूलदेहोऽयमात्मनः ॥

"He by His Maya, conjoined with kama and Karma, because of the Samskara of past experience, and the ripeness of time and karma, and because of non-discrimination of the tattva, be comes desirous of creation. This emanation, O King of mountains, is not preceded by buddhi. This transcendental form of mine that I have described to thee, is the undifferentiated avyakta, and the maya-coloured; in all the Shastras is it described as the cause of all causes, and the first element of all the elements, the embodiment of sat-chit-ananda, compacted of all Karma, the base of ichchha, jnana and kriya. It is declared by the mantra Hrim, and is called the Adi-Tattva.

"From it was born akasha, in the form of the tanmatra of sound. Thereafter arises vayu, of the nature of touch. Then tejas, of the nature of vision. Then water, of the nature of taste. And then Earth, of the nature of smell... From them arose the great thread, which is called the linga. It is declared to possess the nature of all. It is the Sukshma Deha of the Atma. The avyakta is the Karana Deha, declared before, in which the world exists as a seed, from which the linga arises, wherefrom (arise) the gross elements in the way of Panchikarana... The result of that is the Virat Deha, which is the Sthula Deha of the Atma."

The first emanation is here the Adi-tattva; then the Buddhi-tattva, sometimes called Mahat-tattva, said to follow the first; then the five tattvas in order. The terms used, denoting the first two, vary in different accounts; they are sometimes represented as Mahat and ahamkara, or as Adi-Bhuta and Mahat. In any case, the materials from which the worlds are made are seven, and these seven are spoken of in Manu as the source of all:

तेपोमिदं तु सप्तानां पुरुषाणां महौजसाम् ।
सूक्ष्माक्यो मातमात्राभ्य: सम्भवाति...॥[71]

"Verily, this becomes from the subtile formative particles of these seven very mighty beings."

We shall now see that the creative process within a Brahmanda follows on the same lines.

Brahma is surrounded by homogeneous matter, called Pradhana,

---

[71]*Loc. cit*, i, 19.

in the *Vishnu Purana*—in which the gunas are in equilibrium; His energy disturbing this tamasic condition, Rajoguna prevails and there is rapid motion. Then He puts forth the principle of Mahat-buddhi, pure reason—which, entering matter, being invested by it, and causing the predominance of the Sattva-guna, the motion becomes rhythmical, harmonious. Then follows ahamkara, the individualising principle, separating the homogeneous matter into particles, anus, atoms. Ahamkara, causing the tamo-guna to prevail in prakriti, forms successively the five tanmatras, or subtle elements, and the senses: hearing, touch, sight, taste, smell, with their appropriate gross elements: akasha, rayu, agni, apa, prithivi—ether, air, fire, water, earth. Causing Rajo-guna to prevail, ahamkara gives rise to the ten indriyas: the 5 ideal types of sense-organs and the 5 ideal types of action-organs. Causing Sattva-guna to prevail, ahamkara calls out the ten Deities connected with the sense-and-action-organs, and manas, the centralising organ of the indriyas. These three creations are called respectively the भूतादि, Bhutadi, that of the elements; तैजस, Taijasa, that of the fiery, the active energies; and वैकारिक, Vaikarika, the directing, administrative, powers.

The points to remember here are: in what is usually called matter, Tamo-guna predominates; in the Indriyas, Rajo-guna predominates; in the presiding Deities, Sattva-guna predominates.

The work of creation proceeded by calling into existence the Suras or Devas, described by Manu as कर्मात्मान्: "whose nature is action," that vast multitude of intelligent beings, of very varying power and authority, who guide the whole course of nature, and direct all its activities.

It is of course, clearly understood by all Hindus that this vast host of Devas no more obscures the unity of Ishvara, in His triple form as Brahma, Vishnu and Shiva, than do the vast hosts of men animals, plants, and minerals. As said in the shruti:

इन्द्रं मित्रं वरुणमग्निमाहु
रथो दिव्य: स सुपर्णो गरुत्मान् ।
एकं सद्विप्रा बहुधा वदन्ति
अग्निं यमं मातरिश्वानमाहु:॥[72]

---
[72] *Rigveda.* clxiv. 46.

"Indra, Mitra, Varuna, Agni, they call Him, and He is golden-feathered Garutman. Of what is One, sages speak as manifold; they call Him Agni, Yama, Matarishva."
So also the smriti:

आत्मैव देवता: सर्वा: सर्वमात्मन्यवस्थितम्।[73]

"All the Gods (are) even the self: all rests on the self."

एतमेके वदन्त्यग्निं मनुमन्ये प्रजापतिम्।
इन्द्रमेकेऽपरं प्राणमपरे ब्रह्म शाश्वतम्।।[74]

"Some call Him Agni, others Manu, (others) Prajapati, some Indra, others Life-Breath, others the eternal Brahman."

But the Devas have their own place in nature, as the ministers of the will of Ishvara, ruling, protecting, adjusting, guiding, with intelligence and power far greater than human, but still limited. The name, Deva, shining or radiant, very well describes their resplendent appearance, their bodies being formed of a subtle luminous matter, and hence flashing out light. They are concerned with the matter-side of nature, and the guidance of its evolution, and all the constructive energies studied by science are the energies of the Devas. On their work depend the fruits of all human activities concerned with production, in all its branches. Those who seek for material prosperity need their continual co-operation, and this co-operation is granted under quite definite laws. It may be obtained by a scientific knowledge of their methods of working, man falling in with their activities and thus sharing the result. Or it may be obtained from them by what is literally exchange, man supplying them with objects which facilitate their work, or which they enjoy, and they, in return, directing their energies, the energies of "nature," to suit his ends—as a strong man may help a weak man in the performance of a task. Or their increased co-operation may be won by prayers, accompanied by such acts as they approve, such as feeding the hungry, clothing the naked, etc. Or their services may be commanded by great rishis and yogis, who, by purity, knowledge, and austerity, have risen above them in the scale of being. Sometimes a man wins the favour

---

[73] *Manu*, xii, 119.
[74] *Ibid*, 123.

of a Deva by some service done in this or a previous birth, and then all his efforts prosper, and he succeeds where others fail, and he is called "lucky." "Good luck" is the result of the working of Devas, and as their working is invisible, men think the result is a chance, or accident. But it must be remembered that all Devas work within law, and not by arbitrary fancies. The sacrifices and offerings prescribed in the Vedas form a great occult system for obtaining and regulating this co-operation between Devas and men, whereby the work of both was carried on with the largest results.

देवान्भावयतानेन ते देवा भावयन्तु व:।
परस्परं भावयन्त: श्रेय: परमवाप्स्यथ ॥
इष्टान्भोगान्हि वो देवा दास्यन्ते यज्ञभाविता: ।[75]

"With this nourish ye the Devas, (and) may the Devas nourish you: thus nourishing each other ye shall obtain the greatest good."

"Nourished by sacrifice, the Devas shall give you (all) desired enjoyments."

And the reason is given:

अन्नाद्भवन्ति भूतानि पर्जन्यादन्नसम्भव: ।
यज्ञाद्भवति पर्जन्य: ।[76]

"From food creatures become; from rain is the production of food; from sacrifice rain proceedeth."

कांक्षंत: कर्मणां सिद्धिं यजन्त इह देवता:।[77]

"They who desire success in action here worship the Devas."

But the benefits obtained from them are transient:

अन्तवत्तु फलं।[78]

"Transient indeed the fruit."

Hence the worship of the Devas is not practised by men whose hearts are set on spiritual things. They worship Ishvara, rather than His ministers, either as Brahman, or as revealed in the Trimurti, or in the

---

[75]*Bhagavad-Gita.* iii. 11, 12.
[76]*Ibid.* 14.
[77]*Ibid.* IV. 12.
[78]*Ibid.* vii. 23.

Shaktis, or in such a Deva as Ganesha for learning, or in the Avataras. But this will be fur ther dealt with in Part II, Chapter V.

The Devas of the elements—ether, air, fire, water and Earth—Indra, Vayu, Agni, Varuna and Kubera, are the five Devarajas, Deva Kings, of these great departments of nature, Indra being the chief ruler. Under them are divided the great hosts of Devas. Thus the Sadhyas, Vasus, Adityas and Apsaras are specially connected with Indra; the Maruts with Vayu; the Yakshas, Gandharvas, Vidyadharas, and Kinnaras with Kubera. Some have charge of the animal kingdom, as the Nagas and Sarpas of snakes, the Suparnas of birds, etc.

Four great Gods rule the four quarters: Indra, Yama, Varuna and Kubera, as the protectors of mankind. Yama is the Lord of Death, the wise and gracious Deva who instructed Nachiketa. The Asuras, the beings who are opposed to the Suras, or Deras, in their activity, embody the destructive energies of nature; they are as necessary and as useful as the constructive, though on the surface opposed to them. They hinder and obstruct evolution, embodying the very essence of matter, Tamo-guna, inertia, resistance, and by that very resistance make progress steady and durable.

These creations belong to the invisible worlds, although, in their activities, they were to be closely connected with the visible—the worlds visible and invisible, indeed, forming the field of a vast evolutionary process—Samsara, the World Process.

The order of the process in the physical world at its origination was: minerals, plants, animals, men. In the *Vishnu Purana* it is stated that while Brahma was meditating on creation—the three primary Prakrita creations of Mahat, the elements and the indriyas, being over—the immovable creation, minerals and plants, appeared. Then followed the animal kingdom, called Tiryaksrotas. The creation of some Devas followed here, according to the Purana, but they do not belong to the physical world, with which we are here dealing. Then came the creation of men. It must be remembered that while this is the fundamental order of evolution many varieties occur in different kalpas, and accounts in the different books vary, within certain broad limits, since these great classes of beings overlap each other, so that new kinds of animals and plants appear long after man, The world in fact is ever-becoming along the four great lines, however much we may separate them for purposes of exposition.

The stages of evolution are very plainly given in the *Aitareya Brahmana*.

तस्य य आत्मानमाविस्तरां वेदाश्नुते हाविर्भूय: ।
मो पधिवनस्पतयो यच्च किञ्च प्राणभृत् स आत्मानमा- विस्तरां वेद । ओषधि वनस्पतिषु हि रसो दृश्यते । चित्तं प्राणभृत्सु । प्राणभृत्सु स्वेवाविस्तरामात्मा । तेषु हि रसोऽप दृश्यते । न चित्तमितरेषु । पुरुषे त्वेवा विस्तरामात्मा । स हि प्रज्ञानेन सम्पन्नतम: । विज्ञातं वदति । विज्ञातं पश्यति । वेदश्वस्तनम् । वेद लोकालोकौ । मर्त्य नामृतम् ईप्सति । एवं सम्पन्न: । अथेतरेषां पशूनामशना पिपासे एवाभिविज्ञानम् । न विज्ञातं वदन्ति । न वि ज्ञातं पश्यन्ति । न विदु:श्वस्तनम् । न लोकालोको । त एतावन्तो भवन्ति । यथाप्रशं हि सम्भवा:॥[79]

"He who knows the Atma as Him (the Purusha) in manifestation, he most enjoys that manifestation. Herbs and trees and all that bears life, he knows as the self in manifestation. In herbs and trees Rasa (sap, life) is seen, and mind in them that have prana. In them that have prana, the Atma is (more) manifest. In them, Rasa also is seen, while mind is not seen in the others. In man, the Atma is (most) manifest; he is most supplied with knowledge. He speaks that which he knows; he sees that which he knows; he knows what occurred yesterday; he knows the visible and the invisible; by the mortal he desires the immortal, Thus supplied is he. But of the others, animals, hunger and thirst are the only knowledge. They speak not the known; they see not the known; they know not what belongs to yesterday, nor the visible and the invisible. Only this much have they. According to the knowledge are the births."

On this Sayana comments as follows;

"सच्चिदानन्दरूपस्य जगत्कारणस्य परमात्मन: कार्यभूता:
सर्वेऽपि पदार्थाः आविर्भावोपाधय: । तत्राचेत नेषु मृतपाषाणादिषु
सत्तामात्रमाविर्भवति न चात्मनो जीवरूपत्वम् ।
ये तु ओषधिवनस्पतयो जीवरूपा: स्थाव-रा: ये च श्वासरूपप्राणधारिणो जीवरूपा जङ्गमा: ते उभये अतिशयेन आविर्भवस्थानम् इति........."॥

---

[79] *Aitareyaranyaka*. II. iii. 2.

"All objects whatsoever, being of the nature of effects, are Upadhis for this manifestation of the Supreme self, sat, chit, ananda, the cause of the universe. In the unconscious, Earth, stones, etc., only sat is manifest, and the Atma has not yet attained to the form of jiva. The unmoving jivas, namely the herbs and trees, and also the moving jivas, which have prana as breath; both these are stages of manifestation in a higher degree."

The student should note these passages, as it is currently supposed that the idea of evolution is of modern birth.

The work of Brahma consisted in producing all the materials, as we have seen, and by His tapas, or meditation, he formed the archetypes of all living things. But we learn from the *Shiva Purana* and the *Vishnu Bhagavata* that He needed the help of Vishnu in order to endow these forms with life, Vishnu being that aspect of Ishvara from whom the sustaining life, प्राण:, pranah, that is the life that holds forms together and preserves them as forms, together with चित्, chit, consciousness, comes forth.

Moreover, it is further stated in the S*hiva Purana* that when these forms had been fully developed, Mahadeva was appealed to, and He gave immortality; that is, He linked to the forms the Jivatmas evolved in previous kalpas. This is generally referred to in the ascription of ahamkara to Rudra. These three great stages in the building of worlds—the work of Brahma, creative of materials and of the ideal forms of all living beings; the work of Vishnu, in breathing prana and chit into these forms, and maintaining them in life; the work of Shiva in giving the eternal jivatmas—should be clearly understood.

In *Manusmriti* nothing but hints of these details are given, only the name Brahma being used; but it is indicated that He changed His form, divided Himself and produced Virat, who produced Svayambhuva Manu, who then called forth the ten Maharshis, they in turn producing seven Manus. After that, these became the active and direct agents in creation, Brahma himself disappearing after creating the worlds, a class of Devas (those connected with the great elements), and some other general fundamental principles and beings, and giving the Vedas. The account is very brief, and from its brevity somewhat difficult, but this summary of the world-process is only introductory to the main object of the book.

The S*hiva Purana,* as mentioned, gives the following details:

He (Brahma) emanated water first and therein sowed a handful of the seed which was His. The same grew up as an egg, made up of the 24 tattvas. Brahma, who appeared as Virat, perceived the egg becoming hard. This caused doubt in His mind and He gave Himself up to tapas. Thus He spent twelve years, concentrating His thought on Vishnu. Then Vishnu appeared and said: "I am pleased with thee; ask what boon thou desirest." Brahma said: "O Lord! it is just as it should be, for I have been placed by Shiva in your charge. The world which Shiva commanded me to create is here, but I see it is motionless (jada-rupa) and material. So be thou, O Lord, as life (prana) unto it, and make it conscious (chetana). Thus Brahma spoke, and Vishnu, following the directions Shiva gave, entered the egg—His form being one of a thousand heads, a thousand ears, a thousand feet and hands the universal purusha who touched heaven and Earth and pervaded the Egg.

As Vishnu entered it, that Egg of 24 tattvas became full of life and consciousness (sachetana) from Patala to Satya loka.

Hari, the best of all purushas adorned the seat that is Satya, which He occupied. Brahma stood in the world of Tapas, while other purushas occupied the other worlds as became them. Brahma first created a number of sons born of the mind. But they all became ascetics. He created more again, but they also renounced the world. So He began to cry, out of annoyance. As He cried, Mahadeva appeared. Because He came forth from Brahma's cry, He is called Rudra. Immediately on His appearance He addressed Brahma saying;

"Brahma, what aileth thee? Tell that to me and I will remove it."

"O Deva," answered Brahma, "there are obstacles in the way of further manifestation. Do thou therefore so ordain it, as may make it free from impediments." When he heard this, Mahadeva, the destroyer of all trouble, resolved to do what Brahma desired and said: "This creation of yours, I will make it everlasting."

So saying, Mahadeva, the Lord who is bliss, although known as Rudra, disappeared to Kailasa with His ganas. Then (with Shiva's help)

Brahma created Bhrigu and six other rishis. He also from his lap caused Narada to be born, from His shadow (chhaya)-Kardama, and from His thumb he made-Daksha. Thus there appeared ten rishis. And after Bhrigu came Marichi, whose son was Kashyapa. It is this Kashyapa who with his progeny filled the world.[80]

In the *Vishnu Bhagavata* the mention is in connection with the making of the World-Egg as an organised form, but, as said before, the process is similar on the large scale or the small. The point to be recognised is that Vishnu is the organiser.

यदैतेऽसङ्गता भावा भूतेन्द्रियमनोगुणाः।
यदायतननिर्माणे न शेकुर्ब्रह्मवित्तम ॥
उदा संहत्य चान्योन्यं भगवच्छक्तिचोदिताः।
सदसत्त्वमुपादाय चोभयं ससृजुर्ह्रदः ॥[81]

"When these separated existences, the bhutas, indriyas, manas and gunas, were unable to create organisms (literally a dwelling-place, an upadhi), O best of Brahma-knowers, then, mixing with each other, they were impelled by the power of Bhagavan (Vishnu), and, becoming both sat and as at, existent and non-existent evolved this."

The ten Maharishis, Marichi, Atri, Angiras, Pulastya, Pulaha, Kratu, Prachetas, Vasishtha, Bhrigu and Narada, were superhuman beings, who having obtained liberation in former kalpas, were called forth to aid in the direction of the world process, and who remain, superintending the destinies of the worlds, and will remain until pralaya. Sometimes only seven are given this rank, Prachetas, Bhrigu and Narada not being included in the list. Sometimes others are added, as Daksha and Kardama.

The Kumaras, variously given as four, five, six and seven, are, as their name implies, virgin beings, ascetics, and they watch over the world. Shiva himself took the form of one—Rudra or Nilalohita. Sanatkumara, Sanandana, Sanaka and Sanatana are the four most often referred to Ribhu, Kapila and Sana are also mentioned. To this brief sketch of the world-process it should be added that the early human

---

[80]*Shiva Purana*, I. vi. 1–20.
[81]*Loc. cit.* II. v, 32, 33.

races preceding the Âryan are often referred to under the names of Danavas and Daityas, huge beings of enormous strength and energy, who carried on many a struggle with the Devas themselves. The Rakshasas were another race, more brutal in nature, usually malformed, huge, cruel, powerful, cannibals, the terror of milder races. They possessed, moreover, many magical secrets of a dark kind, which they used for terrorising and oppressing. All these have long entirely disappeared from the Earth.

Such is the vast field of Samsara, in which the pilgrim Jivatmas wander, until, in some human form, they reach the knowledge of the self, and obtain liberation.

The points to be remembered are:

1. The coming forth of the many from Saguna Brahman and Mulaprakriti by the power of maya, and their return at the close of the day of manifestation.
2. The manifestation of Ishvara as the Tri-murti, in the forms of creation, preservation, and destruction, Brahma, Vishnu and Shiva, with their shaktis, Sarasvati, Lakshmi, and Uma.
3. The work of Brahma, forming the materials of the universe and the ideal types of all beings, Suras, Asuras, minerals, plants, animals and men.
4. The work of Vishnu, giving prana and chit, and hence making living organised forms possible, all such forms being preserved and maintained by Him.
5. The work of Shiva, breathing into these forms, when they arrive at the human stage, jivatmas that have reached in previous kalpas a stage at which such highly organised bodies can be utilised by them, bodies in which avidya can be destroyed, and they can attain vidya.
6. The existence throughout the world-process of lofty superhuman intelligences, such as rishis, and kumaras, intent on human welfare.
7. The past races on the Earth, Danavas, Daityas, Rakshasas.

CHAPTER III

REBIRTH

सर्वाजीवे सर्वसंस्थे बृहन्ते
तस्मिन्हंसो भ्राम्यते ब्रह्मचक्रे।
पृथगात्मानं प्रेरितारं च मत्वा
जुष्टस्ततस्तेनामृतत्वमेति।।[82]

"In the vast Brahman-wheel, the source and support of all jivas, the hamsa (the individual) is made to wander, thinking himself and the ruler different. United with Him, he obtains immortality."

Here, in a single shloka, we are given the reason of rebirth and its ending. Man wanders about in the universe so long as he thinks of himself as different from Ishvara; knowing himself to be one with Him, he obtains liberation.

In shruti and smriti, in purana and itihasa, the self in man is declared to be of the nature of Brahman.

ततः परं ब्रह्म परं बृहन्तं यथा निकायं सर्वभूतेषु गूढं।
विश्वस्यैकं परिवेष्टितारम् ईशं तं ज्ञात्वाऽमृता भवन्ति ।।
...   ...

अङ्गुष्ठमात्रः पुरुषोऽन्तरात्मा सदा जनानां हृदये सन्निविष्टः।[83]

"Then, having known the Supreme Brahman, the Supreme Immensity, as the essence hidden in all creatures, the one pervader of the universe, the Lord, they become immortal.

"The measure of a thumb, the purusha, the inner self, ever dwelling in the heart of men."

स वा अयमात्मा ब्रह्म।[84]

"He, this self, is Brahman."

---

[82]*Shvetashvatarop.* i. 6.
[83]*Ibid.* iii. 7. 13.
[84]*Brihadaronyakop.* IV. iv. 5.

स वा एष महानज आत्मा योऽयं विज्ञानमयः प्राणेषु एषोऽन्तर्हृदय आकाश:।[85]

"He, this great unborn self, (is) He who (is) this intelligence in living creatures, He who (is) this akasha in the heart."

स वा एष महानज आत्माऽजरोऽमरोऽमृतोऽभयो ब्रह्मा-भयं।[86]

"He, this great, unborn, undecaying, deathless, immortal, fearless self, (is) the fearless Brahman."

It is this nature, identical with Brahman as the sparks from a fire are identical with the fire, which evolves, unfolds itself as the jivatma in all living beings. As a seed grows to be a tree like its parent, so the jivatmic seed grows into self conscious Deity, Samsara exists that the jivatma may learn to realise himself. The jivatma differs from Brahman only as the seed from the tree that bears it.

शाऽज्ञो द्वावजावीशानीशो।[87]

"Wise and unwise, both unborn, powerful and powerless."

Therefore, although unwise and powerless, the jivatma can become wise and powerful; to this end he must evolve, and his evolution is on the wheel of births and deaths.

Transmigration is the word usually given to this journey, for the jivatma transmigrates from one body to another; as one grows old and wastes away he takes another.

वासांसि जीर्णानि यथा विहाय नवानि गृह्णाति नरोऽपराणि ।
तथा शरीराणि विहाय जीर्णा-न्यन्यानि संयाति नवानि देही ।।[88]

"As a man throws away old garments and takes others that are new, so the embodied casts away old bodies and puts on new ones." The word "re-incarnation" is also very generally used in modern days, the stress being here laid on the body rather than on the jivatma; it again takes a fleshy covering.

This truth of the evolution of the jivatma from ignorance to wisdom, from feebleness to power, is definitely revealed in the shruti, and a

---

[85]*Ibid.* 22.
[86]*Ibid.* 25.
[87]*Shretashratarop.* i. 9.
[88]*Bhagavad-Gita.* ii. 22.

knowledge of it is necessary as a basis for good conduct and for the wise shaping of life. Man is not a creature of a day, here today and gone tomorrow, but an unborn immortal being, growing into a knowledge of his true nature and powers. Everything is within him, the fulness of divine wisdom and power, but this capacity has to be unfolded, and that is the object of living and dying. Such a view of man's nature gives dignity and strength and sobriety to life. It has been belived in by wise men in all ages, and has been a part of every ancient religion. For the best proof of this great truth by pure reasoning as distinguished from direct experience with Yoga-developed superphysical faculties, the student should consult Vatsyayana's *Bhashya* on the *Nyaya Sutras* of Gautama.

Only in modern times, during a period of great ignorance, was this truth lost sight of in the West, and very irrational and fantastic notions have in consequence grown up there as to the human soul; its nature and destiny, undermining belief in the just and loving rule of Ishvara[89].

The jivatma contains within himself infinite possibilities, but when first thrown down into prakriti, embodied in a rupa made up of the five elements. All these are inherent, not manifest. He passes through the diversified existences of the mineral kingdom, and of the plant and of the animal realms,—the उद्भिज्जा: udbhijjah (born by fission in the minerals and plants); the स्वेदजा: swedajah (born by exudation or gemmation, in certain low forms of plants and animals); the अण्डजा: andajah (born first as eggs, the oviparous animals)—before coming into the जरायुजा: Jarayujah (the viviparous higher animals and the human kingdom).

In these many of his lower powers are developed, and his consciousness passes from the latent to the active condition. A double evolution goes on; there is the continued life of the jivatma himself, continually increasing in richness and complexity; and there is a corresponding continuity in the forms he occupies, as each physical form is directly derived from a preceding physical form. Each form,

---

[89]But even in the West such great scientific thinkers as Professor Huxley have begun to recognise the continued existence of the jivatma from life to life. "Like the doctrine of evolution itself," he says, "that of transmigration has its roots in the world of reality; and it may claim such support as the great argument from analogy is capable of supplying." *Evolution and Ethics* P. 16.

however independent it may seem, was once part of another form, whose characteristics it shared, and from which it has been separated off for an independent career. While part of the parent form it shared all the advantages and improvements or the reverse, due to the developing jivatma within that parent form, and thus starts on its separate life on a little higher level than its parent if the jivatma has progressed, or on a little lower level if it has retrograded. For while the general movement is one of progress, there are little ebbs and flows, like the waves that run on and fall back in a rising tide. This unbroken physical inheritance from form to form causes what science calls heredity, the passing on of characteristics from parents to offspring. But it has been observed by scientific men that mental and mortal characteristics do not pass from form to form, and they are puzzled to account for the evolution of consciousness. Their theory needs to be completed by the acceptance of transmigration. For just as physical continuity is necessary for physical evolution, so is the continuity of consciousness necessary for the evolution of mental and moral characteristics. This continuity is the consciousness of the jivatma, which takes a form suitable to his condition—as we shall see presently in Chapter IV.—enlarges his own powers by using the form, and thereby improves the form also; the bodies of the children of the body share these improvements of the form, are improved again by other jivatmas, and pass on still more improved bodies. When the old body is worn out, the jivatma throws it off, and takes another form, as said above.

When the animal stage has been fully experienced, and the jivatma is ready to pass on into the human form, his triune nature, reflection of the triune nature of Ishvara, begins to manifest. The human jivatma—as we may now call him—manifests the three aspects of jnana, ichchha and kriya which have ever been in him, and these begin to evolve as self-consciousness; ahamkara appears, and the recognition of the "I" as opposed to the "not I" rapidly developes. The desire-nature, developed in the animal kingdom, now becomes much more powerful, by seizing on the evolving mind as its slave, and using its growing powers for the satisfaction of its own cravings. As the mind grows stronger, and the jivatma by experience learns the pains that result froin unbridled desires, he begins to exert his strength in checking and directing the desires, and the long struggle commences: between the Jivatma, dimly beginning to feel his own divinity, and the kamic elements of his upadhis. As is written in the *Kathopanishat:*

आत्मानरथिनं विद्धि शरीररथमेव तु।
बुद्धिं तु सारथिं विद्धि मन: प्रग्रहमेव च॥
इन्द्रियाणि हयानाहुर्विषयास्तेषु गोचरान्।
आत्मेन्द्रियमनोयुक्तं भोक्तत्याहुर्मनीषिण:॥
यस्त्वविज्ञानवान् भवत्ययुक्तेन मनसा सदा।
तस्येन्द्रियाण्यवश्यानि दुष्टाश्वा इव सारथे:॥
यस्तु विज्ञानवान्भवति युक्तेन मनसा सदा।
तस्यन्द्रियाणि वश्यानि सदश्वा इव सारथे:॥
यस्त्वविज्ञानवान्भवत्यमनस्क: सदाऽशुचि:।
न स तत्पदमाप्नोति संसारं चाधिगच्छति॥[90]

"Know the self the chariot-owner, the body the chariot; know reason the charioteer, and the mind as the reins; they call the senses the horses, the sense-objects their province. The self, joined to the senses and mind, (is) the enjoyer; thus say the wise. Whoever is ignorant, always with mind loose, his senses (are) uncontrolled, like bad horses of the charioteer. Whoever is wise, always with mind tightened, his senses (are) controlled, like good horses of the charioteer. Whoever is indeed ignorant, thoughtless, always impure, he does not obtain that goal, (but) comes again into Samsara."

When a term of Earth-life is over, the Jivatma withdraws from the physical body, and in a subtle vehicle passes into the invisible worlds. He carries thither the results of the Earth-life, to be enjoyed and suffered as fruits, going to the worlds in which these fruits can be consumed.

In the *Brihad-aranyako-panishat* a description of this is given. The Jivatma leaves the body, taking with him the knowledge he has gained and the result of his work; then:

तद्यथा पेशस्कारी पेशसो मात्रामुपादायान्यन्नवतरं कल्याणतरं रूपं तनुत
एवमेवायमात्मेदं शरीरं निहत्या विद्यां गमयित्वान्यन्नवतरं कल्याणतरं रूपं कुरुते ॥[91]

---

[90]*Kathop*, I. iii. 3-7.
[91]*Loc. cit.* IV. iv. 4.

"As a goldsmith, having taken a piece of gold, makes another form, new and more beautiful, so verily the Atma, having cast off this body and having put away avidya, makes another new and more beautiful form."

In this he goes to the invisible world for which he is fitted—a matter to be dealt with in Chapter VI—and then the Upanishat goes on to say what happens when his fruit in that invisible world is consumed.

प्राप्यान्तं कर्मणस्तस्य यत्किञ्चेह करोत्ययं ।
तस्माल्लोकात्पुनरेत्यस्मै लोकाय कर्मण इति नु काम यमान: ॥[92]

"Having arrived at the end of (the fruit of) that work—(of) whatsoever he here does—this one returns again from that world to this world of action; thus verily (the story of) him who desires."

This process is repeated over and over again as long as he has desires, for these desires bind him to the wheel of transmigration. It is truly "the story of him who desires." So also in the *Devi Bhagavata* the same idea is expressed:

पूर्वदेहं परित्यज्य जीव: कर्मवशानुग: ।
स्वर्गें वा नरकं वापि प्राप्नोति स्वकृतेन वै ॥
दिव्यं देहञ्च संप्राप्य यातनादेइमर्थजम् ।
भुनक्ति विविधान् भोगान् स्वर्गें वा नरकेऽथवा ॥
भोगान्ते च यदोत्पत्ते: समयस्तस्य जायते ।
....
तदैव सञ्चितेभ्यच कर्मभ्य: कर्ममि: पुन:।
योजयत्येव तं काल:..........[93]

"Having abandoned the former body, the jiva, following Karma's rule, obtains either Svarga or Naraka according to his deeds,

"And having obtained a celestial body, or a body of suffering born of objects of desire, experiences varied fruit in Svarga or Naraka.

"At the end of the fruits, when the time for his rebirth arrives... then time unites him again with karmas (selected out) of the Sanchita Karmas."

The development of the chit aspect of the jivatma, and the

---
[92]*Ibid*, 6.
[93]*Loc. cit.* IV. xxi. 22–25.

purification of the ichchha aspect, being the main work of the human stage of evolution, the growth of manas, and later of buddhi, marks out the steps of the journey.

The constitution of the human being is very clearly outlined in the *Mahabharata*,[94] from which we give the following summary:

The self in man, the Jivatma, is identical in nature with the Supreme self, Brahman. From this comes forth the understanding (buddhi) and from the understanding the mind (manas); when to these the senses (indriyas) are added, the man the dweller in the body, is complete; the body, his dwelling, is made up of the five elements. The senses, through the body, come into touch with the outer world; the senses hand on to the mind the results of the contact, giving the attributes or properties of the objects contacted the way in which the objects affect them. The mind receives these reports, and groups them into mental images, and presents these to the understanding; the understanding pierces to the reality in which these mental images, made up of attributes, inhere. This is the outgoing of the Jivatma, and his gathering of experience, the प्रवृत्तिमार्गः, the pravritti margah, the path of going forth.

The first step, or stage, of this evolution is the experiencing of varied sensations; and therefore manas is regarded as the sixth sense, which receives and organises the impressions conveyed to it by the five senses, affected by their contact with the outer world through the sense-organs.

मनःषष्ठानीन्द्रियाणि।[95]

"The senses, manas the sixth."

Or, when the senses and sense organs are taken together:

इन्द्रियाणि दशैकं च।[96]

"The ten senses and the one."

Manas, at this stage, is the slave of Kama, and develops its capacities by directing the search for objects of enjoyment. Evolution is quickened by the instruction of the rishis, who teach man to sacrifice

---
[94]*Loc. cit.* Shanti Parva, ccii.
[95]*Bhagavad-Gita* xv. 7.
[96]*Ibid* xiii. 5.

the objects of enjoyment to the Devas, first to gain increased worldly prosperity, and then to gain the delights of Svarga.

The second stage of evolution is one of continual conflict between manas and kama, manas being now sufficiently developed to recognise that the pleasures longed for by kama usually, in the long run, bring more pain than pleasure.

ये हि संस्पर्शना भोगा दु:खयोनय एव ते।[97]

"The delights that (are) contact-born, these verily (are) only wombs of pain."

Manas, therefore, begins to resist the searching for objects of enjoyment, instead of directing it, and hence conflict, in which manas grows more rapidly. The thwarting of the kamic longings purifies kama, and the higher aspect of ichcha begins to show itself. Ichchha which is will, the shakti of Shiva, who is the destroyer of Kama, the son of Vishnu and Lakshmi; and also the lower aspect of ichchha.[98]

The third stage of the evolution of manas consists in the development of the higher intellectual powers; manas no longer enslaved by, nor even struggling with Kama, has become free, is the pure manas, engaged with ideas, wrought out by his own labour, not with sense-born images. The Jivatma ceases to delight in sense-contacts, or in their mental reproductions, and engages himself in pure thought, in the endeavour to understand the self and the not-self. This stage leads up to the evolution of buddhi, the pure reason or the higher understanding, of which the expression is wisdom, the result of the union of knowledge and love, wisdom which sees and loves the self alone.

श्रेयान्द्रव्यमयाद्यज्ञाज्ज्ञानयज्ञ: परन्तप ।
सर्वं कर्माखिलं पार्थ ज्ञाने परिसमाप्यते ।।
....
येन भूतान्यशेषेण द्रदयस्यात्मन्यथो मयि ।।[99]

---

[97] *Ibid* v. 22.
[98] Dharma is born from the wisdom of Vishnu, kama from his love, which must be developed in man first by desire for material objects; therefore Dharma, kama and Artha are enjoined together on the Pravritti Marga.
[99] *Bhagavad-Gita.* iv. 33, 35.

"Better than the sacrifice of objects is the sacrifice of wisdom, O Parantapa! All actions in their entirety. O Partha, culminate in wisdom. By this thou shalt see all beings without exception in the self, and thus in me."

When the Jivatma reaches this stage, he is on the threshold of liberation. He has long विरता दुश्चरितात् ceased from wicked ways, is शान्त: subdued समाहित: concentrated, शान्तमानस: of pacified mind.[100]

यस्तु विज्ञावान्भवति समनस्क: सदा शुचि:।
स तु तत्पदामाप्नोति यस्माद्भूयो न जायते।।[101]

"Whoever verily is wise, thoughtful, always pure, he obtains that goal whence he is not born again."

For this round of births and deaths is not ever lasting for the Jivatma; bound to it by his own desires, with the ceasing of those desires he becomes free; bound to it by his ignorance of his own nature, with the ceasing of that ignorance he knows himself free.

मृत्यो: स मृत्युमाप्नोति य इह नानेव पश्यति।[102]

"Only he goes from death to death who here sees manyness."

यदा सर्वे प्रमुच्यन्ते कामा येऽस्य हृदि श्रिता:।
अथ मर्त्योऽमृतो भवत्यत्र ब्रह्म समश्नुत इति ।। [103]

"When all the desires hiding in his heart are loosed, then the mortal becomes immortal; here he enjoys Brahman."

तस्मादेवंविच्छान्तो दान्त उपरतस्तितिक्षु: समा हितो भूतात्मन्येवात्मानं पश्यति सर्वमात्मानं पश्यति नैनं पाप्मा तरति सर्वं पाप्मानं तरति नैनं पाप्मा तपति सर्वं पाप्मानं तपति विपापो विरजोऽविचिकित्सो ब्राह्मणो भवत्येष ब्रह्मलोक:।[104]

"Therefore having thus becomes wise, calm, subdued, dispassionate, enduring, collected, he sees the self in the self, he sees the self as all; nor does sin overcome him, he overcomes all sin; nor does sin consume him, he consumes all sin. Free from sin, free from passion, he becomes

---

[100] Kathop. I. ii. 23.
[101] Ibid. iii. 8.
[102] Brihadaranyakop. IV. iv. 19.
[103] Ibid. 7.
[104] Ibid. 23.

a Brahmana (of the nature of Brahman); this the Brahman world."
The return is the reversal of the process of out. going, as is very clearly outlined in the *Mahabharata,* from which we can summarise the return as we summarised the outgoing.

The senses are withdrawn from contact with the outer world through the body, and become tranquil, शान्त. The mind is withdrawn from its study of the images obtained by the senses, and thus also becomes tranquil. The understanding withdraws from the study of the concepts presented by the mind, and, thus tranquil, reflects the self. So long as the mind turns to the senses it finds misery. When it turns to the understanding it finds bliss.

Along this road, the निवृत्तिमार्ग: the nivritti margah, or returning path, the Jivatma returns from his wanderings in Samsara and reaches his true home, the Eternal, paying, while he treads this path, all the debts contracted on the pravritti marga.

To see the self is jnana, wisdom; to love the self is bhakti, devotion; to serve the self is karma, action. Such jnana, bhakti, karma, are the three margas, ways, to moksha, liberation. The Jnana Marga is for those in whom chit predominates; the Bhakti Marga for those in whom ichchha predominates; the Karma marga for those in whom Kriya predominates. But in each path, as each jivatma is triune, the evolution of all of its three aspects must be carried on. The jnani, as he gains wisdom, will find devotion and right activity appear; the bhakta, as devotion is perfected, will find him self possessed of activity and wisdom. The karmanya, as his activity becomes wholly selfless, will achieve wisdom and devotion. The three margas are, in fact, one, in which three different temperaments emphasise one or other of its inseparable constituents. Yoga supplies the method by which the self can be seen and loved and served.

The words spoken by Shri Krishna, as to the sankhya and Yoga darshanas, may well be applied here:

सांख्ययोगी पृथग्याला: प्रवदन्ति न पण्डिता:।
एकमप्यास्थित: सम्यगुभयोर्विन्दते फलम् ॥
यत्सांख्यै: प्राप्यते स्थानं तद्योगैरपि गम्यते ॥[105]

---

[105] *Bhagavad-Gita.* V. 4–5.

"Children, not Pandits, speak of the sankhyaand Yoga as different. (He who is) duly established in one obtaineth the fruit of both.

"The place obtained through the sankhyas is gained also through the Yogas."

The mukta, the man who has reached liberation, may or may not remain active in the three worlds. The rishis are muktas, and are employed in the maintenance and guidance of the worlds. Janaka was a mukta, and was a king, ruling his realm. Tuladhara was a mukta, and was a merchant, weighing out his goods. Many a mukta is spoken of in the itihasa who is surrounded by physical conditions. For mukti is not a change of conditions, but a change of condition; not an alteration of the circumstances surrounding the jivatma, but the attitude of the Jivatma to the self and the not-self.

It was said above that while the general sweep of evolution is upward and onward, temporary retrogression might occur, and in some of the very ancient Âryan books-given when the possibility of such retrogression was much greater than now a good deal of stress is laid on the danger of such reversions. Shri Krishna, speaking in much later days, says that fiyat: "the worst of men" only are thrown आसुरीष्वेव योनिषु "into asuric wombs," are born of evil people, such as He had just been describing as asuric. The law is that when a man has so degraded himself below the human level that many of his qualities can only express themselves through the form of a lower creature, he cannot, when his time for rebirth comes, pass into a human form. He is delayed, therefore, and is .attached to the body of one of the lower creatures, as a co-tenant with the animal, vegetable or mineral jiva, until he has worn out, exhausted, the bonds of these non-human qualities and is fit to again take birth in the world of men. A very strong and excessive attachment to an animal may have similar results, where the man should be far beyond such exaggerated fondness.

The points to be remembered are:

1. The Jivatma is Brahman, as a seed is the tree, and remains as a wanderer in Samsara till he realises his own nature.
2. There is continuity of forms, by a new form separating from an old and leading an independent existence; and continuity

of life in each evolving jivatma.
3. The jivatma, embodied in a form, experiences through that form, throws it away when out-worn, reaps his reward in the invisible worlds, and returns to the visible.
4. The Jivatma may be detained in animal forms by self-degradation.
5. There are three stages of the evolving manas:
    (a) subjection to kama; *(b)* conflict with kama; *(c)* triumph over kama and development of the higher intellectual powers.
6. Buddhi is evolved, and liberation is reached.
7. There are three paths to liberation, jnana, bhakti, and kriya, and these finally blend.

CHAPTER IV

KARMA

Karma literally means action, but as every action is triple, in its nature, belonging partly to the past, partly to the present, partly to the future, it has come to mean the sequence of events, the law of cause and effects, the succession in which each effect follows its own cause. The word Karma, action simply, should however remind us that what is called the consequence of an action is really not a separate thing but is a part of the action, and cannot be divided from it. The consequence is that part of the action which belongs to the future, and is as much a part of it as the part done in the present. Thus suffering is not the consequence of a wrong act, but an actual part of it, although it may be only experienced later. A soldier is sometimes wounded in battle, and in the excitement does not feel any pain; afterwards, when he is quiet he feels the pain; so a man sins and feels no suffering, but later the suffering makes itself felt. The suffering is not separated from the wound, any more than heat from fire, though experienced as a result.

Hence all things are linked together indissolubly, woven and interwoven inseparably; nothing occurs which is not linked to the past and to the future.

अकारणं कथं कार्यं संसारेऽत्र भविष्यति।[106]

"How shall there be in this Samsara an uncaused action?"

The jivatma, then, comes into a realm of law and must carry on all his activities within law. So long as he does not know the law in its various branches, called the laws of nature, he is a slave, tossed about by all the currents of natural energies, and drifting whithersoever they carry him; when he knows them, he is able to use them to carry out his own purposes.

So a boat without oars, sails, or rudder is carried about helplessly by the winds and currents, and the sailor finds himself drifting along

---

[106] *Devi Bhagavata*. I. v. 74

under the press of forces he can neither change nor direct. But a clever sailor, with oars, sails and rudder, can send along his boat in any direction he pleases, not because he has changed the winds and the currents, but because he understards their directions, and can use those that are going in the direction he wants, and can play off, the one against the other, the forces that oppose him. So can a man who knows the laws of nature, utilise those whose forces are going his way and neutralise those which oppose. Therefore is knowledge indispensable; the ignorant are always slaves.

It must be remembered that a law of nature is not a command to act in a particular way, but only a statement of the conditions within which action of any kind can be done. "Water boils at 100° C under normal pressure." This is a law of nature. It does not command a man to boil water, but states the conditions under which water boils at 100°C. If he wants boiling water at that temperature, these are the conditions which are necessary. If he is on a high mountain where the pressure is much less than the normal, his water will boil at a temperature not sufficiently high for cooking purposes. How then does the law help him? It tells him how to get his boiling water at 100°C by increasing the pressure; let him shut his water up in a pot from which the steam cannot escape, and so add to the pressure the weight of the steam given off, till the temperature of the water rises to 100°. And so also with every other law of nature. The laws state conditions under which certain results follow. According to the results desired many conditions be arranged, and, given the conditions, the results will invariably follow. Hence law does not compel any special action, but only renders all actions possible, and knowledge of law is power.

The Jivatma, as we have seen, is three-fold in his nature; he consists of ichchha, jnana and kriya, will, wisdom and activity. These, in the lower world of upadhis, of forms, express themselves as desire, knowledge and action, and these three fashion a man's Karma, and each works according to a definite law.

Desire stands behind thought, stimulating and directing it; thought, energised and determined by desire, stands behind action, expressing itself therein in the world of objects.

काममय एकय पुरुष इति स यथाकामो भवति तत्क्रतुर्भवति ।
यत्क्रतुर्भवति तत्कर्म कुरुते यत्कर्म कुरुते तदिभसम्पद्यते॥[107]

"Man verily is desire-formed; as is his desire, so is his thought, as (his) thought is, so he does action; as he does action, so he attains:"

On which shloka Shankara comments that desire is the root of the world.

We have then to study three laws, which, taken together, make up the Law of Karma. We shall then understand the conditions under which things. happen, and can shape our future destiny according to the results we have chosen.

1. Desires carry the man to the place where the objects of desire exist, and thus determine the channels of his future activities.

तदेव सक्त: सह कर्मणैति लिङ्ग मनो यत्र निषक्त मस्य॥[108]

"So indeed the desirer goes by work to the object in which his mind is immersed."

Desire attaches a man to the objects of desire, binding him to them with links unbreakable; wherever is the object of desire thither must go the man who desires it. The object of desire is called फल, fruit, and the fruit which the man has sought he must consume, in whatever place it is found.

The man

...कामकारेण फले सक्तो निबध्द्यते॥[109]

"impelled by desire, attached to fruit, is bound." Whether the fruit be good or evil, pleasurable or painful, the law is the same. So long as a man desires fruit, he is bound by his attachment to that fruit, and is said to have good or bad Karma according as the fruit is pleasant or painful. When a man understands this law, he can watch over his desires, and allow them to attach themselves only to objects the possession of which will yield happiness; then, in another life, he will leave opportunities of attaining them, for they will come and place themselves in his way.

---

[107]*Brihadaranyakop.* IV. iv. 5.
[108]*Ibid.* 6.
[109]*Bhagavad-Gita.* v. 12.

This is the first law, belonging to the desire-nature.
The second law concerns the mind.

2. Mind is the creative power, and a man be comes that which he thinks.

अथ खलु क्रतुमयः पुरुषो यथाक्रतुरस्मिल्लोके पुरुषो भवति तथेतः प्रेत्य भवति॥[110]

"Now verily man is thoughl-formed[111]; as a man thinketh in this world, so, having gone away hence, he becometh."

As Brahma created by meditation, so does manas, which is His reflection in man, have creation as its essential activity; Brahma embodies kriya, activity, but we find that his activity consisted in meditation, thought, and this gave birth to the worlds; hence action is only thought thrown outwards, objectivised, and a man's actions are only his past thoughts materialised. As Brahma created His world, so manas creates his vehicles, and by the same means, thought. Character, the nature of the man, is thought-created; this is the first of the three factors of Karma. What the man essentially is in himself, that is the outcome of his thinking. As he is thinking now, so hereafter he will himself be. If he thinks nobly, he will become noble; if he thinks basely, he will become base. Thus knowing, a man can deliberately shape his character, by dwelling in his mind on all that is good and pure and elevating, and driving out of it all that is evil, foul, and degrading. This is the second law, belonging to the mind.

The third law concerns action.

3. Circumstances are made by actions.

यथा यथा कर्मगुणं फलार्थी
करोत्ययं कर्मफले निविष्टः।
तथा तथायं गुणसंप्रयुक्तः
शुभाशुभं कर्मफलं भुनक्ति॥[112]

"Devoted to the fruits of acts, whatever kind of acts a person covetous of fruits accomplishes, the fruits, good or bad, that he actually enjoys, partake of their character. Like fishes going against a current of

---

[110] *Chhandogyop.* III. xiv. I.
[111] The word is ऋतु.
[112] *Mahabharata*, Shanti Parva, cci. 23.

water, the acts of a past lifeare flung back on the actor. The embodied creature experiences happiness for his good acts, and misery for his evil ones."

नाबीजाञ्जायते किंचित् नाकृत्वा सुखमेधते ।
सुकृतैर्विन्दते सौख्यं प्राप्य देहक्षयं नर: ॥[113]

"Nothing can sprout forth without a seed. No one can obtain happiness without having accomplished acts capable of leading to happiness."

If a man spreads happiness round him, he will reap happiness hereafter; if he spreads misery, he will reap misery. Thus knowing the law, he can prepare for himself favourable or unfavourable circumstances, as he prepared a good or bad character, and pleasure-giving or pain-giving objects. This is the third law, belonging to actions.

These three laws cover the making of Karma, for the Jivatma consists of will, wisdom and activity, and these show themselves in the world by desires, thoughts and actions. When we have divided the factors in a man's destiny into opportunities, character-or capacities-and surrounding circumstances, we have covered them all. Nothing else remains.

We find, then, that we are always making new Karma, and experiencing what we have made in the past. We are obliged to act now in the conditions we have created in our past; we have only the opportunity of obtaining the objects then desired; of using the capacities then created; of living in the circumstances then made. But the living jivatma, that then desired; thought and acted, is still the same powerful agent as he then was, and can put out his powers within the limits he has made, can modify and slowly change them, and create better conditions for the future. Therefore Bhishma places exertion above destiny.

A view of Karma that paralyses human efforts is a crude and mistaken one, and men should see in Karma a guide, and not a paralyser, of action.

One very commonly felt difficulty in connection with Karma is this: men ask: "If I am destined by my Karma to be bad or good, to

---

[113]*Ibid,* ccxci. 12.

do this or not to do it, it must be so; why then make any effort?" The fallacy of this line of thought should be very clearly understood, if the above has been grasped, for it turns upon a complete misunderstanding of the nature of Karma. The effort is part of the Karma, as much as the goodness or badness; Karma is not a finished thing awaiting us, but a constant becoming, in which the future is not only shaped by the past but is being modified by the present. If a man desires to be good, he is putting forth an energy which presently will make him good, however bad he may be now. A man is not a helpless being, destined by his Karma to he either bad or good, but he becomes that which he daily chooses as desirable—badness or goodness. He always is, and always must be, making efforts, merely because he is alive, and his only choice lies in making an effort to move in one direction rather than in another; his quietude is merely a choice to let past choices have their way, and to go in accordance with them. He does not eliminate the element of choice by doing nothing; he simply chooses doing nothing. A man has only to desire, to think, to act, and he can make his Karma what he chooses. Thus the Gods have risen to their high estate, and thus may others rise.

कर्मणेन्द्रो भवेज्जीवो ब्रह्मपुत्रः स्वकर्मणा ।
स्वकर्मणा हरेर्दासो जन्मादिरहितो भवेत् ॥
स्वकर्मणा सर्वसिद्धिममरत्वं लभेद् ध्रुवम् ।
लभेत् स्वकर्मणा विष्णोः सालोक्यादिचतुष्टयम् ॥
सुरत्वञ्च मनुत्वञ्च राजेन्द्रत्वं लभेन्नरः ।
कर्मणा च शिवत्वञ्च गणेशत्वं तथैव च ॥[114]

"By his Karma may a jiva become an Indra, by his Karma a son of Brahma. By his Karma he may become Hari's servant, and free from births.

"By his Karma he may surely obtain perfection, immortality. By his Karma he may obtain the fourfold (mukti), Salokya and the rest, connected with Vishnu.

"Godhood and manhood and sovereignty of a world-empire may a man obtain by Karma, and also the state of Shiva and of Ganesha."

---

[114]*Devi Bhagavata* IX. xxvii. 18–20.

The main thing is to see in Karma not a destiny imposed from without, but a self-made destiny, imposed from within, and therefore a destiny that is continually being re-made by its maker.

Another mistake sometimes made as to karma is that which leads a person to say respecting a sufferer : "He is suffering his Karma; if I help him I may be interfering with his Karma." Those who thus speak forget that each man is an agent of the Karma of others, as well as an experiencer of his own. If we are able to help a man, it is the proof that the Karma under which he was suffering is exhausted, and that we are the agent of his Karma bringing him relief. If we refuse to carry the karmic relief, we make bad Karma for ourselves, shutting ourselves out from future help, and some one else will have the good Karma of carrying the relief and so ensuring for himself aid in a future difficulty. Further, "ifs" and "maybes" are no ground for action; "If I do not help him I may be interfering with his Karma," is as valid an argument as "If I help him." Action should be based on what we know, and we know it is right and good to help others; it is constantly commanded by the wise. Only a full and clear knowledge of the causes in the past resulting in the suffering of the present could justify refusal to help on karmic grounds.

Karma is said to be the three kinds—प्रारब्धं, Prarabdham, सञ्चितं, Sanchitam, and वर्तमानं Vartamanam, called also आगामि, Agami. Prarabdha Karma is that which is ripe for reaping and which cannot be avoided; it is only exhausted by being experienced. Sanchita Karma is the accumulated Karma of the past, and is partly seen in the character of the man, in his powers, weaknesses and capacities. Vartamana Karma is that which is now being created.

अनेकजन्मसंजातं प्राक्तनं सञ्चितं स्मृतम् ॥
....
क्रियमाणश्च यत् कर्म वर्तमानं तदुच्यते ॥
सञ्चितानां पुनर्मध्यात् समाहृत्य कियत् किल ।
देहारम्भे च समये काल: प्रेरयतीव तत्।
प्रारब्धं कम विज्ञेयं...।[115]

---

[115]*Devi Bhagavata.* VI. x. 9, 12, 13, 14.

"That which was in the olden time (आक्तन) produced in many births, is called Sanchitam...

"That Karma which is being done, that is called Vartamana.

"Again, from the midst of the Sanchitas is selected a portion, and, at the time of the beginning of the body, time energises this: it is known as Prarabdha Karma."

The Sanchita Karma is the Karma which is gathered, collected, heaped together. It is the mass which lies behind a man, and his tendencies come from this. The Vartamana Karma is the actual, that which is now being made for the future, or the Agami, the coming Karma; while the Prarabdha Karma is that which has begun, is actually bearing fruit.

Now this Prarabdha Karma is, as said in the shloka above-quoted, selected out of the mass of the Sanchita Karma. In Vedantic literature it is sometimes compared to an arrow already shot. That which is sufficiently congruous to be worked out in one physical body is selected by the Devas who rule this department of nature, and a suitable physical body is built for it, and placed with the parents, nation, country, race, and general surroundings, vecessary for the exhaustion of that Karma.

Prarabdha Karma, as said above, cannot be changed; it must be exhausted by being experienced. The only thing that can be done is to take it as it comes, bad or good, and work it out contentedly and patiently. In it we are paying our past debts, and thus getting rid of many of our liabilities.

प्रारब्धकर्मणां भोगादेव क्षय:।

"The exhaustion of Prarabdha Karma is possible only by the suffering of the consequences of it..."

Sanchita Karma may be largely modified by the additions we make to it: vicious tendencies can be weakened, virtuous ones can lie strengthened, for with every thought, desire and action we are adding to that which will be the Sanchita Karma in our next birth.

Vartamana Karma may, to a great extent, be destroyed in the same life, balanced up, by one who deliberately expiates a wrong done by restitution, voluntarily paying a debt not yet due, in stead of leaving it to fall due at a future time.

There remains the question: how can a man become free from Karma?

From the general Karma of the universe he cannot be freed so long as he remains in the universe; Devas, men, animals, plants, minerals, all are under the sway of Karma; no manifested life can escape from this everlasting law, without which the universe would be a chaos.

ब्रह्मादीनां च सर्वेषां तद्वशत्वं नराधिप ॥[116]

"All, Brahma and the rest, are under its sovereign rule, O king!" If a man would escape this universal Karma, he must go out of the universe—that is he must merge in the Absolute.

But a man may escape from the wheel of births and deaths, and yet remain manifested so long as Ishvara chooses to manifest, by ceasing to create fresh Karma and by exhausting what already exists. For the tie that binds man to the wheel is desire, and when desire ceases man creates no more bonds:

यदा सर्वे प्रमुच्यन्ते कामा येऽस्य हृदि श्रिताः।
अथ मर्त्योऽमृतो भवत्यत्र ब्रह्म समश्नुते॥[117]

"When all the desires hidden in the heart are loosed, then the mortal becomes immortal, then he here enjoys Brahman."

Such is the re-iterated teaching of the shruti. Again, we read in the *Bhagavad Gita:*

यस्य सर्वे समारम्भाः कामसंकल्पवर्जिताः ।
ज्ञानाग्निदग्धकर्माणं तमाहुः पण्डितं बुधाः ।
गतसंगस्य मुक्तस्य ज्ञानावस्थितचेतसः ।
यज्ञायाचरतः कर्म समग्रं प्रविलीयते ॥[118]

"Whose works are all free from the moulding of desire, whose Karma is burned up in the fire of wisdom, him the wise have called a sage..."

"From one with attachment dead, free, with his thoughts established

---
[116]*Devi Bhagavata.* IV. ii. 8.
[117]*Kathop.* II. vi. 14.
[118]*Loc. cit.* iv. 19. 23.

in wisdom, working for sacrifice (only), all Karma melts away."
Then freedom is achieved, and the man may either remain, as the rishis have remained, to aid in the evolution going on in the Brahinanda or may sink to rest.

The points to be remembered are:

1. The nature of action and its consequence.
2. The nature of law.
3. The three laws which make the Karma of the Jivatma.
4. The relation between exertion and destiny.
5. The three kinds of Karma.
6. The ceasing of individual Karma.

CHAPTER V

SACRIFICE

As far-reaching as the law of karma is the law of sacrifice, the law by which the worlds were built, the law by which they are maintained. All lives can only be supported by absorbing other lives: जीवो जीवस्य जीवनम्; all forms can only be preserved by absorbing other forms. Sacrifice permeates all religion as it permeates the universe.

Says Shri Krishna:—

नायं लोकोऽस्त्ययज्ञस्य कुतोऽन्य: कुरूसत्तम॥[119]

"This world is not for the non-sacrificer: how then the other? O best of the Kurus!"

The Sanâtana Dharma has incorporated this law into its very essence; all the Shrutis declare it; all the smritis inculcate it; the Puranas and the itihasa are full of it; the shadangas circle round it; the six darshanas lay it down as the pathway to be trodden ere knowledge can be gained.

We shall see in Part II how sacrifices pervade the whole life of the true Âryan; we are here concerned with the general principle, not with the specific applications:

Creation began with sacrifice:

ॐ उषा वा अश्वस्य मेध्यस्य शिर:॥[120]

"Om! The dawn verily (is) the head of the sacrificial horse."

The dawn is explained as the beginning of the day of Brahma, the day of creation. Then is the great horse sacrifice, the horse, whose body is the universe, the sacrifice of the One who carries the many—devas, gandharvas, asuras, men—as the next shloka says. And then the Upanishat goes on to describe the beyond, when there was not anything, and the building of the universe.

So also in the *Rigveda* the splendid purusha sukta describing the

---
[119]*Bhagavad Gita.* iv, 31.
[120]*Brihadaranyakop.* I. i. 1.

sacrificial slaying of purusha[121] tells how all creatures were formed by one-fourth of Him offered up as "victim" in "that great general sacrifice," three-fourths remaining in heaven as the Eternal Life.

The great sacrifice involved in creation is beautifully described in the S*hata-patha Brahmana.*

ब्रह्म वै स्वयम्भूस्तपोऽतप्यत।
तदैक्षत न वै तपस्यानन्त्यमस्ति हन्त अहं
भूतेष्वात्मानं जुहवानि भूतानि च आत्मनि इति ।
तत्सर्वेषु भूतेष्वात्मानं हुत्वा भूतानि च आत्मनि
सर्वेषां भूतानां श्रेष्ठ्यं स्वाराज्यमाधिपत्यं पर्यैत् ।[122]

"Brahma, the self-existent, performed tapas. He considered: 'In tapas there is no infinity. Come let me sacrifice myself in living things and all living things in myself.' Then having sacrificed himself in all living things and all living things in himself, he acquired greatness, self-effulgence and lordship."

Manu also declares that Brahma created यज्ञं सनातनम्[123] "the eternal sacrifice" ere He drew forth the Veda.

This profound teaching, that Ishvara sacrificed Himself in order to create His universe, means that He limited Himself in matter,—technically died—in order that His life might produce and sustain a multiplicity of separate lives. Every life in His universe is a part of His life ममैवांशः: "a portion of Myself."[124] Without this sacrifice, the universe could not come into existence. As a fourth part only of purusha is said to suffice for the bringing forth of all beings, so Shri Krishna says:

विष्टभ्याहमिदं कृत्स्नमेकांशेन स्थितो जगत् ।।[125]

"Having pervaded all this universe with a portion of Myself, I remain."

Ishvara is far more than His universe, but it is wholly contained in Him, lives in His life, is composed of His substance.

---

[121]*Loc. cit.* X. 90.
[122]*Loc. cit.* XIII. vii. l.
[123]*Loc. cit.* i. 22.
[124]*Bhagavad-Gita.* xv. 7.
[125]*Ibid.* x. 42.

Shri Krishna tells how Prajapati सहयज्ञा: प्रजा: मृष्ट्वा,[126] "having emanated mankind together with sacrifice," bade man find in sacrifice his kamadhuk, the cow whence each could milk the objects he desired. So action is essentially rooted in sacrifice:

भूतभावोद्भवकरो विसर्ग: कर्मसंज्ञित:।[127]

"The pouring out which caused the birth of beings is called Karma."

"The pouring out" is the pouring out of life, which alone enabled separate beings to live, and this pouring out is that same sacrifice described in the purusha sukta. So thoroughly has this been recognised that karma has become the general name for sacrifices, and karma-kanda is the name which covers all sacrificial rites.

The essential idea of sacrifice, then, is the pouring out of life for the benefit of others; such pouring out is the law by which life evolves: it is imposed on the lower creation by strife and continual combats; its voluntary acceptance by self-sacrifice is the crowning glory of man. Hence all man's higher evolution is marked out by self-sacrifice, by sacrificing himself and all his actions to the supreme man obtains liberation.

यत्करोषि यदश्नासि यज्जुहोषि ददासि यत् ।
यत्तपस्यसि कौंतेय तत्कुरुष्व मदर्पणम् ॥
शुभाशुभफलैरेव मोक्ष्यसे कर्मबन्धनै: ॥[128]

"Whatsoever thou doest, whatsoever thou eatest, whatsoever thou offerest, whatsoever thou givest, whatsoever thou doest of austerity, O Kaunteya, do thou that as an offering unto Me.

"Thus thou shalt be liberated from the bonds of action, (yielding) good and evil fruits."

Let us see how the law of sacrifice is seen in the physical world.

The life in the mineral kingdom evolves as the mineral forms in which it dwells are broken up to nourish plants of every kind. The mineral forms perish to feed the life in the vegetable kingdom, and the life in the mineral forms has grown more complex and developed by this sacrifice.

---

[126] *Ibid.* iii. 10.
[127] *Ibid.* viii. 3.
[128] *Bhagavad-Gita.* ix. 27–28

The life in the vegetable kingdom evolves by the sacrifice of the lower plants to nourish the higher, the countless annual plants perishing to enrich the soil in which trees grow. Myriads of others are eaten by animals, and their forms go to build up animal bodies, in which the life has fuller scope.

The life in part of the animal kingdom evolves by the sacrifice again of the lower forms to the higher, and also to the maintenance of the human kingdom, within which also the weak are devoured by the strong in the savage state. But here gradually, with increasing development of the animals to keen sensibility, and with the development of conscience and sympathy in man, another form of the law appears, and man begins to refuse to sacrifice to the support of his own life those who share with him the feelings of pleasure and pain. He first revolts against cannibalism—eating his own kind—and then against eating his weaker brothers in the animal kingdom. He realises that the divine nature in him developes by sacrifice of himself to others, and not by the sacrifice of others to himself, he lessens as much as he can his demands on the lives of others, and increases as much as he can his own sacrifices for them. So long as a man identifies himself with his body, he is always trying to take, to absorb, because the body continues only by such taking and absorbing. When he identifies himself as the self, he is always trying to give, to pour out, because the joy of the self is in forth pouring. On the pravritti marga he takes; on the nivritti marga he gives. Thus evolves the life of man.

The alphabet of the lesson of sacrifice was taught to man by the rishis who watched over the Âryan race in its infancy. They did not attempt to teach men the full lesson of self-surrender, but merely laid down for them a system of sacrifices, in which they should sacrifice some of their possessions with a view to their large increase in the future; the firm grasp with which a man grips the objects on the maintenance of which his life in the body depends was slowly loosened by the sacrifice of some of them, the return for this not being immediate but lying in the future.

आवां राजानावध्वरे ववृत्यां हव्येभिरिन्द्रावरुणा नमोभि: ।
अस्मे इन्द्रावरुणा विश्ववारं रयिं धत्तं वसुयन्तं पुरुक्षुम्॥
इयमिन्द्रं वरुणमष्ट मे गी: प्रावत्तोके तनये तूतुजाना ।[129]

"O Kings! Indra, Varuna, to this our sacrifice be ye turned by offerings and homage: ...

"O Indra, Varuna, plenteous wealth and food and blessing give us: ...

"This my song may it reach Indra, Varuna, and by its force bring sons and offspring."

Such prayers are found on every page of the Samhitas, and thus were men taught to sacrifice what they valued for a future gain.

By these sacrifices they were also taught to see that man is part of a great whole, and related to all around him; and that as his own life was maintained by the sacrifice of other lives, so he must repay that debt by sacrificing to others some of his possessions, sacrificing to the Devas in the fire which was "the mouth of the Gods," or Falt[130] "the eater of food," and to men by charitable gifts. In this way the sense of obligation was impressed on them, and the interdependence of lives.

The next step was to train them to sacrifice these same possessions, immediately valuable, for happiness on the other side of death, a far-off invisible reward. स्वर्गकोमा यजेत्; "let him sacrifice who desireth svarga."

एतेषु यश्चरते भ्राजमानेषु यथाकालं चाहुतयो ह्याददायन् ।
तन्नयन्त्येता: सूर्यस्य रश्मयो यत्र देवानां पतिरको ऽधिवास:॥
एह्येहीति तमाहुतय: सुवर्चस:सूर्यस्य रश्मिभिर्यजमानं वहन्ति ।
प्रियां वाचमाभिवदन्त्योर्चयन्त्य एष व: पुण्य: सुकृतो ब्रह्मलोक:॥[131]

"Whoever works (sacrifices), pouring libations into the shining of these [the seven flames previously mentioned], at the proper time, him these sun-rays lead where dwells the one Lord of the Devas.

"Saying to him 'come, come,' these resplendent libations carry the sacrificer by the sun-ray, worshipping him and saying the sweet words; this is your pure well deserved Brahma-world."

A great step forward was made in this sacrificing of the visible to

---

[129]*Rigveda*. VII, lxxxiv 1, 4, 5.
[130]*Brihdaranyakop*. I. iv. 6.
[131]*Mundakop* I. ii. 5, 6.

the invisible, of the present to a far-off future. But the object of this training in sacrifices was no more the enjoyment of svarga than the enjoyment of wealth on Earth. They had learned to curb their greed for possessions by the practice of giving, and to recognise themselves as owing their lives to the larger life around them; they were thus prepared for the third stage, that of sacrifice as duty, for which no reward should be sought.

Men now began to see that the sacrifice of the lower to the higher was right, a duty that was owed in return for the perpetual sacrifice of the higher to the lower, of the life of Ishvara for the maintenance of His children; and further that the body also owed a debt to the lower creatures who supported it, that ought to be paid by helping and serving them in turn. Then they were ready for the lesson:

कर्मण्येवाधिकारस्ते मा फलेषु कदाचन ।
मा कर्मफलहेतुर्भूर्मा ते संगो ऽस्त्वकर्मणि ॥
योगस्थ: कुरु कमाणि संगं त्यक्ता धनंजय ॥[132]

"Thy business is with the action only, never with its fruits; let not the fruit of action be thy motive, nor be thou to inaction attached.

"Perform action, O Dhananjaya, established in Yoga, having renounced attachment."

The wheel of life which is ever turning, this interdependence of lives, being thoroughly understood, men see it as an obvious duty to help in the turning, and readily see the unworthiness of trying to live without doing their share of work:

एवं प्रवर्तितं चक्रं नानुवर्तयतीह य: ।
अघायुरिन्द्रियारामो मोघं पार्थ स जीवति ॥[133]

"He who on Earth does not follow the wheel thus revolving, sinful of life and rejoicing in the senses, he, O Partha! liveth in vain."

This, practised for long, led up to the last lesson, the complete self-surrender of the man to Ishvara, recognising himself only as an instrument of the divine will carrying out in the physical world the purposes of that will.

---

[132] *Bhagavad Gita.* ii. 47-48.
[133] *Ibid.* vi. 16.

मन्मना भव मद्भक्तो मद्याजी मां नमस्कुरु ।
मामेवैष्यसि सत्यं ते प्रतिजाने प्रियोऽसि मे ॥
सर्वधर्मान्परित्यज्य मामेकं शरणं व्रज ।[134]

"Merge manas in Me, be My devotee, sacrifice to Me, worship Me, thou shalt come to Me; I pledge thee My troth; thou art dear to Me. Abandoning all dharmas, come unto Me alone for shelter."

Thenceforth the whole life is a sacrifice, and the man lives only to do the divine will. Hence he abandons all separate dharmas as dharmas, as having over him no binding force. He has but the one dharma, of carrying out the divine will, and if he fulfils all family and other relationships more perfectly than he ever did before, it is not because they in themselves bind him, but because Ishvara having placed him amid these surroundings as part of Himself, as His representative, he must fully meet all the necessities of the case in this representative character.

During this long training, men were gradually led to see that outer sacrifices of wealth were less valuable than inner sacrifices of virtue, and that the purification of the heart and mind were of more real importance than the external purifications.

While these should not be neglected, the neglect of the other was fatal.

यस्यैते चत्वारिंशत्संस्कारा: न चाटावात्मगुणा: न स छहण: सायुज्यं सालोक्यं च गच्छतियस्य तु खलु चत्वा-रिंशत्संस्काराणामेकदेशोऽप्यष्टावात्मगुणा अथ स ब्रह्मण: सायुज्यं सालोक्यं च गच्छति ॥[135]

"He who has the forty-two samskaras, but has not the eight virtues of the self, will not obtain Brahman, nor will he go to Brahmaloka. But he who has only a part of the forty-two samskaras, but has the eight virtues of the self, he will attain to Brahman and go to Brahmaloka." The object of sacrifice is purification, and this has been insisted on over and over again. Says Shri Krishna:

---

[134]*Ibid.* xviii, 65, 66.
[135]*Gautama Dharma Sutra,* viii. 24, 25.

यामिमां पुष्पितां वाचं प्रवदन्त्यविपश्चित: ।
वेदवादरता: पार्थ नान्यदस्तीति वादिन: ॥
कामात्मान: स्वर्गपरा जन्मकर्मफलप्रदाम् ।
क्रियाविशेषबहुलां भोगैश्वर्यगतिं प्रति ॥
भोगैश्वर्यप्रसक्तानां तयापहृतचेतसाम् ।
व्यवसायात्मिका बुद्धि: समाधौ न विधीयते ॥[136]

"Flowery speech is uttered by the foolish, rejoicing in the letter of the Vedas, O Partha, saying 'There is naught but this.'

"With kama for self, with Svarga for goal, they offer rebirth as the fruit of action, and prescribe many and various ceremonies for the attainment of pleasure and lordship.

"To those who cling to pleasure and lordship, whose minds are captivated by such, cometh not this determinate reason, on samadhi steadily bent."

And again:

श्रेयान्द्रव्यमयायज्ञाज्ज्ञानयज्ञ: परन्तप।
...   .
नहि ज्ञानेन सदृशं पवित्रमिह विद्यते॥[137]

"Better than the sacrifice of any objects is the sacrifice of wisdom, O Parantapa...

Verily there is no purifier in this world like wisdom."

Bhishma speaking of truth and declaring it to be sacrifice of a high order, says:

अश्वमेधसहस्रं च सत्यं च तुलया धृतं ।
अश्वमेधसहस्राद्धि सत्यमेव विशिष्यते ॥[138]

"Once on a time a thousand horse-sacrificesand truth were weighed against each other in the balance. Truth weighed heavier than a thousand horse-sacrifices."

With regard to abstention from cruelty he says:

---

[136] *Bhagavad Gita.* ii. 42, 44.
[137] *Ibid.* iv. 33, 38.
[138] *Mahabharata.* Shanti Parva. clxii. 26.

सर्वयज्ञेषु वा दानं सर्वतीर्थेषु चाप्लुतं ।
सर्वदानफलं चापि नैतत्तुल्यमहिंसया ।
अहिंस्रस्य तपोऽक्षय्यमहिंस्रो यजते सदा ।।[139]

"Gifts made in all sacrifices, ablutions performed in all sacred waters, and the merit acquired by making all the possible kinds of gifts—all these do not come up to abstention from cruelty. The penances of a man that abstains from cruelty are inexhaustible. The man who abstains from cruelty is regarded as always performing sacrifices."

To destroy the sense of separateness is to gain the ultimate fruit of all sacrifices purification and union with the Supreme. This is the road along which the great rishis have led the true followers of the Sanatana Dharma.

The points to be remembered are:

1. The world was created and is maintained by a divine sacrifice.
2. Sacrifice is essentially giving, pouring forth.
3. Sacrifice is the law of evolution; compulsory in the lower kingdoms, becoming voluntary in the human.
4. Man rises by definite stages from vaidika sacrifices to self-sacrifice.
5. Sacrifices of virtue and wisdom are more effective than the sacrifices of external objects.

---

[139]*Ibid*, Anushasana Parva, cxvi. 40-41.

CHAPTER VI

THE WORLDS—VISIBLE AND INVISIBLE

We have followed the jivatma in his evolution, and have seen the laws of his growth, the unfolding of his consciousness. We have now to consider the upadhis in which he dwells, and the worlds that he inhabits during his long pilgrimage. These upadhis are related to the worlds, and by them the Jivatma comes into contact with these worlds, and is able to gain experience from them and to act in them. The upadhis are only brought into existence to serve the purposes of the jivatma, moved by desire to taste these worlds. That the Jivatma's own desire is at the root of his embodiment is very plainly stated in the *Chhandogyopanishat.*

First comes the statement;

मघवन्मर्त्यं वा इदं शरीरमात्तं मृत्युना तदस्यामृत स्याशरीरस्यात्मनोऽधिष्ठानम् ।[140]

"O Maghavan, this body truly is mortal, controlled by death. It is the dwelling of the immortal bodiless Atma."

Then the wish to experience is said to lead the Atma to form organs for receiving and transmitting to himself the experiences. His wish lies at the root of each, and matter obeys his impulse, and obediently moulds itself into a form suitable for the exercise of the life-function. (Science, in these later days, proves over and over again that an organ is formed under the pressure of the life seeking to function in a particular way).

यो वेदेदं जिघ्राणीति स प्रात्मा गन्धाय घ्राणमथ यो वेदेदमभिव्याहरणीति स आत्माऽभिव्याहाराय वागथ यो वेदेदं शृण्वानीति स आत्मा श्रवणाय धोत्रमथ यो वेदेदं मन्वानाति स आत्मा मनोऽस्य दैवं चक्षुः ॥[141]

"He who has the consciousness, 'may I smell,' he the Atma, in order to smell, (makes) the organ of smell; he who has the consciousness, 'may I speak,' he, the Atma, in order to speak, (makes) the voice; he who has the consciousness, 'may I hear,' he, the Atma, in order to hear,

---

[140]*Chhandogyop.* VIII. xii. 1.
[141]*Ibid.* 4, 5.

(makes) the organ of hearing; he who has the consciousness, 'may I think,' he, the Atma, (makes) the mind, his divine eye."

It is by this subtle organ, the mind, that he sees and enjoys, for the grosser matter cannot affect his fine essence; the shruti proceeds:

स वा एष एतेन दैवेन चक्षुषा मनसैतान्कामान्पश्यन् रमते।

"He, verily, this (Atma), by this divine eye, the mind, sees and enjoys these (objects of) desires."

Here is, at once, the psychology and physiology connected with the jivatma. He is a conscious being, and that consciousness, seeking external experiences, fashions senses and sense-organs for contact with the outer worlds, and a mind of nature more akin to itself as a bridge between the outer and the inner. It is these and the worlds to which they are related, that we have now to study.

Shri Krishna speaks on exactly the same lines, reminding us further of the essential identity between the jivatma and the Supreme Ishvara:

ममैवांशो जविलोके जीवभूत: सनातन: ।
मन:षष्ठानीन्द्रियाणि प्रकृतिस्थानि कर्षति।।

...   .

श्रोत्रं चक्षु: स्पर्शनं च रसनं घ्राणमेव च ।
अधिष्ठाय मनश्चायं विषयानुपसेवते ।।[142]

"A portion of Myself, transformed in the world of life (into) an immortal jiva, draws round itself the senses with manas as the sixth, placed in prakriti...

"Enshrined in the ear, the eye, the organs of touch, taste and smell, and the mind, he enjoyeth the objects of the senses."

There are three worlds in which the jivatma circles round on the wheel of births and deaths.

These are भूलोक: Bhulokah or Bhurloka, the physical Earth; भूर्वलोक: Bhuvarlokah, the world next the physical, and closely related to it but of finer matter; स्वर्लोक: Svarlokah, or Svarga, the heavenly world. Beyond these are four other worlds, belonging to the higlier evolution of the

---

[142] *Bhagavad-Gita.* xv. 7, 9.

jivatma: महर्लोक: Maharlokah, जनलोक: Janalolkah, तपोलोक: Tapolokah, and सत्यलोक: Satyalokah. The first three lokas, or worlds perish at the end of a day of creation, a day of Brahma, and are reborn at the dawn of the succeeding day. The others persist, but as Maharloka is rendered untenable and deserted by all its inhabitants, four lokas may be regarded as perishing at the night of Brahma, while three—Janaloka, Tapoloka, and Satyaloka remain. All these seven lokas are within the Brahmanda; two others, Vaikuntha and Goloka, lie beyond it, but can be reached from it.[143]

Other lokas—such as Indraloka, Suryaloka, Pitsiloka, etc.—are special regions situated within these seven great lokas, as countries make up a continent.

There are seven other worlds, usually called talas, literally surfaces, which have to do with regions "within" the Earth, that is of grosser matter than the Earth. The student may remember that the sons of Sagara, after hunting all over the surface of the Earth for the stolen horse, penetrated the lower regions, and came to Rasatala.[144] The names of these are: पातालं Patalam; महातलं Mahatalam रसातलं Rasatalam; तलातलं Talatalam; सुतलं Sutalam; वितलं Vitalam; and अतलं Atalam. They correspond to the lokas, as an image corresponds to an object, and are on a descending scale, as the lokas are on an ascending.

These lokas mark the stages of evolution of the consciousness of the Jivatma; as his powers unfold, he becomes conscious of these lokas one after the other, and becomes able to feel, think, and act in upadhis made out of the भूतानि bhutani, the bhutas or elements, which correspond to these stages of consciousness. Each loka, as a state, represents a form of the consciousness of Ishvara; and, as a place, represents a modification of prakriti, expressing that state of consciousness. As the jivatma is of the nature of Ishvara, he is capable of realising these seven states of consciousness, and of thus living in touch with the seven worlds or modifications of prakriti, which correspond to them. These seven, as said above, make up the Brahmanda, the world egg, within which the creative work of Brahma proceeds.

---

[143] See *Vishnu Purana*. I. iii.
[144] See *Ramayana*. I. xl. 22.

पातालाद् ब्रह्मलोकान्तं ब्रह्माण्डं परिकीर्तितम् ॥
तत ऊर्ध्वं च वैकुण्ठो ब्रह्माण्डाद् बहिरेव स: ।
तत ऊर्ध्वं च गोलोक: पञ्चाशत्कोटियोजन: ॥
नित्यसत्यस्वरुपश्च यथा कृष्णस्तथाप्ययम् ।
...   .
ऊर्ध्वं धराया भूर्लोको भुवाकस्तत: पर: ।
तत: परश्च स्वर्लोको जनलोकस्तत: पर: ।
तत: परस्तपोलोक: सत्यलोकस्तत: पर: ॥
तत: परो ब्रह्मलोकस्तप्तकाञ्चनसन्निभ:।
...   .
एवं सर्वं कृत्रिमञ्च बाह्याभ्यन्तरमेव च ।
तविनाशे विनाशश्च सर्वेषामेव नारद ।
जलबुबुवत् सर्वं विश्वसंघमनित्यकम् ॥
नित्यौ गोलोकवैकुण्ठौ प्रोक्तौ शश्वदकृत्रिमौ ॥[145]

"From Patala to Brahmaloka is called the Brahmanda. Then beyond is Vaikurtha, outside the Brahmanda. Yet beyond is Goloka, extending over fifty crores of Yojanas. It is eternal and of the nature of truth. Whatever Krishna is, such is it.

"Above the Earth is Bhurloka, then Bhuvarloka beyond. Then next is Svarloka, and Janaloka beyond. Yet beyond is Tapoloka, and again beyond Satyaloka. Then beyond is Brahmaloka, like burning gold.

"All this is made, one within the other; when that perishes, all perish, O Narada! All this collective universe is like a water-bubble, transient. Goloka and Vaikuntha are called everlasting, ever-uncreate."

Here "Patala" is made to cover the seven Talas and Maharloka is omitted, Brahmaloka being added at the end to make up the seven.

Let us examine these words more closely.

The first three, Bhur, Bhuvar and Svar Lokas, are those in which the jivatma lives during his long evolution, in which he dwells while on the wheel of births and deaths. The *Brihadaranyakopanishat* says:

अथ त्रयो वाव लोका मनुष्यलोक: पितृलोको देवलोक इति।[146]

---

[145]*Devi Bhagavata*, IX. 8–10, 12–16. A similar statement is made in the *Vishnu Bhagavata*. III. x. 7–9, xi. 28–31.
[146]*Loc. cit.* I. v. 16.

"Now verily there are three worlds, the world of men, the world of the pitris, the world of the Devas."

These three are called the त्रिलोकी Triloki, the three worlds.

Each of these worlds is a definite region, marked off by the nature of the matter of which it is composed. The Tattva that predominates in Bhurloka, or Prithvi, the Earth, is the Prithvi Tattva; there are seven modifications of it, Prithvi, Apah, Agni, Vayu, Akasha-solid, liquid, gaseous, radiant matter, etheric, super-etheric and atomic. In all the combinations which make up these modifications of prakriti, the various aggregations of the Anu, the Prithvi Tattva is predominant.

In Bhuvarloka the Apah Tattva is predominant and in the seven corresponding modifications there the aggregations of the Anu of that world, this Apah Tattva, is the most prominent characteristic,

In Svarloka the Agni Tattva is the ruling power, and all the combinations bear the stamp of this fiery Anu. All the bodies of the beings belonging to that region are flashing and luminous, and from this comes the name of Deva, the shining.

We then come to Maharloka, in which also the Agni Tattva is predominant, a world composed only of the three finest and subtlest aggregations of the fiery Anu.

The three higher lokas, Jana-Tapa and Satya-lokas, are not reached by the Jivatma till he is very highly evolved. In Janaloka and Tapoloka the Vayu Tattva predominates, hence all the combinations interpenetrate each other without any difficulty, as gases do down here, and the sense of unity predominates over the sense of separateness.

In Satyaloka the Akasha Tattva predominates, and the jivatma here attains the Shabda-Brahma-world, and is on the threshold of mukti. He has reached the limit of the Brahmanda. Beyond it lie Vaikuntha and Goloka, composed of the two highest tattvas, the Mahat Tattva—sometimes called Anupadaka, because it has as yet no upadaka, receptacle or holder—and the Adi-Tattva, the root of all.

These seven lokas correspond to seven states of consciousness of the Jivatma. The life in man which is consciousness is that of the self; it is written:

आत्मन एष प्राणो जायते।[147]
"Of Atma this life is born."
and

तस्मादेता: सप्तार्चिषो भवन्ति।[148]
"From this these seven flames become."

Again, in the *Mundakopanishat*, the seven worlds are connected with the seven flames, and these flames take the departed soul to the heavenly worlds.[149]

And the *Devi Bhagavata* says:

सप्त प्राणार्चिषो यस्मात् समिध: सप्त एव च
होमा: सप्त तथा लोकास्तस्मै सर्वात्मने नम: ॥[150]

"From whom the seven prana-flames, and also the seven fuels, the seven sacrifices and worlds: to that all-self we bow."

The seven pranas, or life-breaths, of the body are the representatives of the seven great pranas, the true life-breaths, of the self, consciousness seven-fold divided in man.

This is plainly stated in the *Chhandogyopanishat,* where it is said that there are five gates out of the heart which lead to heaven, the five pranas, or life-breaths, each of these leading to a special region, that to which each belongs. Thus prana itself, the chief life-breath, leads to the sun, here standing for the chief, or highest loka, Satyaloka. Vyana, leading southwards, carries to the moon here to the dark side of the moon, connected with Bhuvarloka. Apana leads to the fire region, Maharloka, and Samana, "which is the mind," to Svarloka. Udana leads to the air region, that of Vayu which includes Janaloka and Tapoloka.

The pranas in man correspond to thc kosmic Pragnas, for man is related to, and reflects in every part, the image of Ishvara and His universe.

In the *Mandukyopanishat,* the self is said to have four states, the जाग्रत, Jagrat, waking, in which he is called Vaishvanara; the स्वप्न:

---

[147]*Prashnop.* iii. 3.
[148]*Ibid.* 5.
[149]*Loc. cit.* I. ii, 3, 6.
[150]*Loc. cit.* VII. xxxiii. 49.

"dreaming" in which he is called Taijasa; the third सुषुप्ति: Sushuptih, "well sleeping," in which he is called Prajna; and the fourth, that which is Brahman. These three states belong to the seven lokas, as will be clearly seen, if we now consider the देहा: Dehah, bodies, in which the aspects of consciousness are manifested, We shall return to the aspects of consciousness when we consider them in their several material sheaths.

There are three chief bodies which the Atma uses as upadhis: (1) The स्थूलशरीरम् Sthula-shariram, sense or gross body; this is the upadhi of the Vaishvanara consciousness. (2) The सूक्ष्मशरीरम् Sakshma-shariram, subtle body; this is the upadhi of the Taijasa consciousness. (3) The कारणशरीरम् Karana shariram, or causal body; this is the upadhi of the prajna consciousness.

प्राज्ञस्तु कारणात्मा स्यात् सूक्ष्मदेही तु तैजस:।
स्थूलदेही तु विश्वास्यास्त्रिविध: परिकीर्तित: ॥
एवमीशोऽपि संप्रोक्त ईश्वसूत्रविरारपदै: ।
प्रथमो व्यष्टिरूपस्तु समष्टयात्मा पर: स्मृत: ॥[151]

"Atma in the Karana is Prajna; He is Taijasa in the Sukshma body; in the Sthuladeha he is named Vishva. Threefold he is thus called."

"The Lord also is thus spoken of as threefold, by the names Isha, Sutra and Virat. The first (jivas) is the distributive form, while the collective self is the Supreme."

As every man has, then, three upadhis and uses them as the organs of three different forms of consciousness, the Lord has three Dehas, upadhis, and three different forms of universal consciousness; these are called Isha, Satra and Virat respectively, corresponding to the three human forms of consciousness—Prajna, Taijasa, and Vaishvanara.

These Upadhis may be considered as expressions in matter of the three aspects of the self: will, wisdom and activity. The Sthula-sharira is the organ of activity; the Sukshma-sharira is the organ of wisdom; the Karana-sharira is the organ of will. And just as these three aspects express themselves in higher and lower states of consciousness—will and desire, wisdom and knowledge, creation and generation—so are

---

[151]*Devi Bhagavata*. VII. xxxii. 47, 49.

the Shariras made up of sleaths, composed of differing densities of matter, according to the subdivision of the consciousness working in each sheath. The three shartras are related to the seven lokas as follows: The Sthula-sharira is the upadhi in Bhurloka.

The Sukshma-sharira	⎧ Bhurloka. ⎨ Bhuvarloka. ⎩ Svarloka. Maharloka,
The Karana-sharira	⎧ Janaloka. ⎨ Tapoloka. ⎩ Satyaloka.

The Shariras, as said above, are made up of sheaths, and here the vedantic division of the five कोषा: koshah, sheaths, is very helpful.

The first kosha is that which is built of the particles of food, and is therefore named अन्नमयकोष: Annamaya-koshah, food-sheath. This is identical with the Sthula-sharira, the dense body, and is composed of solids, liquids, and gases, in which the Prithvi Tattva predominates. Here the outer expressions of the Karmendriyas, the organs of action-hands, feet, voice, generation and evacuation-have their place. Here is the nervous system, with its central organ, the brain, through which Vaishvanara, the waking consciousness, acts, and comes into touch with Bhurloka.

The second, third and fourth koshas—the प्राणमयकोष: pranamaya-koshah, life-breath sheath; the मननियकोष: manomaya-koshah, mind sheath; and the विज्ञानकोष: vijnanamaya-koshah, knowledge sheath-make up the Sakshma-sharfra, the subtle body.

ज्ञानेन्द्रियाणि पश्चैव पाच कर्मेन्द्रियाणि च ।
प्राणादिपञ्चकञ्चैव धिया च सहितं मन: ॥
एतत् सुस्मं शरीरं स्वात् मम लिंग बदुच्यते ॥[152]

"The five jnanendriyas, the five karmendriyas, and the five pranas, and manas with vijnana, this is the Sukshma-sharira, which is called my type."

---

[152] *Devi Bhagavata.* VII. xxxii. 41. 42.

The student must here notice the word "karmendriyas." The absolute organs—hands, feet, etc.—belong obviously to the Sthulasharira, but the centres which govern them, the true motor centres, are in the Sukshma-sharira, as are the sense centres which have as their organs in the Sthula-sharira the eye, ear, nose, tongue and skin. Each Indriya is essentially a subtle centre in the Sukshma-sharira, and has an organ in the Sthala-sharira. If this be grasped, the student will not be puzzled by the verbal contradictions that he may meet with in his reading.

The Sukshma-sharira is connected with Bhurloka—see above table—by that part of it which is called the pranamaya-kosha; this kosha is composed of the subtle ethers of the physical world, Bhurloka, and the Pranas move in this etheric sheath, the life-currents which carry on all the functions of the body; of these there are five at work—the remaining two being latent—and these are: प्राण: Pranah, the outgoing breath; अपान: Apanah, the incoming breath: व्यान: Vyanah, the held-in breath; उदान: Udanah, the ascending breath; समान: Samanah, the equalising breath, which distributes the digested food throughout the body. In these pranas the magnetic energies of the body exist, and all bodily energies are modifications of these.

अहमेवतत्पञ्चधात्मानं प्रविभज्यतद्प्राणमवष्टभ्य विधारयामीति।[153]

"I, indeed, fivefold dividing myself, by my support maintain this (body)."

यस्मात्कस्माच्चाङ्गात्प्राण उत्क्रामति तदेव तच्छुष्यति।[154]

"From whatever limb prana departs, that indeed becomes dried up."

And, as we shall presently see, when prana leaves the body, the body dies. For the purusha asks:

कस्मिन्नहमुत्क्रान्त उत्क्रान्तो भविष्यामि कस्मिन्वा प्रतिष्ठित प्रतिष्ठास्यामीति । सप्राणमसृजत ॥155

"Who is it in whose going I shall go, in whose slaying I shall stay? He created prana."

---
[153] *Prashnop.* ii. 3.
[154] *Brihadaranyakop.* I. iii. 19.
[155] *Prashnop.* vi. 3.

Modern science, it may be remarked, has come to the conclusion that all these energies are movements in ether, and it is this ether, as said above, which forms that Pranamaya-kosha.

The part of the Sukshma-sharira connecting it with Bhuvarloka and Svarloka is the Manomaya-kosha, or mind-sheath. This Manomaya-kosha is composed of matter from these two worlds, and is the upadhi of the lower mind, manas affected by, mingled with, Kama. This mind, which is never separated from desires, has in this sheath matter of Bhuvarloka, in which desires work, and matter from Svarloka, in which thoughts work,

Lastly, the Sukshma-sharira, by its finest particles, is connected with Maharloka, to which pure manas, manas free from kama, belongs, and these particles, of the matter of Maharloka, form the Vijnanamaya-kosha.

This body, it will be seen, is a very complicated one, yet it is necessary to understand it, if the path of the man after death is to be followed. It is the upadhi of the Taijasa consciousness, in which the self comes into touch with the permanent invisible worlds, the consciousness spoken of sometimes as that of dream. It includes, however, far more than is indicated by the modern use of the word dream, for it includes the high states of trance, attainable by Yoga, in which a man may reach Maharloka.

The third Sharira, the Karana-sharira, is composed of the matter of the three higher and relatively permanent lokas, Jana, Tapo, and Satya Lokas.

The Anandamaya-kosha of the Vedantins is the same as this Karana-sharira, and this is composed of the materials of the three lokas just named. The name covers the three—as there are really three sheaths under one name; in the bodies of the dwellers in Janaloka, the material of that world predominates and wisdom specially characterises them, that world being the abode of the Kumaras, the Beings whose pure wisdom is untouched by any desire. In the Tapoloka the great ascetics and devotees live, and in their bodies the materials of Tapoloka predominate, ananda being their chief characteristic. Satya or Brahmaloka is the home of those whose peculiar functions are in activity, closely allied to the nature of Brahma.

In this third Sharira the prajna consciousness works, not affecting the lower bodies; beyond this is the Brahmanda, and the Atma, rising beyond it, unites with Ishvara.

Consciousness, in the Annamaya-kosha, works in the brain and is concerned with external activities; it uses at the same time the Pranamaya-kosha, to carry on the life-functions of the body, and affects, by this, all the objects with which it comes into contact; these two koshas leave minute particles of themselves on all the objects they touch, and the rules of physical purity are based on this fact.

Consciousness, in the waking state, also uses the Manomaya-kosha, by which it desires and thinks, and these three sheaths are active during all waking consciousness. A deep thinker, a philosopher or metaphysician, also uses the Vijnanamaya-kosha in working out his thoughts, but ordinary men do not get beyond the Manomaya-kosha.

When the time of death comes, the Pranamaya-kosha separates from the Annamaya-kosha, and leaves the latter inert and helpless, fit only for the burning-ghat. Its elements are scattered, and go back into the general store. The presence of prana is necessary for its life.

यावद्ध्यस्मिन्छरीरे प्रायो वसति तावदायु:॥[156]

"As long as prana dwells in the body, so long life."

This same Upanishat describes a dying man, and tells how all the powers of the waking consciousness are gathered up in prana, so that when prana goes out all these accompany it, and the man, the self, going out, all these powers go with him.

He is then in the Karana and Sukshma Shariras.

The Pranamaya-kosha, the part of the subtle body made of ethers, soon drops away, and the man enters the pretaloka, the world of the departed, a special region in Bhuvarloka; if he has been a bad man, the coarser part of the Manomaya-kosha is rearranged to form the ध्रुवं शरीरं, Dhruvam-shariram, the strong body,[157] called also the Yatana-sharira, in which he suffers the results of his evil deeds; if he be a good man, these coarser particles gradually drop away, and in the partially purified

---

[156]*Kaushitaki Br. Up.* iii. 2.
[157]*Manu.* xii. 16.

Manomaya-kosha he goes to the peaceful Pitriloka, the "watery world," still a region in Bhuvarloka. When the Manomaya-kosha is quite freed from its desired particles, he goes on into the division of Svarga; allotted to the departed, sometimes called the moon.

ये वैके चास्माल्लोकात्प्रयन्ति चन्द्रमसमेष ते सर्वे गच्छन्ति...
स्वर्गस्य लोकस्य द्वारं यश्चन्द्रमाः।[158]

"They who depart from this world, they all go to the moon... The moon is the gate of Svarga."

And again we read in the *Brihadaranyakopanishat* that the departed go to

पितृलोकं पितृलोकाच्चन्द्रं।।[159]

"Pitriloka, from Pitriloka to the moon."

The Manomaya-kosha is called the lunar body, and, as we shall see in a moment, is also called Soma, the moon.

This path, from the Earth to Pitriloka, from Pitriloka to the moon, or the part of Svarga allotted to ordinary men between death and birth other than Indraloka, Saryaloka, etc., divisions of Svarga gained by special merits—is called Pitriyana, the path of the Pitris.[160] From this moon they return to the Earth, the first stage being that in which a new Manomaya-kosha is obtained; this is the Soma-raja, brought out of the fire region—Svarga—by the Devas. Then the Devas put the Soma-raja into the fire of Parjanya, the "watery world," once more, and the watery particles are built into the Manomaya-kosha, those belonging to kama, to desire. This is brought down to Bhurloka, where the Pranamaya and Annamaya-koshas are formed, and so rebirth is gained.[161]

The Devayana, the path of the Devas, is only trodden by those who do not compulsorily return to the Earth during this kalpa. They depart as do the others, but they pass on from the moon, casting off the Manomaya-kosha, to the Deva world, and from that to the Sun and the lightning, to Brahmaloka:

---

[158]*Kaushilaki Br. Up.* i. 2.
[159]*Loc. cit.* VI. ii. 16.
[160]See *Ibid. 2; Prashnop.* I. 9. and *Chhandogyop.* V. x. 4.
[161]*Chhandogyop.* V. iv–viii.

तेषु ब्रह्मलोकेषु परा: परावतो वसन्ति।[162]

"In those Brahma-worlds they dwell immemorial years."
Shankara remarks that these are not absolutely free from transmigration, but that they will not be reborn within this kalpa. These are they of whom the *Vishnu Purana* says that they dwell in the higher lokas while Brahma sleeps.[163]

One other matter of importance remains in connection with man's bodies and the seven lokas. By Yoga, a man may, during his life-time, separate himself from his lower sheaths and rise into the higher worlds; and, far more, he may reach the vidya which liberates.

अथ यदिदमस्मिन्ब्रह्मपुरे दहरं पुण्डरीकं वेश्म दहरोऽस्मिन्नन्तराकाश:।[164]

"Now within this Brahmapura (the body) there is a minute lotus-like chamber, and within it a minute inner space."
Therein dwells the Atma, unobserved by ordinary men;

यथापि हिरण्यनिधिं निहितमक्षेत्रज्ञा उपर्युपरि सञ्चरन्तो न विन्देयुरेवमेवेमा: सर्वा: प्रजा अहरहर्गच्छम्त्य एतं ब्रह्मलोकं न विन्दन्ति ।[165]

"As those ignorant of the nature of the field pass over a hidden gold-mine and do not find it, so all men daily go to this Brahmaloka and do not find it."
Leaving the body in sleep, they as it were, walk over it, but do not know it. But he who knows it, daily retires to this region in the heart, and

अस्माच्छरीरात्समुत्थाय परंज्योतिरुपसम्पद्य स्वेन रूपेणाभिनिष्पद्यत एष आत्मेति।[166]

"Having risen from this body, he attains a splendid body of light, and dwells in his own form. This is the Atma."
By Yoga this separation is effected, and it is written:

तरस्वाच्छरीरात्प्रहेन्मुदिवेषीकां धैर्येण।[167]

"That (purusha) let him draw out from his own body with self-

---

[162]*Brihadaranyakop.* VI. ii. 15. and see *Chhandogyop.* V. x. 2.
[163]*Loc. cit.* I. iii.
[164]*Chhandogyop.* VIII. i. 1.
[165]*Ibid.* iii. 2.
[166]*Ibid.* 4.
[167]*Kathop.* II. vi, 17.

possession, like a grass-stalk from its sheaths."
This is not the place to enter into details as to Yoga. Enough to know that such high possibilities are within the reach of man, and may be realised by purity, by knowledge and by love.

The following points should be remembered :

1. The Jivatma, seeking experience, forms bodies.
2. He dwells in three worlds, during the cycle of births and deaths,
3. There are seven Lokas within the Brahmanda, and seven Talas.
4. There are three great Shariras, corresponding to three main states of consciousness, and these are subdivided into seven, corresponding to the seven lokas.
5. At and after death, the jivatma throws off the lower koshas, dwelling finally in Svarga in the purified Manomaya-kosha, after leaving Pitriloka.
6. The jivatma may, by Yoga, free himself from the lower koshas during physical life.

Names of Jivatma	States of Consciousness	Sub-States or Consciousness	Shariras or Bodies	Koshas or Sheaths	Lokas
Vaishvanara	Jagrat	Physical or waking	Sthula-sharira,	Annamaya	Bhurloka
Taijasa	Svapna	Physical Dream Trance Highest Trance	Sukshma-sharira,	Pranamaya Manomaya Vijnanamaya	Bhurloka Bhuvarloka Svargaloka Maharloka.
Prajna	Sushupti	Kumara, Narada Manu (Prajapatya)	Karana-sharira	Anandamaya triple i.e. Jana-An, Tapa-An Satya-an	Janaloka, Tapoloka Satyaloka

PART II

GENERAL HINDU RELIGIOUS CUSTOMS AND RITES

CHAPTER I

THE SAMSKARAS

Certain general principles pervade all religious ceremonies, and these principles must be clearly grasped, otherwise these ceremonies will be unintelligible, and the mind will, sooner or later, revolt against them.

These principles are:

1. Man is a composite being, a jivatma enclosed in various sheaths; each sheath is related to one of the visible or invisible worlds, and therefore also to its inhabitants. He is thus in touch with these worlds, and in continual relations with them.
2. The Jivatma and prakriti are in a state of unceasing vibration; these vibrations vary in rapidity, regularity and complexity.
3. The vibrations of the Jivatma are rapid and regular, becoming more and more complicated as he unfolds his powers.
4. The vibrations of the matter of the sheaths are continuously affected by those of; the jivatma, and non-continuously by the various vibrations which reach each from the world to which its materials belong. In addition, each vibrates continuously according to the fundamental vibration of its world.
5. The jivatma endeavours to impose his own vibrations on his sheaths, so that they may respond to him, and work harmoniously with him.
6. He is constantly frustrated in these attempts by the vibrations that reach his sheaths from outside, and set up vibrations in them that are independent of him.
7. He may be very much assisted in his labour by the setting up of vibrations which are in harmony with his own efforts.

These principles must be studied carefully and thoroughly understood.

Then we come to certain special facts, a know ledge of which is also necessary:

A mantra is a sequence of sounds, and these sounds are vibrations, so that the chanting, loud or low, or the silent repetition, of a mantra sets up a certain series of vibrations. Now a sound gives rise to a definite form, and a series of pictures is made by successive musical notes; these may be rendered visible, if suitable scientific means are taken to preserve a record of the vibrations set up by the sounds. Thus the forms created by a mantra depends on the notes on which the mantra is chanted; the mantra, as it is chanted, gives rise to a series of forms in subtle matter. The nature of the vibrations—that is their general character, whether constructive or destructive, whether stimulating love, energy, or other emotions—depends on the words of the mantra. The force with which the mantra can affect outside objects in the visible or invisible worlds depends on the purity, devotion, knowledge and will-power of the utterer. Such vibrations are included among the "various vibrations" mentioned under Principle 4 as affecting the sheaths, and are also referred to under Principle 7.

The repeated recitation of a mantra, that is, the repeated setting up of certain vibrations, gradually dominates the vibrations going on in the sheaths, and reduces them all to a regular rhythm, corresponding to its own. Hence the feeling of peace and calm which follows on the recitation of a mantra.

The name of a Deva, or other being, mentioned in a mantra, sets up vibrations similar to those present in the Deva and his sheaths, and, as the mantra is repeated many times with cumulative effects, the sheaths of the utterer—or of any hearer—gradually repeat these vibrations with ever increasing force.

यस्य यस्य च मन्त्रस्य प्रोद्दिष्टा या च देवता ।
तदाकारं भवेत् तस्य दैवतं देवतोच्यते ॥[168]

"Whatever the Devata concerned with a mantra, his is the form of it; the mantra of the Deva is said to be the Deva."

Pingala, the writer on Vaidika mantras, divides the metres according to the seven fundamental vibrations, and gives the name of the Devata corresponding to each vibration,

As the matter of the sheaths thus vibrates, it becomes easily penetrable by the influence of the Deva, and very impervious to other

---
[168] *Yogi Yajnavalkya,* quoted in the *Ahnika Sutravali.* p. 13.

influences. Hence the Deva's influence reaches the Jivatma, and other influences are shut out.

If the sheaths contain much coarse matter which cannot vibrate in answer to the subtle and rapid vibrations set up by the mantra, the repetition of the mantra may cause pain, disease, death. It is therefore dangerous for an impure person to recite a mantra, or to listen to the recitation of a mantra, or even for a mantra to be inaudibly recited in his presence.

If the sheaths contain some coarse matter, and some pure, the coarse matter will be shaken out, as the sheaths vibrate in answer to the mantra, and pure matter will be drawn in to replace that which is shaken out.

But one important fact must be remembered, since, in a mantra, the sound and rhythm are all important:

मन्त्रो हीन: स्वरतो वर्णतो वा मिथ्याप्रयुक्तो न तमर्थमाह
स वाग्वज्रो यजमानं हिनस्ति यथेन्द्रशत्र: स्वरतोपराधात्।।[169]

"When the mantra is defective in Svara or Varna, it is incorrectly directed and does not declare the true meaning. That lightning-word (then reacts upon and) slays the performer (of the sacrifice) himself as (the word) 'Indra-Shatru' for fault of Svara (slew Vrittra, the performer of the sacrifice, and the enemy of Indra, instead of slaying Indra the enemy of Vrittra, as intended)."

A good knowledge of Samskrit is therefore necessary.

The magnetic properties of objects are also important in this matter of vibrations. *All* objects are always vibrating, and thus affect the sheaths of other objects near them. To affect the sheaths in any particular way, it is necessary to choose objects which have the desired vibrations.

All rites and ceremonies ordained by seers and sages are based on these principles and facts, which govern the mantras and the objects used with them. They are all intended to aid the jivatma in reducing his sheaths to obedience, in purifying them, and in making them strong against evil; or else to shape external conditions to man's benefit, protection and support.

If these principles and facts are understood, the student will see

---

[169] *Vyakarana—Mahabhashya* I. i. l.

clearly the reason of many injunctions and prohibitions which he finds in the Sanâtana Dharma as to by whom and in whose presence mantras may be recited, what substances should be used in different ceremonies, what offerings should be made, and so on. Instead of a meaningless labyrinth of ceremonies, sounds, objects and gestures, he will see an ordered system, intended to help the jivatma to unfold his powers more rapidly, and to overcome the obstacles in his way.

The संस्कारा: Samskarah, are variously given, some lists enumerating only ten, others rising to a higher and higher number up to fifty-two. Among those which are specially called the ten Samskaras, some mark the important stages of a man's life up to and including his marriage; the remainder are ceremonies which may be performed daily or on special occasions, or are subsidiary to some of the Ten.[170]

The Ten principal and generally recognised Samskaras are:

1. गर्भाधान — Garbhadhanam.
2. पुंसवनं — Pumsavanam.
3. सीमन्तोन्नयन — Simantonnayanam.
4. जातकर्म — Jatakarma.
5. नामकरणं — Namakaranam.
6. अन्नप्राशनं — Annaprashanam.
7. चूड़ाकरणं — Chudakaranam.
8. उपनयन — Upanayanam.
9. समावर्तनं — Samavartanam.
10. विवाह: — Vivahah

वैदिकै: कर्मभि: पुण्यैर्निषेकादिद्विजन्मनाम् ।
कार्य: शरीरसंस्कार: पावन: प्रेत्य चेह च ॥[171]

"With sacred Vaidika rites should be performed the Samskaras of the body, namely, Nisheka and the rest, of the twice-born, which purity here and here-after."

The whole life of the Âryan is thus guarded from conception to cremation.

---

[170]In the Introduction to Mandlik's edition of the *Yajnavalkya Smriti* several lists are given, pp. xxx–xxxii.
[171]*Manusmriti*, ii. 26.

The Garbhadhanam sanctifies the creative act, not to be undertaken carelessly, lightly, nor during the presence of any evil emotion in the mind of husband or wife, nor for the sake of mere enjoyment, but with the purpose of exercising the divine power of creation, the creating of a human body. The husband prays that a child may be conceived. Thus the first dawning of the new life is amid the vibration of a mantra (*Rigveda.* X. lxxxv. 21, 22).

The Annamaya-kosha and Pranamaya-kosha are being formed within the mother's womb, and in the third month the Pumsavanam is performed with mantras—*Rigveda.* I. i. 3; III. iv. 9; V. xxxvii. 2; II. iii. 9—for the forming of a male child.

At the seventh month takes place the Simanton-nayanam, or parting of the hair of the mother, at which the *Rigveda* mantras, X. cxxi. 10; clxxxiv. I; II. xxxii. 4–8, are recited, guarding her from evil influences, and bringing to bear on the growing sheaths the most harmonious and health-giving vibrations.

These three Samskaras protect both mother and child, and to the latter bring all helpful vibrations to shape the developing body. The occult knowledge, which was thus utilised for the health and beauty of the evolving form, having disappeared for the most part, these useful and beautiful ceremonies have fallen into desuetude, to the great loss in health and vigour of the race.

The next Samskara, the ceremony performed at birth, is the Jatakarma, the father welcoming his new-born child, praying for its long life, intelligence, wisdom, and well-being, and feeding it with gold, honey and butter.[172]

Shankhayana *Grihya Sutras* (i. 24), Ashvalayana *Grihya Sutras* (i. 15), and Apastamba *Grihya Sutras* (i. 15) refer to this ceremony. Ashvalayana gives *Rigveda.* II. xxi. 6. and III. xxxvi. 10. to be recited at the conclusion of the Jatakarma ceremony.

When the child is eleven days old, or on the tenth or twelfth day, the Namakaranam, the naming ceremony, is performed, with the *Rigveda* mantra, I. xci. 7. The name given should be according to caste:

---

[172]*Manusmriti*, ii. 29.

मङ्गल्यं ब्राह्मणस्य स्यात् क्षत्रियस्य बलान्वितम् ।
वैश्यस्य धनसंयुक्तं शूद्रस्य तु जुगुप्सितम् ॥
शर्मवद् ब्राह्मणस्य स्याद्राज्ञो रक्षासमन्वितम् ।
वैश्यस्य पुष्टिसंयुक्तं शूद्रस्य प्रेष्यसंयुतम् ॥
स्त्रीणां सुखोद्यमक्रूरं विस्पष्टार्थ मनोहरम् ।
मङ्गल्यं दीर्घवर्णान्तमाशीर्वादाभिधानवत् ॥[173]

"Let a Brahmana be auspicious, a Kshattriya full of power, a Vaishya connected with wealth, and a Shudra with lowliness.

"A Brahmana's implying happiness; a Kshattriya's protection; a Vaishya's prosperity; a Shudra's service.

"Women's easily pronounceable, not harsh, with a clear meaning, pleasing, auspicious, ending in a long vowel, (soft) like the utterance of a benediction."

In the sixth month comes the Annaprashanam, the first feeding with solid food, with the *Rigveda* mantras, IV, xii. 4, 5; IX, lxvi. 19; and I. xxii. 15.

In the first or third year—or, according to the Grihya Sûtras, in the fifth for a Kshattriya and the seventh for a Vaishya—the Chudakaranam, the tonsure, or shaving of the head, is performed.

The Karnavedha, or ear-boring ceremony, is performed at the fifth or seventh year, or even later. In Southern India it is sometimes performed on the twelfth day after birth or at the close of the first year, or with the Chuakaranam. It is not mentioned in the authoritative lists of Samskaras, but in modern Indian life it is regularly performed.[174]

By these ceremonies the young body is constantly harmonised and guarded, and says Yajnavalkya:

एवमेन: शमं याति बीजगर्भसमुद्भवम् ॥[175]

"Thus is the sin (hereditary defect) arising from defect of seed and embryo allayed."

These Samskaras belong to the child-stage of life. With the next, the Upanayanam, the stage of youth may be said to begin. The lad

---

[173] *Ibid.* 31–33.
[174] See *Parashara Grihya-Sutra*, II, i, and *Gadadhara-Bhashya* thereon.
[175] *Loc. cit.* i, 13.

is now to put away the toys of childhood, and is to begin the life of study which is to fit him to take his place in the world.

The Upanayanam is the ceremony of the investiture with the sacred thread, the initiation which is the "second birth," given by the Acharya, and which constitutes the boy a fost:, Dvijah, twice-born.

कामान्माता पिता चैनं यदुत्पादयतो मिथ:।
संभूति तस्य तां विद्याद्यद्योनावभिजायते ।।
आचार्यस्त्वस्य यां जातिं विधिवद्वेदपारग:।
उत्पादयति सावित्र्या सा सत्या साऽजराऽमरा।।[176]

"That the father and mother give birth to him from mutual desire, so that he is born from the womb, let this be known as his physical birth.

"But that birth which is given, according to the ordinance, through the Savitri, by the preceptor who has mastered the Vedas, that is the true birth, the unaging and immortal."

The word Upanayana or Upanayana, means bringing near—bringing near to the preceptor, who initiates the boy, by giving him the sacred mantra called गायत्री Gâyatrî.[177] Shankhayana, Ashvalayana and Apastamba agree with Yajnavalkya in their age limits. Manu gives the age at the fifth year for a Brahmana, the sixth for a Kshattriya and the eighth for a Vaisya, making the limit, up to which initiation may be given, the sixteenth, twenty-second and twenty-fourth years respectively.[178] Yajnavalkya puts the lower limits at the eighth, eleventh and twelfth years, and the higher at the same ages as Manu.[179]

The boy is dressed in a kaupina, and then in a new garment, and wears a girdle of Munja grass, if a Brahmana; of a bowstring, if a Kshattriya; of woollen thread, if a Vaishya. The Acharya puts on him according to his caste an antelope skin, a spotted deer skin, or a cow skin, and knots the girdle round him.[180] He then invests him with the यज्ञोपवीतं, Yajnopavitam, the sacrificial thread, and after certain questions and answers he sprinkles him with water, recites certain formulas and

---

[176]*Manusmriti.* ii. 147, 148.
[177]So named because it protects him who chants it: गायन्तं त्रायते इति।
[178]*Loc. cit.* ii. 37, 38.
[179]*Loc. cit.* i. 14, 37.
[180]These significant symbols have been dropped in modern India, and all castes wear the same.

mantras, and, placing his hand on the pupil's heart, he says : 'Under my will I take thy heart; my mind shall thy mind follow; in my word thou shalt rejoice with all thy heart; may Brihaspati join thee to me." He then teaches him the Gâyatrî, and gives him a staff, the length and the wood of which vary according to the caste of the boy.[181]

The whole ceremony represents the spiritual birth of the Arya, and all its parts are significant. As spirits are sexless, the kaupina symbolically makes him sexless, and being such the Brahmachari is bound to lead a life of chastity or celibacy. The new garment represents the new body. The girdle is wound round thrice to show that the boy has to study the Samhitas, the Brahmanas and the Upanishats. The skin represents the ascetic life he should lead.

The sacrificial thread consists of three threads, knotted together, and signifies the various triads which exist in the universe: the triple nature of spirit, sat, chit, ananda; the triple nature of matter, sattva, rajas, tamas; the Trimurti; the triple Jivatma, jnana, ichchha, kriya; the three words, bhuh, bhuvah, svah; mind, speech and body, each again divided into three as regards action; and so on. And he who wears the thread should exercise a triple control, over his mind, speech and body.[182]

The staff represents, as a rod, like the triple wand of the Sannyasi the control that a student should exercise over thoughts, words and actions.

वाग्दण्डोऽस्थ मनोदण्ड: कर्मदण्डस्तथैव च ।
यस्यैते निहिता बुद्धौ त्रिदन्डीति स उच्यते॥
त्रिदण्डमेतनिक्षिप्य सर्वभूतेषु मानव: ।
कामक्रोधौ तु संयम्य तत: सिद्धि निगच्छति ॥[183]

"The rod that rules the voice, the rod that rules the mind, the rod that rules the acts,—he in whose buddhi these are maintained is called a Tridandi.

"The man who exercises this triple rod in respect to all creatures, controlling desire and anger, he attains perfection."

Then came the end of the student stage, the Samavartanam; the pupil presented his teacher with a gift, and received permission to take

---

[181] See, for full details, the *Shaukhayana Grihya Sutra*, II. i–vi.
[182] See *Manusmriti*, xii, 4–11.
[183] *Manusmriti*, xii. 10, 11.

the formal bath, which marked the close of his pupil age.

गुरवे तु वरं दत्त्वा स्थानीत तदनुज्ञया।
वेदं व्रतानि वा पारं नीत्वा हाभयमेव वा॥[184]

"To the teacher having given what is wished for, let him bathe with his permission, having completed the Vedas, the Vratas, or both." Then he returned home and performed the Samavartanam, the returning ceremony. He was then called a Snataka, and was ready to marry and enter the household state.

गुरूणानुमतः स्नात्वा समावृत्तो यथाविधि।
उद्वहेत द्विजो भार्या सवर्णीं लक्षणान्विताम्॥[185]

"Having bathed, with the permission of his teacher, and having become Samavritta (returned) according to rule, let a twice-born man marry a wife of his caste, endowed with auspicious marks."

Thus closed the student stage, and with the Vivaha, the marriage, the life of the householder began. Now he was to take up his duties as man and begin the payment of his debts by sacrifice, by study and by begetting children.

The ceremonies accompanying marriage vary much with local custom, and the simple and dignified original ceremony has become much overlaid by show and pomp. The Vaidika mantras show the spirit in which marriage should be undertaken, and it is these which the true Âryan should lay stress on, not the modern glitter and show.

The Sukta of Surya's bridal gives a picture of the marriage ceremony.

गृहान् गच्छ गृहपत्नी यथासो
वशिनी त्वं विदथमा वदासि ॥
इह प्रियं प्रजया ते समृध्यता-
मस्मिन् गृहे गार्हपत्याय जागृहि ।
एना पत्या तन्वं संसृजस्वा-
धाजिवी विद्यमावदाथः॥[186]

---

[184]*Yajnavalkya*, i. 51.
[185]*Manumriti*, iii. 4.
[186]*Rigveda*, X. lxxxv. 26, 27.

"Go to the house as the house's mistress; as ruler, speak thou to the household folk.

"Here be thou beloved with thy children; in this house be vigilant to rule thy household. With this man, thy husband, be productive; speak ye to your household-folk full of years."

The bridegroom speaks to the bride:

गृभ्णामि ते सौभंगत्वाय हस्तं मया पत्या जरदष्टिर्ययास:॥[187]

"I take thy hand for good fortune; may'st thou grow old with me, thy husband."

They walk round water and the sacred fire hand-in-hand, and the bride sacrifices grains in the fire, praying:

आयुष्मानस्तु मे पतिरेधन्तां ज्ञातयो मम।[188]

"May my husband live long; may my kinsfolk increase."

Agni is said to give the bride to the bridegroom, he who is ever the Lord of the Hearth.

The Sukta prays, when the bride goes to her new home:

इहैव स्तं मा वियोटं विश्वमायुर्व्यश्नुतम् ।
क्रीडन्ती पुत्रैर्नसृभिर्मोदमानौ स्वे गृहे ॥[189]

"Here dwell ye, be not parted; enjoy full age, play and rejoice with sons and grandsons in your own house."

And it prays that the bride, lovely and gentle hearted, may bring bliss to the home, to men and animals, ruling the home, pious, mother of heroes.

The law of marriage is given by Manu:

अन्योन्यस्याव्यभीचारो भवेदामरणान्तिक: ।
एष धर्म: समासेन ज्ञेय: स्त्रीपुंसयो: पर: ॥
तथा नित्यं यतेयातां स्त्रीपुंसौ तु कृतक्रियो ।
यथा नातिचरेतां तौ वियुक्कावितरेतरम् ॥[190]

Let there be faithfulness to each other until death; this, in short,

---

[187]*Ibid*, 36.
[188]Shankhayana's *Grihya Sutras*, I. xiv. I.
[189]*Rigveda*, X. lxxxv. 42.
[190]*Manusmriti*. ix. 101, 102.

should be known as the highest duty of husband and wife.

"So let husband and wife ever strive, doing all their duties, that they may not, separating from each other, wander apart."

Such was the Âryan ideal of marriage, perfect faith of each to each till death, and Âryan literature shows how nobly that ideal was fulfilled. Let the student look on marriage in the old light, and we may see men and women again of the old type.

Thus, in the ancient days, was the young man launched into manhood, with mantras and with prayers; but Gautama's saying already quoted[191] must ever be laid to heart :

"He who has the forty-two Samskaras, but has not the eight virtues of the self, will not obtain Brahman, nor will he go to Brahmaloka. But he who has only a part of the forty-two Samskaras but has the eight virtues of the self, he will attain to Brahman and go to Brahmaloka.

---

[191] P. 135.

CHAPTER II

SHRADDHA

The longer lists of Samskaras include the various ceremonies performed on behalf of those who have departed from the physical world, the ceremonies that fall under the general name of श्राद्धम् shraddham. The Âryan has never felt the presence of a thick barrier between the visible and invisible worlds, between the living and the dead. All his religion brings the invisible worlds into continual contact with the visible, the Devas are as real as the men And he recognises the continued existence of the jivatma so vividly that the death of the body is not to him a matter of terror and anxiety, but a habitual thought, and the dead are never regarded as dead, but merely as living elsewhere. The habitual thought of transmigration, linking life with life, reduces any particular death to a mere incident in an indefinite series, and the jivatma, not the body, assumes predominant importance. Still more vividly is this idea that the Jivatma is the man impressed on the minds of Âryans by the recurring shraddhas, in which the continued existence of those who have left the physical world is brought before the eyes of the present dwellers upon Earth.

The duties an Âryan owes to the dead commence from the moment the life departs, and are divided into two classes—preta-kriya and Pitri-kriya or shraddhas—funeral and ancestral ceremonies. The dead is called the प्रेत: pretah, the departed, till the Sapindikarana is performed, when he becomes a pitri.

At death the man, clothed in the Pranamaya-kosha, leaves the Annamaya-kosha, and as all the Vaidika Samskaras have been framed to help the processes of nature, the preta-kriya is intended to neutralise the tendency of the Pranamaya-kosha to hang about the Annamaya-kosha as long as the latter is whole, and thus to retain the real man in Bhurloka after the normal course of nature requires him to leave it.

The first important thing to be done is to destroy the Annamaya-kosha, and this is done by cremation. In the words of the *Chhandogyopanishat:*

तं प्रेतं दिष्टमितोऽग्नय एव हरन्ति यत ऐवेतो यत: सम्भूतो भवति ।[192]

"They carry him who has departed, as ordained, to the fire whence he came, whence he was born."

Before the fire is applied to the corpse, the celebrant walks three times round the spot where it is laid, and sprinkles water on it with the verse *Rigveda* X, xiv. 9:

अपेत वीत विच सर्पतात: ...।

"Go away, withdraw, and depart from here. While the body is burning, *Rigveda* X. xiv. 7:

प्रेहि प्रेहि पथिमि: ...।

"Go on, go on, on the ancient paths" is to be recited.

On the third day after the cremation the remnants of the bones are gathered and buried, or thrown into running water, thus completing the disintegration of the Annamaya-kosha. The Pranamaya-kosha then rapidly disintegrates.

The next work to be done is to help to disintegrate the lowest part of the Manomoya-kosha and thus change the preta, the departed, into the pitri, the ancestor.

For this purpose have been framed the Ekoddishta-shraddha and the Sapindana-shraddha. The Ekoddishta-shraddha is one directed to a single dead person, whereas a shraddha proper is directed to three generations of pitris or to all pitris, The offerings connected with it are intended to be offered (during a whole year. No avahana, inviting, takes place in this ceremony, nor the putting of food into the fire, nor do the Vishvedevas take part in it.[193]

The Ekoddishta-shraddhas are completed by the performance of the Sapindikarana, the reception of the preta, into the community of the pitris. According to Shankhayana, the celebrant fills four water-pots with sesamum, scents, and water—three for the fathers, one for the newly dead person—and pours the pot that belongs to the newly dead person into the pots of the pitris with the two verses, *Vajasaneya*

---

[192] V. ix. 2.
[193] Shaukhayana's *Grihya Sutras* iv. 2, 5.

Samhita. xix. 45, 46.[194]

If these ceremonies should be properly performed, the subtle parts of the offerings made during their performance feed the deceased till he goes to Pitriloka. The mantras facilitate his passage thereto and he takes his place among the pitris.

Then "the fourth is dropped," *i. e.*, in the ceremonies the great-grandfather of the deceased person is not invoked, the deceased, his father and grandfather forming the three pitris.

The numerous periodical ceremonies that are performed to the pitris proper are technically shraddhas. At a shraddha the pitris are the deities to whom the sacrifice is offered; the Brahmanas who are fed represent the Ahavaniya fire.[195]

The Abhyudayika-shraddhas or Nandi-shraddhas are performed on the occassions of rejoicings, such as the birth of a son, the marriage of a son or daughter, Namakarana, Jatakarma, Chudakarana etc. In this ceremony the Nandimukha pitris, glad-faced ancestors, those that have gone to the Svarga-loka, are invoked, and an even number of Brahmanas are fed in the forenoon.

Of all the ancient ceremonies, shraddhas alone are still perfomed with any appreciable degree of religious fervour and it is hoped that an intelligent understanding of the rational basis of them will increase the shraddha, faith, without which a shraddha cannot properly deserve the name.

We shall see, in studying the Five Daily sacrifices—Chapter IV— that the Pitri-yajna has its place among them. On the new-moon day this is followed by the monthly shraddha ceremony, called the पिण्डान्वाहार्यकं, Pindanvaharyakam, and पार्वणश्राद्धम्, Parvarashraddham, one of the seven पाकयज्ञा, Pakayajnah, or sacrifices with baked offerings.

Sacrifices to the pitris are offered in the afternoon, facing south,[196] and the ground should slope southwards.[197] On the new moon-day, Kusha or Darbha grass is arranged for seats, and an odd mumber of Brahmanas are invited. Great stress is laid on the character and learning

---

[194]*Ibid.* iv. 3.
[195]Apastamba's *Dharma Sutras*, II. vii. 16 (3).
[196]Apastamba's *Yajna Paribhasha*, Sutra LX.
[197]*Manusmriti.* iii. 206.

of these Brahmanas.

यथेरिणे बीजमुप्ता न वप्ता लभते फलम्।
तथानृचे हविर्दत्त्वा न दाता लभते फलम् ॥[198]

"As the sower having sown seed in barren soil, obtains no harvest, so the giver, having given sacrificial food to one ignorant of the richas, obtains no harvest."

नश्यन्ति हव्यकव्यानि नराणामविजानताम्।
भस्मभूतेषु विप्रेषु मोहाद्दत्तानि दातृभिः॥[199]

"The offerings of ignorant men to Devas and pitris perish, being gifts from deluded givers to Brahmanas who are ashes."

ब्राह्मणो ह्यनधीयानस्तृणाग्निरिव शाम्यति ।
तस्मै हव्यं न दातव्यं न हि भस्मनि हूयेत ॥[200]

"A Brahmana who is ignorant goeth out like a grass fire; to him sacrificial food ought not to be given; offerings are not poured into ashes."

So, also, Hiranyakeshin says that the Brahmanas invited to the shraddhas must be pure and versed in the mantras.[201]

Having gathered these and prepared the materials for the sacrifice, and offered Havih in the Dakshinagni, the sacrificer calls to the pitris, and sprinkles water. According to Manu, he should make three cakes, offering them to his father, grandfather and great-grandfather, pour out water near the cakes, and give to the Brahmanas very small portions of them; after this the Brahmanas should be fed in the afternoon.[202] In the *Grihya Sutra*s it is directed that the Brahmanas are first fed, and that then the offerings are to be made to the pitris. The domestic Bali offerings should follow the shraddha.[203]

Similar ceremonies may be performed in the dark fortnight, and the Ashtaka ceremony is sometimes offered to the pitris.

---

[198]*Ibid.* 142.
[199]*Ibid.* 97.
[200]*Ibid*, 168.
[201]*Grihya Sutras* II. iv. 10.
[202]*Manusmriti*, iii, 208–237.
[203]*Ibid.* 265.

It must be remembered that Pitriloka and Pretaloka, or Yamaloka, are both regions in Bhuvarloka (see Part I. ch. vi.) and influence from the Earth, Bhurloka, reaches both of these. The influence of pinda offerings reaches throughout Pretaloka; the three higher generations (fourth, fifth and sixth) are affected by offerings of remnants of food. Including the offerer, only seven generations can mutually influence each other by the giving and receiving of food. Three generations beyond these can receive only libations of water. Influence from below can go no further, for by that time an average man is supposed to have passed into Svarga, and the whole object of shraddha is to facilitate his passage thither.

The general principles of the shraddha of a person recently departed are adaptations of the principles underlying all Samskaras.

Shraddhas may, generally speaking, be regarded as serving the same purpose with reference to the subtler bodies, as is served by the pre-natal and natal Samskaras with reference to the gross physical body. Having helped the jivatma going from here to a fair birth in the other world, the human helper has completed his duty, and cannot go any further or give other help. The agencies of the other world thereafter take up the jivatma into their own exclusive charge.

CHAPTER III

SHAUCHAM

The rules for purifying the body are based on scientific facts as to the Annamaya and Pranamaya-koshas.

The Annamaya-kosha is composed of solids, liquids and gases, and infinitesimal particles of these are constantly passing off from the body. Apart altogether from the obvious daily losses sustained by the body in the excrements and sweat, there is this ceaseless emission of minute particles alike in night and day, whether the body is waking or sleeping. The body is like a fountain, throwing off a constant spray. Every physical object is in this condition, stones, trees, animals, men; all are ceaselessly, throwing off these tiny particles, invisible because of their extreme minuteness, and are, as ceaselessly, receiving the rain of particles from others which fills the air in which they live, and which they breathe in with every breath. A continual interchange is thus going on between all physical bodies; no one can approach another with out being sprinkled by the other, and sprinkling him in turn, with particles from their respective bodies. Everything a man goes near receives some particles froin his body; every object he touches retains a minute portion of his body on its surface; his clothes, his house, his furniture, all receive from him this rain of particles, and rain particles from themselves on him in turn.

The Pranamaya-kosha, composed of the physical ethers and animated by the life-energies, affects all around it, and is affected by all around it, not by emitting or receiving particles, but by sending out, and being played upon by, vibrations, which cause waves, currents, in the etheric matter. The life-waves, magnetism-waves, go out from each man as ceaselessly as the fine rain of particles from his Annamaya-kosha. And similar waves from others play upon him, as ceaselessly as the fine rain of particles from others falls on him.

Thus every man is being affected by others, and is affecting them, in the physical world, in these two ways: by a rain of particles given off from the Annamaya-kosha, and by waves given off from the Pranamaya-kosha.

The object of the rules of Shaucham is to make this inevitable influence of one person on another a source of health instead of a source of disease, and also to preserve and strengthen the bodily and mental health of the performer. The Annamaya-kosha is to be kept scrupulously clean, so that it may send off a rain of health on everyone and everything that is near it; and the Pranamaya-kosha is to be reached by the mantra-produced vibrations in the etheric matter which permeates the things used in the ceremonies—as etheric matter permeates everything—so that these vibrations may act beneficially on it, and may cleanse and purify it.

The rules affecting bodily cleanliness are definite and strict. On rising, the calls of nature are first to be attended to,[204] plenty of water being used for cleansing purposes, and then the mouth and teeth are to be washed, and a bath taken. A man is to be careful that no unclean matters remain near his dwelling;

दूरादावसथान्मूत्रं दूरात् पादावसेचनम् ।
उच्छिष्टान्नं निषेकं च दूरादेव समाचरेत् ।।[205]

"Far from his dwelling let him cast excrement, far the water used for washing his feet, far the leavings of food, and bath-water."

Much disease is caused by the neglect of this rule, the filthy surroundings of dwellings causing ill-health and general loss of vigour. In modern city life, the community takes on this duty by an organised system of drainage, but this should be on the same principle of conveying noxious matters far away from all habitations; and it is part of the duty of a good citizen to see that rivers in the neighbourhood of cities are not poisoned, nor filth allowed to accumulate to the injury of the public health.

A man must wash, in some cases bathe the whole body, before taking part in any religious ceremony, and sip water with appropriate mantras.

---

[204]*Manusmriti*, iv. 43–52, 56–152.
[205]*Ibid.* iv. 131.

आचम्य प्रयतो नित्यमुभे संध्ये समाहित: ।
शुचौ देशे जपञ्जप्यमुपासीत यथाविधि ॥[206]

"Being purified by sipping water, he shall always daily worship in the two twilights with a collected mind, in a pure place, performing Japa according to rule."

He must wash before and after meals;

उपस्पृश्य द्विजो नित्यमन्नमद्यात्समाहित: ।
भुक्त्वा चोपस्पृशेत्सम्यगद्भि: खानि च संस्पृशेत् ॥[207]

"Having washed, the twice-born should eat food always with a collected mind; having eaten, let him wash well with water, sprinkling the sense organs."

If a man has touched anything impure, a person or an object,

स्नानेन शुध्यति।[208]

"by bathing he is purified."

मृत्तोयै: शुध्यते शोध्यं।[209]

"By Earth and water that which should be made pure is purified."

These are the two great purifiers, though alkalies and acids may be used for cleaning copper, iron, brass, pewter, tin and lead; earthen vessels can be purified by burning, houses by sweeping, cowdung and whitewash; other methods are given for special substances. So long as any smell or stain remains on an object it is not to be considered pure.[210]

ज्ञानं तपोऽग्निराहारो मृन्मनो वार्युपाञ्जनम् ।
वायु: कर्मार्ककालौ च शुद्धे: कर्तृणि देहिनाम् ॥211

"Wisdom, austerity, fire, food, Earth, mind, water, plastering, wind, rites, the sun and time, are the purifiers of human beings."

But no body can be truly pure unless the mind and heart be pure:

---

[206] *Manusmriti.* ii. 222.
[207] *Ibid.* 53.
[208] *Ibid.* v. 85.
[209] *Ibid.* 108.
[210] *Ibid.* 105–127.
[211] *Ibid* 105.

अद्भिर्गात्राणि शुध्यन्ति मनः सत्येन शुध्यति ।
विद्यातपोभ्यां भूतात्मा बुद्धिज्ञानेन शुध्यति ॥[212]

"The body is purified by water, the mind by truth, the soul by knowledge and austerity, the reason by wisdom."

Besides the impurities due to obvious causes, the birth or death of sapindas, or of relatives not sapindas, causes impure magnetic currents in the Pranamaya-kosha and therefore sullies the Annamaya-kosha. In the case of sapindas, the impurity lasts from ten days to one month according to the caste of the parties concerned. In the case of the death of little children the impurity lasts for a very short time.

The relationship of sapinda ceases with the seventh remove of relationship through males. In the case of relations not sapindas, the impurity lasts 3 days, or less, decreasing according to the remoteness of the relationship. During the period of impurity sacrificial oblations, recitation of mantras, and some other religious duties have to be given up. No one must eat the food of, or touch, one impure. But the customs vary much in these respects in the different parts of the country and even the word sapinda is differently interpreted.

Further details may be studied in the smritis, and may be applied by the student to his own life, in conformity with caste and family customs and having regard to the changed conditions of life. Infectious diseases of all kinds run riot where the rules of individual purity are disregarded, and where houses, clothes and articles in daily use are not scrupulously cleaned. Modern science is re-establishing, with infinite labour and pains, the facts on which these ancient rules were based, and a clear understanding of the reason for their imposition will render obedience to them willing and cheerful.

---

[212] *Manusmriti.* v. 109.

CHAPTER IV

THE FIVE DAILY SACRIFICES

The application of the great law of sacrifice to the daily life of the Âryan was made by the laying down of rules for making sacrifices, by which he gradually learned to regard himself as part of a connected whole, a whole of which the parts were mutually interdependent, owing to each other's mutual aid and support. When this lesson had been thoroughly assimilated, then, and then only, might the man lay aside these duties, entering on the life of the Sannyasi, who having sacrificed all his possessions and himself, had nothing left to offer.

The various bodies or vehicles of man are nourish ed and helped to grow severally, by the initial energy received from parents, by food, by sympathy and help from his fellow-beings, by magnetic influences, and by knowledge and illumination. He therefore owes a fivefold debt to nature and it is but meet and proper that, if he would flourish, he should fully recognise his indebtedness and do his best to pay back his debt. As stated before, he is not an isolated creature, and his whole well-being depends upon his co-operation with nature, which works not so much for the exaltation of individuals as for the steady evolution of all creation. The sacrifices prescribed by Hindu law-givers are nothing more than an enumeration of the duties which thus devolve on every man. They embrace all the planes of his existence, and are therefore conducive to his highest growth.

There are thus five महायज्ञा:, Mahayajnah, great sacrifices, to be offered every day, and seven पाकयज्ञा:, Pakayajnah, literally cooked sacrifices, occurring at stated intervals. In addition to these, there are the fourteen Shrauta sacrifices, divided into हविर्यज्ञ, Havir-yajnah, offering of grains, etc., and सोमयज्ञा:, Soma-yajnah, offerings of Soma. Some of these are of daily, others of occasional, obligation.

The five great sacrifices are as follows:

1. ब्रह्मयज्ञ: Brahma-yajnah, called also: वेदयज्ञ:, Veda-yajnah, sacrifice to Brahman or the Vedas.

2. देवयज्ञ: Deva-yajnah, sacrifice to Devas.
3. पितृयज्ञ: Pitri-yajnah, sacrifice to Pitris.
4. भूतयज्ञ: Bhuta-yajnah, sacrifice to Bhutas.
5. मनुष्ययज्ञ Manushya-yajnah, sacrifice to men.

These are laid down by Manu among the duties of the householder.

अध्यापनं ब्रह्मयज्ञ: पितृयज्ञस्तु तर्पणम् ।
होमो दैवो बलिभौंतो नृयज्ञोऽतिथिपूजनम् ॥
... ...
अहुतं च हुतं चैव तथा प्रहुतमेव च ।
ब्राम्यं हुतं प्राशितं च पञ्च यज्ञान् प्रचक्षते ॥
जपोऽहुतं हुतो होम: प्रहुतो भौतिको बलि: ।
ब्राह्मयं हुतं द्विजाग्न्यर्चा प्राशितं पितृतर्पणम् ॥
स्वाध्याये नित्ययुक्त: स्याछैव चौवेहें कर्मणि ।
दैवे कर्मणि युक्तो हि विभर्तीदं चराचरम् ॥[213]

"Teaching is the Brahma sacrifice, Tarpana (the offering of water) is the pitri sacrifice, Homa (the pouring into the fire) the Deva sacrifice, Bali (food) is the Bhuta sacrifice, hospitality to guests the Manushya sacrifice.

"They call the five sacrifices Ahuta, Huta, Prahuta, Brahmya-huta, and Prashita.

"Japa is Ahuta, Homa is Huta, the Bali given to Bhutas is Prahuta, respectful reception of the twice-born is Brahmya-huta, and the pitri-tarpana is Prashita.

"Let a man ever engage in Veda study, and in the rites of the Devas; engaged in the rites of the Devas, he supports the movable and immovable kingdoms."

And again—

ऋषय: पितरो देवा भूतान्यतिथयस्तथा ।
आशालते कुटुम्बिभ्यस्तभ्य: कार्य विजानता ॥
स्वाध्यायेनार्चयेतीन होमवान्यथाविधि ।
पितृच्छ्राद्धेन नृनन्नैभूतानि बलिकर्मणा ॥[214]

---

[213] *Manusmriti.* iii 70, 73–75.
[214] *Ibid.* 80.

"The Rishis, the pitris, the Devas, the Bhutas and guests expect (help) from the householders: hence he who knows should give to them.

"Let him worship, according to the rule, the Rishis with Veda study, the Devas with Homa, the pitris with shraddhas, men with food, and the Bhutas with Bali."

We have here very plainly indicated the nature of the sacrifices to be offered; the sacrifice to Brahman, called also that of the Vedas and the Rishis, is study and teaching: this is a duty every inan owes to the Supreme to cultivate his intelligence and to share his knowledge with others. Every day the Âryan should devote a portion of time to study; the man who lives without daily study becomes frivolous and useless. This duty is enjoined by the first of the great sacrifices.

Then comes the sacrifice to the Devas—the recognition of the debt due to those who guide nature, and the "feeding" them by pouring ghee into the fire, the Homa sacrifice. The Devas are nourished by exhalations as men by food, their subtle bodies needing no coarser sustenance.

The sacrifice to the pitris follows, consisting of the offerings of cakes and water. The pitris are the sons of Marichi and the Rishis produced by Manu, and are of many classes, the progenitors of the various divine and human races. From the Somasad pitris the Sadhyas and pure Brahmanas are descended, and from the Agnishvatta pitris the Devas and also some Brahmanas. The Daityas, Danavas, Yakshas, Gandharvas, Uragas, Rakshasas, Suparnas and Kinnaras descend from the Barhishad pitris, as do also some Bralmanas. The pitris of Kshattriyas are the Havirbhuks, of Vaishyas the Ajyapas, of Shudras the Sukalins. Countless descendants become associated with them, so that the sacrifice may be said to be to ancestors. In this a man is taught to remember the immense debt he owes the past, and to regard with loving gratitude those whose labours have bequeathed to him the accumulated stores of wealth, learning and civilisation. He is reminded also of the time when he will pass into the great ancestral host, and of his duty to hand down to posterity the legacy he has received, enriched, not diminished, by his life. The full meaning of descent from pitris is ascertainable only by study of occult science.

The sacrifice to Bhutas consists of Bali, or offerings of food placed on the ground in all directions, intended for various beings of the invisible worlds, and also for stray animals of all kinds and wandering outcasts and diseased persons. The injunction as to this should be remembered;

शुनां च पतितानां च श्वपचां पापरोगिणाम् ।
वायसानां कृमीणां च शनकैर्निर्वपेद्भुवि ॥215

"Let him gently place on the ground (food) for dogs, outcasts, Shva-pachas, those diseased from sins, crows and insects"

It is not to be thrown down carelessly and contemptuously, but put there gently, so that it may not be soiled or injured. It is a sacrifice, to be reverently performed, the recognition of duty to inferiors, however degraded.

Lastly comes the sacrifice to men, the feeding of guests—or generally of the poor—the giving of food to the houseless and the student:

कृत्वैतद्बलिकमैवमतिथिं पूर्वमाशयेत् ।
भिक्षां च भिक्षवे दद्याद्विधिवद् ब्रह्मचारिणे ॥216

"The Bali offering made, let him feed first the guest, and let him give food, according to rule, to a beggar and a student."

In this man is taught his duty to his brother-men, his duty of brotherly help and kindness. He feels humanity in feeding some of its poorer members; and learns tenderness and compassion. The giving of food is illustrative of all supply of human needs. Manushya-yajna includes all philanthropic actions. As in the old days, want of food was the chief want of man, that is mentioned prominently. The complexities of life have given rise to other wants now. But they, are all included in the Manushya-yajna, provided they are legitimate wants, and it becomes the duty of each man to remove them, so far as lies in his power.

Thus these five great sacrifices embrace man's duty to all the beings round him; and the man who truly performs them in spirit as well as in letter, day by day, is doing his share in turning the wheel of life

---
[215] *Manusmriti*, ii. 92.
[216] *Ibid*, iii. 94.

and is preparing for himself a happy future. We may glance briefly at the other sacrifices.

The Paka-yajnas are seven in number:

1. पितृश्राद्धं   Pitri-shraddham
2. पार्वणश्राद्धं   Parvana-shraddham
3. अष्टका   Ashtaka
4. श्रावणी   Sravani
5. अध्वयुजिः   Ashvayujih
6. आग्रहायणी   Agrahayani
7. चैत्री   Chaitri

The first two of these are ceremonies in honour of the pitris, and have been dealt with in Chapter II under Shraddha. The remainder, except the fourth, are now rarely met with.

The fourteen Shrauta sacrifices are as follows.

The seven Haviryajnas:

1. अग्न्याधेय   Agnyadheyam
2. अग्निहोत्र   Agnihotram
3. दर्शपूर्णमासं   Darsha-purnamasam
4. आग्रयण   Agrayanam
5. चातुर्मास्यं   Chaturmasyam
6. निरूढपशुबन्धः   Nirudha-pashu-bandhah
7. सोचामणिः   Sautramanih

In these milk, ghee, grains of various kinds, and cakes were offered, and Manu says that a Brahmana should daily offer the Agnihotra in the morning and evening, the Darsha and Purnamasa at the end of each fortnight, the Agrayana with new grain-before which the new grain should not be used- the Chaturmasya at the end of the three seasons, the Nirudha-pashu-bandha at the solstices.[217]

The seven Somayajnas are:

1. अग्निष्टोमः   Agnishtomah
2. अत्याग्निष्टोमः   Atyagnishtomah

---

[217] *Manusmriti*, iv. 25–26

3. उक्थ्यः   Ukthyah
4. षोडषी:   Shodashi
5. दाजपेयः   Vajapeyah
6. अतिरात्रः   Atiratrah
7. आप्तोर्यामः   Aptoryamah

In these sacrifices Brahmana priests must be employed, the number varying with the sacrifice, the man on whose behalf they are offered being called the 7417:, Yajamanah; the husband and wife light the three sacred fires—the Ahavaniya fire on the east, for offerings to the Devas; the Dakshina fire on the south, for performing the duties to the pitris; the Garhapatya fire on the west; sometimes a fourth is mentioned, the Anvaharya—and these are not allowed to go out; this is the Agnyadhana ceremony. All the Shrauta sacrifices are offered in these.

According to some authors the domestic or household—the Avasathya or Vaivabika—fire is lighted by the student on his return home when his pupilage is completed, but on this point there are many varieties of custom. The Paka-yajnas are offered in the household fire.

A description of the daily life of a Brahmana is given in the *Ahnika Sutravali*,[218] and may be summarised as follows:

He should wake up in the Brahma-muhurta[219] and think of Dharma and Artha, of the evils of the body, and of the Vedas. At the dawn he should rise, follow the Shaucha rules, and take his bath, then performing Sandhya. Then he should perform the Agnihotra, and worship the Devas and the Gurus (teacher and parents). After this he should study the Vedas and Vedangas. Then he should work for those dependent on him—parents, guru, wife, children, relatives, friends, the aged, infirm, and friendless poor, and those who have no means. Then he should bathe, perform the mid-day sandhya, feed the Pitris, Devas, men and animals, and take his own meal. After this he should read Puranas, itihasa, and Dharmashastras, avoiding idle talk and discussion. Then he should go out, visit temples and friends, returning to his evening Sandhya and Agnihotra. After this he should eat, attend to any family

---

[218] Edited by Pandit Vaidyanarayana Vitthala
[219] There are thirty Muhurtas in 24 hams, a Muhurta being 48 minutes.

duties, and finally, after a brief reading of the Vedas, retire to bed. Any special duty should be attended to when it presents itself; as to these no rule can be laid down.

The general principle of this is that a man's life should be orderly, regulated, and balanced, due time being given to each part of his duty so that none should be slighted or omitted, and none allowed to monopolise his time. Above all he should realise the idea that man has no separate individual existence, but is indissolubly linked with the universe, and his whole life must be a life of sacrifice and duties, if he is to fulfil the very law of his being. Such deliberate regulation of life is wise—necessary, even, is the most is to be made of life—and conduces to peacefulness and absence of hurry. In modern life the details cannot be carried out but the general principle of regularity, balance and a sustained spirit of self-sacrifice and duty should be maintained, so that all-round and harmonious progress may be made.

CHAPTER V

WORSHIP

We have already seen that the work of the Devas was recognised and duly honored among the Âryans, and that the duty of sacrificing for their support was regularly performed. But the truly religious man's relations with the invisible powers are not confined to these regular and formal sacrifices. Ishvara Himself, the Supreme Lord, will attract the heart of the thoughtful and pious man, who sees, beyond these many ministers, the King Himself, the ruling Power of His universe, the life and support of Devas and men alike. It is towards Him that love and devotion naturally rise—the human spirit, who is His offspring, a fragment of Himself, seeking to rise and unite himself to his parent. These feelings cannot find satisfaction in sacrifices offered to Devas, connected as they are with the outer words, with the not-self; they seek after the inner, the deepest, the very self, and remain craving and unsatisfied until they rest in Him.

Worship is the expression of this craving of the part for the whole, of the separate for the one, and is not only due from man to the source of his life, but is a necessary stage in the evolution of all those higher qualities in the jivatma which make possible his liberation and his union with the Supreme. An object of worship is therefore necessary to man.

That object will always be, to the worshipper, the Supreme Being. He will know intellectually that the object of his worship is a form of manifestation of the Supreme, but emotionally that form is the Supreme—as in truth it is, although the Supreme includes and transcends all forms.

Now a form is necessary for worship. The Nirguna Brahman, the absolute, the all, cannot be an object of worship. It is not an object, but is beyond all subject and object, including all, in separate. But from that

वाचो निवर्तन्त अप्राप्य मनसा सह॥[220]

"Words return with the mind, not having reached."
Words fall into silence, mind disappears, it is all in all.

The Saguna Brahman may be the object of worship for those whose minds are of a metaphysical nature, and who find rest and peace in the contemplation of Brahman in his own nature as Sat-Chit-Ananda, the universal self, the one, the Supreme. Such contemplation is worship of a lofty kind, and is peculiarly congenial to philosophic minds, who find in it the sense of peace, rest, unity, which they cannot feel in any more limited conception. But to most it is easier to rise to Him through His manifestation as the Lord and life of His worlds, or through one of the manifestations, as Mahadeva Narayana, or more concrete yet, Shri Rama or Shri Krishna, or other embodiment. These arouse in them the bhakti, the love and devotion, which the other conception fails to stir, and all the tendrils of the human heart wind themselves round such an image, and lift the heart into ananda, into bliss unspeakable.

Whether one of these two ways is the better is an oft-disputed question, and the answerers on either side are apt to be impatient with those on the other, intolerant of the uncongenial way. But the answer has been given with perfect wisdom and all-embracing comprehension by Shri Krishna himself. Arjuna was troubled by the question, five thousand years ago, and put it to his divine teacher:

एवं सततयुक्ता ये भक्तास्त्वां पर्युपासते ।
ये चाप्यचरमव्यक्तं तेषां के योगवित्तमा: ॥
श्रीभगवानुवाच ।
मय्यावेश्य मनो ये मां नित्ययुक्ता उपासते ।
श्रद्धया परयोपेतास्ते मे युक्ततमा मता: ॥
ये त्वक्षरमनिर्देश्यमव्यक्तं पर्युपासते ॥
सर्वत्रगमचिंत्यं च कूटस्थमचलं ध्रुवम् ॥
सीनयम्यन्द्रिय ग्रामं सर्वत्र समबुद्धय: ।
ते प्राप्नुवन्ति मामेव सर्वभूतहिते रता: ॥
क्लेशोऽधिकतरस्तेषामव्यक्तासक्तचेतसाम् ।
अव्यक्ता हि गातदु:खं देहवद्भिरवाप्यते ।

---
[220]*Taittiriyop.* 11, iv, I.

ये तु सर्वाणि कर्माणि मयि संन्यस्य मत्पराः।
अनन्येनैव योगेन मां ध्यायत उपासते ॥
तेषामहं समुद्धर्ता मृत्युसंसारसागरात् ।
भवामि न चिरात्पार्थ मय्यावेशितचेतसाम् ॥[221]

"Those Bhaktas, who, ever controlled, worship thee, and those also (who worship) the indestructible, the unmanifested, of these which are the more skilled in Yoga?

"The Blessed Lord said:

"They who with manas fixed on me, ever controlled, worship me, with faith Supreme endowed, these I hold as best in Yoga.

"They who worship the indestructible, the ineffable, the unmanifested, the omnipresent, the unthinkable, the unchangeable, the immutable, the eternal.

"Renouncing and subduing the senses, everywhere equal-minded, in the welfare of all creatures rejoicing, these also come unto Me.

"Greater is the difficulty of those whose minds are set on the unmanifested, for the path of the unmanifested is hard for the embodied to reach.

"Those verily who, renouncing all actions in Me and intent on Me, worship, meditating on Me with whole-hearted Yoga,

"These I speedily lift up from the ocean of death and existence, O Partha, their minds being fixed on Me."

This is the final answer; both achieve, both gain mukti, but the worship of Ishvara in a form is easier than the worship of Him without a form, and escape from the cycle of rebirth is easier for those who thus worship.

The simplest form of worship is that generally spoken of as paja, in which an image representing some divine form is used as the object, and the being thus represented is adored; flowers are used, as beautiful symbols of the heart-flowers of love and reverence; water is sanctified with a mantra, poured on the image, and sprinkled over the worshipper; a mantra, in which the name of the object of worship occurs, is repeated inaudibly a certain number of times, and the invisible bodies are thus rendered receptive of His influence, as before explained (see p. 168).

---

[221] *Bhagavad-Gita.* xii. 1–7.

Then the worshipper passes on according to his nature into spontaneous praise or prayer, aspiration and meditation, and becoming oblivious of the external object, rising to the one imaged in that object, and often feeling His presence, becomes suffused with peace and bliss. Such worship steadies the mind, purifies and ennobles the emotions, and stimulates the unfolding of the germinal spiritual faculties.

The use of an image in such worship is often found most helpful, and is well-nigh universal. It gives an object to which the mind can at first be directed and thus steadiness is obtained. If it be well chosen, it will attract the emotions, and the symbols, always present in such an image, will direct the mind to the characteristic properties of the object of worship. Thus the lingam is the symbol of the great pillar of fire, which is the most characteristic manifestation of Mahadeva, the destroying element which consumes all dross but only purifies the gold. The four-armed Vishnu represents the protecting support of the deity, whose arms uphold and protect the four quarters, and the objects held in the hands are symbols of His creative, ruling, destroying, forces, and of the universe He governs. The Shalagrama is used in the household as the symbol of Vishnu. But all these are already familiar.

When the worshipper passes from the external worship to the internal, the image is reproduced mentally and carries him on into the invisible world, where it may change into a living form, animated by the one it represents. Further, a properly prepared image—sanctified by mantras and by the daily renewed forces of the worshipper's devotion—becomes a strong magnetic centre from which issue powerful vibrations, which regularise and steady the invisible bodies of the worshipper, and thus assist him in gaining the quiet and peaceful conditions necessary for effective prayer and meditation.

Apart from these definite uses, the bhakta feels a pleasure in contemplating such an image, similar in kind to, but greater in degree than, any one finds in having with him the picture of a beloved but absent friend.

For all these reasons, no one should object to the use of images in religious worship by those who find them helpful; nor should any one try to force their use on those who are not helped by them. Tolerance in these matters is the mark of the truly religious man.

The special form to which puja is addressed is sometimes the Kula-deva, or Kula-devi, the family Deva or Devi, and sometimes is the one chosen for the worshipper by his Guru, or chosen by himself as the one which most appeals to him. This Form is the Ishta-deva, the Deva sacrificed to, or desired.

Other forms of worship are generally classed under the name Upasani. Flowers are not employed, nor is an image necessary, though it is often used, for the reasons already given. The daily sandhya is a form of such worship in which all students should be properly instructed. It is of two types, Vaidika and Tantrika, and varies according to caste and family customs. The complicated sandhya ceremony as performed nowadays in various parts of India does not exactly represent the oldest form of it, as taught in the *Taittiriya Brahmana*, and the early smritis. But the Arghya-pradana to the Sun and the meditation on and recitation of the Gayatri, which form the heart of the ceremony, are the oldest parts of it too. Unless it is performed at the proper sandhyas it cannot be of much profit to the performer. A sandhya is the meeting point of two periods of time, great or small, or of two different states of one and the same subject. It is the teaching of the ancient rishis of India that at sandhyas there is always a special manifestation of force which vanishes when the sandhya is past.

The broad features are:

1. Achamana and Marjana, purifying the body with water sanctified by a mantra.
2. Pranayama, control of the breath.
3. Agha-marshana, expiatory of all sins to which the ego, not the personality, is attached; the worshipper goes back in mind to the time when there was no manifestation and no sins.
4. Gâyatrî, either Vaidika or Tantrika, followed by
5. Worship of the Sun-God—Arghya and Upasthâna.
6. Japa, recitation, a certain number of times, of the Mantra of the Ishta-deva, including adoration and salutation.

The Vaidika sacrifices and samskaras are mostly out of use, but this sandhya Vandana is a living thing, the last remnant, and the student must jealously keep to it and must perform it every day.

Another kind of Upasana is meditation, and the treatise of Patanjali, the *Patanjala-sutrani,* should here be carefully studied, when the time for systematic meditation arrives. In student days the due performance of sandhya and of some form of Puja may suffice, but the theoretical outline of the practice of meditation may be given. Says Patanjali;

यमनियमासनप्राणायामप्रत्याहारधारणा
ध्यानसमाययोऽष्टावङ्गानि।[222]

"Yama, Niyama, Asana, Pranayama, Praty ahara, Dharana, Dhyana, Samadhi—the eight limbs."

The first two of these, Yama and Niyama, have to do with conduct, for without good conduct and purity there can be no meditation.

तत्राहिंसासत्यास्तेय ब्रह्मचर्याऽपरिग्रहा यमाः[223]

"Harmlessness, truth, honesty, chastity, absence of greed—(these are) Yamas."

शोचसंतोषतपः स्वाध्यायेश्वरप्रणिधानानि नियमाः।[224]

"Purity, contentment, austerity, Veda-study, yearning after Ishvara—(these are) Niyamas."

These qualities acquired, a man may sit for meditation. There are two preliminaries. Any posture which is steady and pleasant is suitable :

स्थिरसुखमासनम्।[225]

"Firm, pleasant—(that is) Asana."

Pranayama is the regulation of the breath, and this has to be learned from a teacher.

Then comes the immediate preparation, the closing of the senses against external objects, and the drawing of them and placing them in the mind: this is Pratyahara.

---

[222]*Op. rit.* ii. 29.
[223]*Ibid.* 30.
[224]*Ibid.* 32.
[225]*Ibid.* 46.

Now follows meditation proper, consisting of three stages, Dharana, Dhyana and Samadhi.

देशबन्धश्चित्तस्य धारणा।[226]

"The binding of the mind to (one) object is Dharana."

This is concentration, the steadying of the mind on one point, in one place, so that it is fixed, one pointed. Only such a mind can pass on to Dhyana.

तंत्र प्रत्ययैकतानता ध्यानम्।[227]

"The steady (and uninterrupted) flow of cognition towards that (object) is Dhyana."

When this is reached, the mind, fixing itself thus, loses the consciousness of itself and remains identified with the object of thought, and this state is samadhi.

तदेवार्थमात्रनिर्भासं स्वरूपशून्यमिव समाधिः।[228]

"That same (Dhyana) showing the object only, and devoid, as it were, of self-consciousness, (is) Samadhi."

These are the preparations for and the stages of meditation. By this a man rises to knowledge, by this he loses himself in the divine Being he worships; by this he disengages himself from the bonds of action. Without meditation no truly spiritual life is possible.

Manu has declared, after describing the life of the Sannyasi :

ध्यानिकं सर्वमेवैतद्यदेतदभिशब्दितम् ।
न ह्यनध्यात्मवित्कश्चित्क्रियाफलमुपाश्नुते ॥

"All this that has here been declared depends on meditation; for no one who does not know the Supreme self can fully enjoy the fruit of rites."

It is therefore a thing to be looked forward to and prepared for, and every student who desires the higher life should begin his preparation by practising Yama and Niyama.

---

[226]*Ibid.* iii. 1.
[227]*Ibid.* 2.
[228]*Ibid.* 3.

CHAPTER VI

THE FOUR ASHRAMAS

The student will have noticed the extremely systematic and orderly arrangement of life which characterises the Sanâtana Dharma. It is in full keeping with this, that the whole life should be arranged on a definite system, designed to give opportunity for the development of the different sides of human activity and assigning to each period of life its due occupations and training. Life was regarded as a school in which the powers of the Jivatma were to be evolved, and it was well or ill spent according as this object was well or ill achieved.

The life was divided into four stages, or Ashramas: that of the ब्रह्मचारी, Brahmachari, the student, bound to celibacy; that of the गृहस्थ:, Grihasthah, the householder; that of the वानप्रस्थ:, Vanaprasthah, the forest-dweller; that of the Hearai Sannyasi, the ascetic, called also the यति, Yatih, the controlled, or the endeavourer.

ब्रह्मचारी गृहस्थश्च वानप्रस्थो यतिस्तथा
एते गृहस्थप्रभवाश्चत्वार: पृथगाश्रमा: ||[229]

"The Student, the Householder, the Forest dweller, the Ascetic—these, the four separate orders, spring from the Householder."

A man should pass through these regularly, and not enter any prematurely. Only when each had been completed might he enter the next.

वेदानधीत्य वेदो वा वेदं वापि यथाक्रमम् ।
अविप्लुतब्रह्मचर्यो गृहस्थाश्रममावसेत् ||[230]

"Having studied the Vedas, or two Vedas, or even one Veda, in due order, without breaking celibacy, let him dwell in the householder order."

गृहस्थस्तु यदा पश्येद्वलीपलितमात्मन: ।
अपत्यस्य तथापत्यं तदारण्यं समाश्रयेत् ||[231]

---

[229] *Manusmriti*.vi. 87.
[230] *Ibid*. iii. 2.
[231] *Ibid*. vi. 2.

"When the householder sees wrinkles (in his skin) and whiteness (in his hair) and the son of his son, then let him retire to the forest."

वनेषु तु विहृत्यैवं तृतीयं भागमायुष: ।
चतुर्थमायुषो भागं त्यक्त्वा सङ्गान् परिव्रजेत् ।।[232]

"Having passed the third portion of life in the forests, let him, having abandoned attachments, wander (as an ascetic) the fourth portion of life."

This succession is regarded as so important for the due development of the Jivatma, and the proper ordering of society, that Manu says:

अनधीत्य द्विजो वेदाननुत्पाद्य तथा प्रजाम् ।
अनिष्ट्वा चैव यज्ञैश्च मोक्षमिच्छन् व्रजत्यध: ।।[233]

"A twice-born man who seeketh Moksha without having studied the Vedas, without having produced offspring, and without having offered sacrifices, goeth downwards."

The offering of sacrifices, we shall see, is the chief duty of the forest-dweller, and therefore indicates the Vanaprastha state.

In rare and exceptional cases a student was allowed to became a Sannyasi, his debts to the world having been fully paid in a previous birth; but these rare cases left the regular order unshaken. Strictly speaking, indeed, even he was not called a Sannyasi, and did not receive the initiations of Sannyasa proper; but was called a Bala or Naishthika Brahmachari, like Shuka and the Kumara Rishis. The great multiplication of young Sannyasis found in modern days is directly contrary to the ancient rules, and causes much vice and trouble and impoverishment of the country.

We will now consider the Ashramas in order.

The student life began, as we have seen, with the Upanayana ceremony, the boy being then committed to the care of his teacher, with whom he lived while his pupilage continued. His life there after was simple and hardy, intended to make him strong and healthy, independent of all soft and luxurious living, abstemious and devoid of ostentation. He was to rise before sunrise and bathe and then perform sandhya

---

[232]*Ibid.* 33.
[233]*Ibid.* 37.

during the morning twilight till the sun rose; if it rose while he was still sleeping, he had to fast during the day, performing Japa. Then he went out to beg for food which was placed at his teacher's disposal, and was to take the portion assigned to him cheerfully:

पूजयेदशनं नित्यमद्याच्चैतदकुत्सयन् ।
दृष्ट्वा हृष्येत्प्रसीदेच्च प्रतिनन्दच्च सर्वश: ॥
पूजितं ह्यशनं नित्यं बलभूर्जं च यच्छति ।
अपूजितं तु तद्भुक्तमुभयं नाशयदिदम् ॥[234]

"Let him ever honour (his) food, and eat it with out contempt; having seen it, let him be glad and pleased, and in every way welcome it.

"Food which is honoured ever gives strength and nerve-vigour; eaten unhonoured, it destroys both these."

The day was to be spent in study and in the service of his teacher:

नोदितो गुरुणा नित्यमप्रणोदित एव वा।
कुर्यादध्ययने योगमाचार्यस्य हितेषु च ॥[235]

"Directed or not directed by his teacher, let him ever engage in study, and in doing benefits to his preceptor."

At sunset he was again to worship till the stars appeared. Then the second meal was taken. Between these two meals he was generally not to eat, and he was enjoined to be temperate as to his food.

अनारोग्यमनायुष्यमस्वर्यं चातिभोजनम् ।
अपुण्यं लोकविद्विष्टं तस्मात्तत्परिवर्जयेत् ।[236]

"Over-eating is against health, long life, (the attainment of) heaven and merit, and is disapproved by the world; therefore let him avoid it."

The rules laid down as to his general conduct show how frugality, simplicity and hardiness were enforced, so that the youth mnight grow into a strong and vigorous man; it was the training of a nation of energetic, powerful, nobly-mannered and dignified men.

वर्जयेन्मधु मांसं च गन्धमाल्यं रसांस्त्रिय:।
शुक्तानि चैव सर्वाणि प्राणिनां चैव हिंसनम् ।

---

[234] *Manusmriti.* ii. 54, 55.
[235] *Manusmriti.* ii. 191.
[236] *Ibid.* 57.

अभ्यङ्गमञ्जनं चाक्षणोरुपानञ्छत्तधारणम् ।
कामं क्रोधं च लोभं च नर्तनं गीतवादनम् ।
द्यूतं च जनवादं च पारवादं तथानृतम् ।
स्त्रीणां च प्रेक्षणालम्भमुपघातं परस्य च ॥
एक: शयीत सर्वत्र न रेत: स्कन्दयेत् कचित् ।
कामाद्धि स्कन्दयन् रेतो हिनस्ति व्रतमात्मन: ॥
स्वप्ने सिक्त्वा ब्रह्मचारी द्विज: शुक्रमकामत: ।
स्नात्वार्कमर्चयित्वा त्रि: पुनार्मामित्यूचं जपेत् ॥[237]

"Let him refrain from wine, meat, perfumes, garlands, tasty and savoury dishes, women, all acids, and from injury to sentient creatures.

"From unguents, collyrium to the eyes, the wearing of shoes and umbrellas, from lust, anger and greed, dancing, singing and playing on musical instruments.

"Dice-playing, gossip, slander and untruth, from staring at and touching women, and from striking others.

"Let him always sleep alone, and let him not waste his seed; he who from lust wastes his seed, destroys his vow (and its valuable fruits.)

"A twice-born Brahmachari who loses seed in sleep without lust, having bathed and worshipped the sun, should repeat the rik, पुनर्मांम् etc., three times."

The student will see that all the injunctions of Manu above quoted apply perfectly to the present day, except the prohibition as to shoes and umbrellas. Changed social conditions make modifications necessary on this point, as well as on certain other matters not included in the quotation.

The great stress laid upon chastity and purity during youth is due to the fact that the vigour and strength of manhood, freedom from disease, heal thy children, and long life, depend more on this one virtue of complete continence than on any other one thing, self-abuse being the most fertile breeder of disease and premature decay. The old legislators and teachers therefore made a vow of celibacy part of the obligation of the student, and the very name of the student, the Brahmachari, has become synonymous with one who is under a vow of celibacy. The injunction quoted above, to avoid dancing, singing, playing on musical

---

[237]*Manusmriti.* ii. 177–181.

instruments, dicing, gossip, staring at and touching women, has as aim to keep the lad out of the company and the amusements that might lead him into forgetfulness of his vow, and into temptations for its breach. The simple food, the hard work, the frugal living, all build up a robust body, and inure it to hardships.

Over and over again Manu speaks on this:

इन्द्रियाणां विचरतां विषयेष्वपहारिषु ।
संयमे यत्नमातिष्ठेद्विद्वान्यन्तेव वाजिनाम् ॥[238]

"Let the wise man exercise assiduity in the restraint of the senses, wandering among alluring objects, as the driver (restrains) the horses,"

वशे कृत्वेन्द्रियग्रामं संयम्य च मनस्तथा ।
सान्संसाधयेदर्थानक्षिण्वन्योगतस्तनुम् ॥[239]

"Having brought into subjection all his senses, and also regulated his mind, he may accomplisli' all his objects by Yoga, without emaciating his body,"

The *Chhandogyopanishat* declares that Yajna, Ishta, the feeding of the poor, the dwelling in forests, are all summed up in Brahmacharya, and that the third heaven of Brahma is only thus obtained.[240]

The practice of self-control and complete continence was rendered much more easy than it would otherwise have been, by the care bestowed on the physical development and training of youth by physical exercises and manly games of all kinds. In the *Ramayana* and the *Mahabharata,* we read of the way in which the youths were practised in the use of weapons, in riding and driving, in sports and feats of skill. These physical exercises formed a definite part of their education, and contributed to the building up of a vigorous and healthy frame.

Having thus fulfilled, in study and strict chastity, the student period, the youth was to present his teacher with a gift, according to his ability, and return home to enter the household life.

Then, and then only, he was to take a wife, and the responsibilities of man's estate. After marriage, great temperance in sexual relations

---

[238] *Manusmriti.* ii. 88.
[239] *Manusmriti.* ii. 100.
[240] *Loc. cit.* VIII. iv. 3 and v. I-4.

was enjoined, marital connexion being only permissible on any one of ten nights in a month (see *Manu,* iii. 45–49). Women were to be honoured and loved, else no welfare could attend the home:

पितृभिर्भातृभिश्चैताः पतिभिर्देवरैस्तथा॥
पूज्या भूषयितव्याश्च बहुकल्याणमीप्सुभिः॥
यत्र नार्यस्तु पूज्यन्ते रमन्ते तत्र देवताः।
यत्र तास्तु न पूज्यन्ते सर्वास्तत्राफलाः क्रियाः॥
शोचन्ति जामयो यत्र विनश्यत्याशु तत्कुलम् ।
न शोचन्ति तु यत्रैता वर्धते तद्धि सर्वदा॥241

"They must be honoured and adorned by fathers brothers, husbands and brothers-in-law, desiring, welfare.

"Where women are honoured, there verily the Devas rejoice; where they are not honoured, there indeed all rites are fruitless.

"Where the female relatives grieve, there the family quickly perishes; where they do not grieve, that family always prospers."

संतुष्टो भार्यया भर्ता भर्ना भार्या तथैव च ।
यस्मिन्नेव कुले नित्यं कल्याणं तत्र वै ध्रुवम् ॥242

"In the family in which the husband is contented with his wife, and the wife, with the husband, there happiness is ever sure."

The Grihastha is the very heart of Âryan life; every thing depends on him.

यथा वायु समाश्रित्य सर्वे जीवन्ति जन्तवः ।
तथा गृहस्थमाश्रित्य वर्तन्त इतराश्रमाः ॥243

"As all creatures live supported by air, so the other orders exist supported by the householder."

सर्वेषामपि चौतेषाम् वेदश्रुतिविधानतः ।
गृहस्थ उच्यते श्रेष्ठः स त्रीनेतान्बिभर्ति हि ॥
यथा नदीनदाः सर्वे सागरे यान्ति संस्थितिम् ।
तथैवाश्रमिणः सर्वे गृहस्थे यान्ति संस्थितिम् ॥244

---

[241] *Manusmriti.* iii. 55–57.
[242] *Manusmriti.* iii. 60.
[243] *Ibid.* 77.
[244] *Ibid.* 89–90.

"Of all these, by the precepts of the Veda-shruti, the householder is called the best; he verily supports the other three.

"As all streams and rivers flow to rest in the ocean, so all the Ashramas flow to rest in the householder,"

Hence the householder is the best of the orders, ज्येष्ठाश्रमो गृहीं. He has the duty of accumulating wealth-in this the Vaishya is the typical householder—and of distributing it rightly. Hospitality is one of his chief duties, and in this he must never fail.

तृणानि भूमिरुदकं वाक् चतुर्थी च सूनृता।
एतान्यपि सतां गेहे नोच्छिद्यन्ते कदाचन ॥[245]

"Grasses, Earth, water, the kind word, these four are never lacking in the houses of the good."

He must ever feed first his guests, Brahmanas, his relatives and his servants, and then he and his wife should eat, but even before these he should serve brides, infants, the sick, and pregnant women,[246]

The householder must duly offer the five great sacrifices, and by Brahmana householders the duty of the monthly shraddhas should be observed. The Brahmana should maintain his studies, and not follow occupations which prevent study, but earn his living in some business that does not injure others.[247] Careful rules are laid down for conduct, which will be dealt with in Part III, as they belong to the general conduct of life, the householder being the typical human being. His special virtues are hospitality, industry, truth, honesty, liberality, charity, purity of food and life. He may enjoy wealth and luxury, provided he give alms.

The householder may quit the household life, and become a Vanaprastha, going to the forest when, as before said, he is growing old and has grand-children. His wife may go with him, or remain with her sons, and he goes forth, taking with him the sacred fire and sacrificial instruments. His duty to the world is now to help it by prayer and sacrifice, and he is accordingly to continue to offer the five daily sacrifices, together with the Agni hotra, the new and full moon sacrifices

---
[245] *Ibid.* 101.
[246] *Ibid.* 114–116.
[247] *Ibid.* 2.

and others. The rule of his life is to be sacrifice, study, austerity, and kindness to all:

स्वाध्याये नित्ययुक्त: स्याद्दान्तो मैत्र: समाहित: ।
दाता नित्यमनादाता सर्वभूतानुकम्पक: ॥[248]

"Let him ever be engaged in Veda study, con trolled, friendly, collected; ever a giver, not a receiver, compassionate to all beings."

This simple ascetic life leads him on to the last stage, that of the Sannyasi, the man who has renounced all. He no longer offers sacrifices, having given all his property away; he lives alone, with tree for shelter, his life given to meditation.

अनग्निरनिकेत: स्याद् ग्राममन्नार्थमाश्रयेत्।
उपेक्षकोऽसंकुसुको मुनिर्भावसमाहित: ॥[249]

"Let him be without fire, without dwelling, let him go to a village for food, indifferent, firm of purpose, a muni of collected mind."

Then follows a beautiful description of the true Sannyasi:

नाभिनन्देत मरणं नाभिनन्देत जीवितम् ।
कालमेव प्रतीक्षेत निर्देशं भृतको यथा ॥
दृष्टिपूतं न्यसेत्पादं वस्त्रपूतं जलं पिवेत् ।
सत्यपून वदेद्वाचं मन:पूतं समाचरेत् ॥
अतिवादांस्तितिक्षेत नावमन्येत कंचन ।
न चेमं देहमाश्रित्य वैरं कुर्वीत केनचित् ॥
क्रुध्यन्तं न प्रतिक्रुध्येदाक्रुष्ट: कुशलं वदेत् ।
सप्तद्वारावकीर्णा च न वाचमनृतां वदेत् ॥
अध्यात्मरतिरानीनो निरपेक्षा निरामिष: ।
आत्मनैव सहायन सुखार्थी विचरेदिह ॥[250]

"Let him not wish for death, let hiin not wish for life, let him wait for the time, as a servant for his wages.

"Let him set feet purified (guided) by sight, let him drink water purified by (strained through a) cloth, let him speak words purified by truth, let him do acts purified (governed) by reason.

---

[248] *Manusmriti.* vi. 8.
[249] *Ibid.* 43.
[250] *Manusmriti.* vi. 45–49.

"Let him endure harsh language, and let him not insult any one ; nor, relying on this (perishable) body, let him make an enemy of any one.

"Let him not return anger to the angry, let him bless when cursed ; let him not utter lying speech, scattered at the seven gates (*i.e.* speech showing desire for the fleeting and false objects of the five outer senses and manas and buddhi.)

"Rejoicing in the Supreme self, sitting indiffer ent, refraining from sensual delights, with himself for his only friend, let him wander here on the Earth), aiming at liberation."

He is to meditate constantly on transmigration and suffering, on the Supreme self and Its presence in high and low alike, to trace the Jivatma through its many births, and to rest in Brahman alone. Thus doing, he reaches Brahman.

Such were the four Ashramas of Sanâtana Dharma, designed for the training of man to the highest ends. In modern days they cannot be completely revived in their letter, but they might be revived in their spirit, to the great improvement of modern life. The student period must now be passed in school and college, for the most part, instead of in the Ashrama of the Guru ; but the same principles of frugal, hardy, simple living might be carried out, and Brahmacharya miglit be universally enforced. The Gsihastha ideal, coinmenced at marriage, might be very largely followed in its sense of duty and responsibility, in its discharge of religious obligations, in its balanced ordering of life, in its recognition of all claims, of all debts. The third Ashrama could not be lived in the forest by many, and the fourth Ashrama is beyond the reach of most in these days; but the idea of the gradual withdrawal from worldly life, of the surrender of the conduct of business into the hands of the younger generation, of the making of meditation, study and worship the main duties of life—all this could be carried out. And the presence of such aged and saintly men would sanctify the whole community, and would serve as a constant reminder of the dignity and reality of the religious life, setting up a noble ideal, and raising, by their example, the level of the whole society.

A life which is well-ordered from beginning to end—that is what is implied in the phrase "The four Ashramas." Two of them—namely that of the student and that of the householder-may be said to represent in the life of an, individual that outward-going energy which carries the Jiva into the Pravritti Marga. The two later stages—the life of the Vanaprastha and that of the Sannyasi these are the stages of withdrawal from the world, and may be said to represent the Nivritti Marga in the life of the individual. So wisely did the ancient ones mark out the road along which a man should tread, that any man who takes this plan of life, divided into four stages, will find his outgoing and indrawing energies rightly balanced. First, the student stage, properly lived and worthily carried out; then the householder stage, with all its busy activity in every direction of worldly business; then the gradual withdrawal froin activity, the turning in ward, the life of comparative seclusion, of prayer and of meditation, of the giving of wise counsel to the younger generation engaged in worldly activities; and then, for some at least, the life of complete renunciation.

It must not be forgotten that the passing through these Ashramas and the reaching of liberation has for its object—as we may see from the stories of muktas in the Puranas and Itihasas—the helping on of the worlds, and the co-operating with Ishivara in His benevolent administration, and His guidance of evolution. In the outward life of Sannyasa the Jiyatma learns detachment and in difference, but the highest Sannyasa is that of the inner, not that of the outer life, in which a man, who is completely detached and indifferent, iningles in the life of men for their helping and uplifting.

अनाश्रित: कर्मफलं कार्य कर्म करोति य:।
स सन्यासी च योगीच न निरग्निर्न चाक्रिय:॥[251]

"He who performeth such action as is duty, in dependently of the fruit of action, he is a Sannyasi and Yogi also, not he that is without fire and rites."

Such a man lives in the midst of objects of attachment and is yet without attachment, regarding nothing as his own though possessed of wealth. He then becomes the ideal householder, whom the Grihastha reflects, and verifies in its fullest sense the dictum of Manu, that the

---

[251] *Bhagavad-Gita* iv, i.

householder's order is the highest of all because it is the support of all. And the household life is truly lived only where a man sets before himself that high ideal of administrator rather than owner, servant rather than master of all.

CHAPTER VII

THE FOUR CASTES

Just as the Four Ashramas serve as a school for the unfolding of the Jivatma during a single life, so do the Four Castes serve as a similar school for its unfolding during a part of the whole period of its transmigrations. Looked at in the broadest sense, they represent the complete period, but, as an external system, the Jivatma is in them only for a portion of his pilgrimage. The present confusion of castes has largely neutralised the use they once served. In the ancient days the Jivatma was prepared for entrance into each caste through a long preliminary stage outside India; then he was born into India and passed into each caste to receive its definite lessons; then was born away from India to practice these lessons; usually returning to India, to the highest of them, in the final stages of his evolution.

It is necessary to see the great principles underlying the Caste System in order to estimate its advantages at their proper value; and also in order to distinguish rightly between these fundamental principles and the numerous non-essential, and in many cases mischievous, accretions which have grown up around it, and have become interwoven with it, in the course of ages.

The first thing to understand is that the evolution of the Jivatma is divided into four great stages, and that this is true of every Jivatma, and is in no sense peculiar to those who, in their outer coverings, are Âryans and Hindus. Jivatmas pass into and out of the Hindu Religion, but every Jivatma is in one or other of the four great stages. These belong to no age and to no civilisation, to no race and no nation. They are universal, of all times and of all races.

The first stage is that which embraces the infancy, childhood and youth of the Jivatma, during which he is in a state of pupilage, fit only for service and study, and has scarcely any responsibilities.

The second stage is the first half of his manhood, during which he carries on the ordinary business of the world, bears the burden of household responsibilities, so to say, the accumulation, enjoyment and proper disposal of wealth, together with the heavy duties of organising, training and educating his youngers in all the duties of life.

The third stage occupies the second half of his manhood, during which he bears the burden of national responsibilities, the duty of protecting, guiding, ruling, others, and utterly subordinating his individual interests to the common good, even to the willing sacrifice of his own life for the lives around him.

The fourth stage is the old age of the Jivatma, when his accumulated experiences have taught him to see clearly the valuelessness of all earth's treasures, and have inade him rich in wisdom and compassion, the selfless friend of all, the teacher and counsellor of all his youngers,

These stages are, as said above, universal. The peculiarity of the Sanâtana Dharma is that these four universal stages have been made the foundation of a social polity, and have been represented by four definite external castes, or classes, the characteristics laid down, as belonging to each caste being those which characterise the stage of the universal evolution to which the caste corresponds.

The first stage is represented by the Shudra caste, in which, as we shall see, the rules are few and the responsibilities light. Its one great duty is that of service; its virtues are those which should be evolved in the period of youth and pupilage—obedience, fidelity, reverence, industry and the like.

The second stage is represented by the Vaishya, the typical householder, on whom the social life of the nation depends. He comes under strict rules, designed to foster unselfishness and the sense of responsibility, to nourish detachment in the midst of possession, and to make him feel the nation as his household. His virtues are diligence, caution, prudence, discretion, charity, and the like.

The third stage is represented by the Kshattriya, the ruler and warrior, on whom depends the national order and safety. He also lives under strict rules, intended to draw out all the energy and strength of his character and to turn them to unselfish ends, and to make him feel that everything he possesses, even life itself, must be thrown away at the call of duty. His virtues are generosity, vigour, courage, strength, power to rule, self control, and the like.

The fourth stage is represented by the Brahmana, the teacher and priest, who lives under the strictest of all rules directed to make himn a centre of purifying influence, physically as well as morally and spiritually. He is to have outgrown the love of wealth and power, to be devoted to study, learned and wise. He is to be the refuge of all crea tures, their sure help in time of need. His virtues are gentleness, patience, purity, self-sacrifice, and the like.

The Jivatma who, in any nation, at any tiine, shows out these types of virtues, belongs to the stage of which his type is characteristic, and, if born in India as a Hindu, should be born into the corresponding caste. In this age one can only say "should be," as the castes are now confused and the types are but rarely found. These characteristic virtues form the "Dharma" of each caste, but these Dharmas are now, unhappily, disregarded.

It is easy to see that the broad dividing lines of classes everywhere follow these lines of caste. The manual labour class, the proletariat—to use the Western term—should consist of Jivatmas in the Shudra stage. The organisers of industry, the merchants, bankers, financiers, large agriculturists, traders, should be Jivatmas in the Vaishya stage. The legislators, warriors, the judicial and administrative services, the statesmen and rulers, should be Jivatmas who are in the Kshattriya stage. And the teachers, *savant*s, clergy, the spiritual leaders, should be Jivatmas in the Brahmana stage. There are Jivatmas of the four types everywhere, and there are social offices of the four kinds everywhere; but now, in the Kali Yuga, the four types of Jivatmas and the four departments of national life are mixed up in inextricable confusion, so that every nation presents a whirl of contending individuals, instead of an organised community moving in harmony in all its parts.

Another fundamental principle of caste was that as the Jivatma advanced, his external liberty, as seen above, became more and more circumscribed and his responsibilities heavier and heavier. The life of the Shudra was easy and irresponsible, with few restrictions as to food, amusement, place of residence or form of livelihood. He could go anywhere and do anything. The Vaishya had to bear the heavy responsibilities of mercantile life, to support needful public institutions with unstinted charity, to devote himself to business with the utmost diligence; and he was required to study, to make sacrifices, to be pure in his diet, and disciplined in his life. The Kshattriya, while wielding power, was worked to the fullest extent, and his laborious life, when he was a monarch, would alarm even a diligent king of the present day; the property, the lives of all, were guarded by the warrior caste, and any man's grievance unredressed was held to dishonour the realm. Heaviest burden of all was laid on the Brahmana, whose physical life was austere and rigidly simple, who was bound by the most minute rules to preserve his physical and magnetic purity, and whose time was spent in study and worship. Thus the responsibility increased with the superiority of the caste, and the individual was expected to subordinate himself more and more to the community. The rigid purity of the Brah mana was far less for his own sake than for that of the nation. He was the source of physical health by his scrupulous cleanliness, continually purifying all the particles of matter that entered his body, and sending forth a pure stream to build the bodies of others, for health and gladness are contagious and infectious, for the same reasons as disease and sorrow. The rules which bound him were not intended to subserve pride and exclusiveness, but to preserve him as a purifying force, physical as well as moral and mental. The whole purpose of the caste system is misconceived, when it is regarded as setting up barriers which intensify personal pride, instead of imposing rules on the higher classes, designed to forward the good of the whole community. As Manu said:

समानाद्ब्राह्मणो नित्यमुद्विजेत विषादिव ।
अमृतस्येव चाकाङ्क्षेदवमानस्य सर्वदा ॥[252]

"Let the Brahmana flee from homage as from venom: let him ever desire indignity as nectar."

Let us now study some of the statements made on this subject in the shruti and smriti.

The general principle laid down above as to the universality of the

---

[252] *Manusmriti*, ii. 162.

four great stages and as to their being founded on natural divisions is enunciated by Shri Krishna:

चातुर्वर्ण्यं मया सृष्टं गुणकर्मविभागशः।
तस्य कर्तारमपि मां विद्धि .... [253]

"The four castes were emanated by me, by the different distribution of the energies (attributes) and actions; know me to be the author of them."

This distribution it is which marks out the castes, and it is not, of course, confined to India. But in the land in which settled the first family of the Âryan stock, the Manu established a model polity or social order, showing in miniature the course of evolution, and into this were born Jivatmas belong ing to the different stages, who showed out the characteristics of the several castes, and thus formed a truly model state. This was "the golden age" of India, and the traditions of this still linger, the splendid background of her history.

When humanity is figured as a vast man or when the Ishvara is spoken of as emanating men, then we have the following graphic picture of the four castes:

ब्राह्मणोऽस्य मुखमासाद्बाहू राजन्यः कृतः।
ऊरू तदस्य यद्वैश्यः पद्भ्यां शूद्रो अजायत ॥[254]

"The Brahmana was His mouth; the Rajanya was made His two arms; His two thighs the Vaishya; the Shudra was born from His two feet."

The teacher is the mouth, and the ruling power the arms; the merchants are the pillars of the nation, as the thighs of the body, while all rest on the manual worker. As we see the facts and necessities of social organisation, we cannot but recognise the inevitableness of the division, whether it be represented or not by a system of four castes.

The virtues that constitute the four castes are thus described by Shri Krishna:

---

[253] *Bhagwad-Gita.* iv. 13.
[254] *Rigveda.* X. xc. 12.

ब्राह्मणक्षत्रियविशां शूद्राणां च परंतप।
कर्माणि प्रविभक्तानि स्वभावप्रभवैर्गुणै: ॥
शमो दमस्तप: शौचं क्षांतिरार्जवमेव च।
ज्ञानं विज्ञानमास्तिक्यं ब्रह्मकर्म स्वभावजम् ॥
शौर्यं तेजो धृतिर्दाक्ष्यं युद्धे चाप्यपलायनम् ।
दानीश्वरभावश्च क्षात्रं कर्म स्वभावजम् ॥
कृषिगोरक्ष्यवाणिज्यं वैश्यकर्म स्वभावजम् ।
परिचर्यात्मकं कर्म शूद्रस्थापि स्वभावजम् ॥[255]

"Of Brahmanas, Kshattriyas, Vaishyas and Shudras, O Parantapa! the Karmas have been distributed according to the Gunas born of their own natures.".

"Serenity, self-restraint, austerity, purity, forgiveness, and also uprightness, wisdom, knowledge, belief in God, are the Brahmana-Karma, born of his own nature."

"Prowess, splendour, firmness, dexterity, and also not fleeing in battle, generosity, rulership are the Kshattriya-Karma, born of his own nature."

"Agriculture, protection of kine, and commerce are the Vaishya-Karma, born of his own nature. Action of the nature of service is the Shudra-karma, born of his own nature,"

Thus clearly are outlined the Dharmas of the four castes, the qualities which should be developed in each of the four great stages of the pilgrimage of the Jivatma through Samsara.

Manu explains the occupations of each caste very clearly:

सर्वस्यास्य तु सर्गस्य गुप्त्यर्थं स महाद्युति: ।
मुखबाहूरुपज्जानां पृथकर्माण्यकल्पयत् ॥
अध्यापनमध्ययनं यजनं याजनं तथा ।
दानं प्रतिग्रहं चैव ब्राह्मणानामकल्पयत् ॥
प्रजानां रक्षणं दानमिज्याध्ययनमेव च ।
विषयेष्वप्रसक्तिं च क्षत्रियस्य समादिशत् ॥
पशूनां रक्षणं दानमिज्याध्ययनमेव च ।
वणिकपथं कुसीदं च वैश्यस्य कृषिमेव च ॥

---

[255]*Bhagavad-Gita*. xviii. 41–44.

एकमेव तु शूद्रस्य प्रभु: कर्म समादिशत् ।
एतेषामेव वर्णानां शुश्रूषामनसूयया ।।²⁵⁶

"He, the Resplendent, for the sake of protecting all this creation, assigned separate Karmas to those born of His mouth, arms, thighs and feet."

"Teaching and studying the Veda, sacrificing and also guiding others in offering sacrifices, gifts and receiving of gifts, these He assigned to the Brahmanas."

"The protection of the people, gists, sacrificing, and study of the Vedas, non-attachment amid the objects of the senses, these He prescribed to the Kshattriyas."

"The protection of cattle, gifts, sacrificing, and study of the Vedas, commerce, banking, and agri culture, to the Vaishyas."

"The Lord commanded one Karma only to the Shadras, to serve ungrudgingly these castes."

Thus the Brahmanas alone might teach the Vedas, but the duty of studying them belonged equally to the three twice-born castes.

A man who did not show forth the Dharma of his caste was not regarded as belonging to it, according to the teachers of the ancient days. We have already seen that ignorant Brahmanas were mere ashes, unfit for the discharge of their duties, and even more strongly Manu says,

यथा काष्ठमयो हस्ती यथा चर्ममयो मृग:।
यश्च विप्रोऽनधीयानत्रयस्ते नामधारका: ।।
योऽनधीत्य द्विजो वेदमन्यत्र कुरुते श्रमम्।
स जीवन्नेव शूद्रत्वमाशु गच्छति सान्वय: ।।²⁵⁷

"As a wooden elephant, as a leathern deer, such is an unlearned Brahmana ; the three bear only names.

"The Brahmana who, not having studied the Vedas, labors elsewhere, becomes a Shudra in that very life together with his descendants."

And again:

---

²⁵⁶*Manusmriti*. i. 87–91.
²⁵⁷*Manusmriti*. ii. 157, 168.

THE FOUR CASTES • 155

शूद्रो ब्राह्मणतामेति ब्राह्मणश्चैव शूद्रताम् ।
क्षत्रियाजातमेवन्तु विद्याद्वैश्यात्तथैव च ।।[258]

"The Shudra becomes a Brahman and a Brahmana a Shudra (by conduct). Know this same (rule to apply) to him who is born of the Kshattriya or of the Vaishya."

So also Yudhishthira, taught the fundamental distinctions, without the existence of which caste becomes a mere name :

सत्यं दानं क्षमा शीलमानृशंस्यं तपो घृणा ।
दृश्यन्ते यत्र नागेन्द्र स ब्राह्मण इति स्मृत:।।
शूद्रे तु यद्भवल्लक्ष्यं द्विजे तञ्च न विद्यते।
नैव शूद्रो भवेच्छूद्रो ब्राह्मणो न च ब्राह्मण:।।
यत्रतल्लक्ष्यते सर्प वृत्त स ब्राह्मण: स्मृत: ।
यत्र नैतत् भवेत् सर्प तं शुद्रमिति निर्दिशेत् ।।[259]

"Truth, gift, forgiveness, good conduct, gentleness, austerity, and mercy, where these are seen, O king of serpents, he is called a Brahmana.

"If these marks exist in a Shudra and are not in a twice-born, the Shudra is not a Shudra, nor the Brahmana a Brahmana.

"Where this conduct is shown, O serpent, he is called a Brahmana; where this is not, o serpent, he should be regarded as a Shudra." .

In the V*ishnu-Bhagavata* we read:

यस्य यल्लक्षणं प्रोक्तं पुंसो वर्णाभिव्यञ्जकम् ।
यदन्यत्रापि दृश्येतं तत् तेनैव विनिर्दिशेत् ।।[260]

"What is said as to the marks of conduct indicative of a man's caste, if those marks are found in another, designate him by the caste of his marks (and not of his birth)."

Commenting on this Shridhara Svami says:

"Brahmanas and others are to be chiefly recognised by Shama and other qualities, and not by their birth alone."

जन्मना जायते शूद्र: संस्कारात् द्विज उच्यते।

---
[258]*Ibid.* x. 65.
[259]*Mahabharata*, Vana parva, clxxx, 21, 25, 26.
[260]*Loc. cit*, VII. xi. 35.

"By birth every one is a Shudra. By Samskara he becomes twice-born."

So also we find that the preceptor Haridrumata of the Gotama gotra, approached by Satyakama, desirous of becoming his pupil, asked him his gotra; the boy answered that his mother did not know his gotra, for he was born when she was engaged in waiting on guests, and he could only go by her name; he was therefore merely Satyakama, the son of Jabala. Haridrumata declared that an an swer so truthful was the answer of a Brahmana, and he would therefore initiate him.[261]

Further it must be remembered :

आचारहीनं न पुनन्ति वेदा:।[262]

"The Vedas do not purify him who is devoid of good conduct."

Much question has arisen as to the possibility of a man passing from one caste to another during a single life. It is, of course, universally granted that a man raises himself from one caste to another by good conduct, but it is generally considered that the conduct bears fruit by birth into a higher caste in the succeeding life. The texts quoted in support of passage from one caste to another will mostly bear this interpretation, just as by degradation from one caste to another rebirth in a lower caste was generally meant. But there are cases on record of such passage during a single life. The history of Vishvamitra, a Kshattriya, becoming a Brahmana is familiar to every one,[263] but equally familiar are the tremendous efforts he made ere he attained his object-a proof of the extreme difficulty of the change. Gargya, the son of Shini, and Trayyaruni, Kavi and Pushkararuni, the sons of Duritakshaya, all Kshattriyas, became Brahmanas, as did Mudgala, son of Bharmyashva, also a Kshattriya.[264] Vitahavya, a Kshattriya, was made a Bralimana by Bhtigy, in whose Ashrama he had taken refuge.[265]

The truth probably is that changes of caste were made in the ancient days, but that they were rare, and that good conduct for the most part took effect in rebirth into a higher caste. Even the famous shloka:

---

[261]*Chhandogyop.* IV, iv.
[262]*Vasishtha-Smriti.* vi, 3.
[263]*Ramayana,* Balakanda lvii—lxv.
[264]*Vishnu Bhagavata,* IX. xxi. 19, 20, 33.
[265]*Mahabharata,* Anushasanaparva, xxx.

न योनिनापि संस्कारो न श्रुतं न च सन्ततिः ।
कारणानि द्विजत्वस्य वृत्तमेव तु कारणं ॥[266]

"Not birth, nor Samskaras, nor study of the Vedas, nor ancestry, are causes of Brahmanahood. Conduct alone is verily the cause thereof," may apply as well to rebirth into a higher caste as to transference into it. In ancient days the immediate present was not as important as it is now, the continuing life of the Jivatma being far more vividly kept in mind, and the workings of karmic law more readily acquiesced in. Nor were the divisions of castes then felt to be an injustice, as they now are when the Dharmas of the castes are neglected, and high caste is accompanied by a feeling of pride instead of by one of responsibility and service.

Innumerable subdivisions have arisen within the great castes, which have no foundation in nature and therefore no stability nor justification. By these much social friction is caused, and petty walls of division are set up, jealousies and rivalries taking the place of the ancient co-operation for the general good. The circles of inter-marriage be come too restricted, and local and unimportant customs become fossilised into religious obliga tions, making social life run in narrow grooves and cramping limitations, tending to provoké rebellion and exasperate feelings of irritation. Moreover, many of the customs regarded as most binding are purely local, customs being vital in the South which are unknown in the North, and *vice versa*. Hence Hindus are split up into innumerable little bodies, each hedged in by a wall of its own, regarded as all important. It is difficult, if not impossible, to create a national spirit from such inharmonious materials, and to induce those who are accustomed to such narrow horizons to take a broader view of life. While a man of one of the four castes, in the old days, felt himself to be an integral part of a nation, a man of a small sub-caste has no sense of organic life, and tends to be a sectarian rather than a patriot.

At the present time a man of any caste takes up any occupation, and makes no effort to cultivate the characteristic virtues of his caste. Hence the inner and the outer no longer accord, and there is jangle

---

[266] *Mahabharata*, Vanaparva, cccxiii. 108.

instead of harmony. No caste offers to incoming jivatmas physical bodies and physical environments fitted for one caste more than for another, and the castes consequently no longer serve as stages for the evolving Jivatmas. Hence the great value of the Hindu system as a graduated school, into which Jivatmas could pass for definite training in each stage, has well-nigh ceased, and the evolution of the human race is thereby delayed.

The caste system is one on which the student, when he goes out into the world, will find great difference of opinion among pious and highly educated men, and he will have to make up his own mind upon it, after careful study and deliberation. It is the system which Manu considered best for the fifth, or, Âryan, race, the Panchajanas, and in its early days ensured order, progress and general happiness, as no other system has done. It has fallen into decay under those most disintegrating forces in human society—pride, exclusiveness, selfishness, the evil brood of Ahamkara wedded to the personal self instead of to the Supreme self.

Unless the abuses which are interwoven with it can be eliminated, its doom is certain ; but equally certain is it, that if those abuses could be destroyed and the system itself maintained, Hinduism would solve some of the social problems which threaten to undermine Western civilisation, and would set an example to the world of an ideal social state.

PART III

ETHICAL TEACHINGS

CHAPTER I

ETHICAL SCIENCE, WHAT IT IS

Morality, or Ethic, is the Science of Conduct, the systematised principles on which a man should act. The conduct of man has reference to his surroundings as well as to himself. We have to ascertain what is good in relation to those who form our surroundings, as well as in relation to the time and place of the actor; and we may take a wider and wider view of our surroundings, according to the knowledge we possess. We have also to ascertain what is good for ourselves and in relation to ourselves What is good for one man may not be good for another man. What is good at one time, and at one place, may not be good at another time, and at another place.

Ethical Science is therefore a relative Science—it is relative to the man himself and to his surroundings.

The object of morality is to bring about happi ness by establishing harmonious relations between all the Jivatmas that belong to any special area; harmonious relations between the members of a family; harmonious relations between the families that make up a community; harmonious relations between the communities that make up a nation; harmonious relations between the nations that make up humanity; harmonious relations between humanity and the other inhabitants of the Earth; harmonious relations between the inhabitants of the Earth and those of other worlds of the system. The great cirme goes on spreading outwards indefinitely, and including larger and larger areas within its circumference. But still, whether the area be large or small, Ethic is "the principles of harmonious relations." Thus we have family morality, social morality, national morality, international morality, human morality, inter-world morality, and all these concern us. With the yet wider sweeps of the Science of Conduct we are not yet concerned, but the basic principle is the same throughout.

It is obvious that the establishment of harmonious relations between a man and his surroundings, near and remote, means happiness. We are always suffering from the want of harmony, from jarring wishes, from friction between ourselves and others, from the lack of mutual support, mutual assistance, mutual sympathy. Where there is harmony there is happiness; where there is disharmony there is unhappiness. Morality, then, in establishing harmony establishes happiness, makes families, and communities and nations and humanity and all dwellers in this and other worlds happy. The ultimate object of Morality, of Ethic, of the Science of Conduct, is to bring about universal Happiness, Universal Welfare, by uniting the separated selves with each other and with the Supreme self. All the six Darshanas are agreed as to this *summum bonum* of man.

The student must grasp this thought, and realise it very clearly. Morality brings about Universal Happiness at last. Let us pause for a mo ment on this word, "Happiness." Happiness does not mean the transitory pleasures of the senses nor even the more durable pleasures of the mind, It does not mean the satisfaction of the cravings of the upadhis, nor the joys which are tasted in the possession of outer objects. Happiness meants the deep, inner, enduring bliss which is the satisfaction in the self. It means perfect harmony, lasting peace. Happiness is:

यत्रोपरमते चित्तं निरुद्धं योगसेवया ।
यत्र चैवात्मनाऽऽत्मानं पश्यन्नात्मनि तुष्यति ॥
सुखमात्यंतिकं यत्सद् बुद्धिग्राह्यमतींद्रियम् ।
वेत्ति यत्र न चैवायं स्थितश्चलति तत्त्वत:॥
यं लब्ध्वा चापरं लाभं मन्यते नाधिकं तत: ।
यस्मिस्थितो न दु:खेन गुरुणापि विचाल्यते ॥[267]

"That in which the mind finds rest, quieted by the practice of Yoga; that in which he, seeing the self by the self, in the self is satisfied;

"That in which he findeth the Supreme delight which the buddhi can grasp, beyond the senses, wherein established, he moveth not from the Reality;

"That which, having obtained, he thinketh there is no greater gain beyond it; wherein established, he is not shaken even by heavy sorrow." Nothing less than this is Happiness, and this is the happiness which

---

[267] *Bhagavad-Gita*, vi. 20–22

Morality brings about. The student must not allow his clear vision of this truth to be clouded by superficial appearances, which seem to be at variance with it. However difficult and painful it inay soinetimes be to do right; how ever tiresome and burdensome obedience to moral precepts may sometimes be; none the less, in the long run, doing right means to be happy, and doing wrong means to be miserable. "As the wheels of the cart follow the ox," said the great Indian teacher, the Buddha, "so misery follows sin," Thus also speak all the Shastras.

All this is inevitable, as we shall see later on. We have spoken of harmony, of happiness, of right, of wrong, and of the inhabitants of the Earth and those of other worlds of the system.

But if we are to go to the root of things, to first principles, we cannot but seek the help of Religion. For Religion gives us the ultimate data upon which Ethical Science may be built. Morality has only one basis, on which it is built up, as a house is built on its foundation. And just as a house will become crooked and fall, if it be built on a shaky foundation, so will any morality fall which is not built on that sound basis.

CHAPTER II

THE FOUNDATION OF ETHICS, AS GIVEN BY RELIGION

(1) The *fir*st thing we learn from religion is the Unity of all selves, and this is the foundation of Ethics. Ethics is built upon:

THE RECOGNITION OF THE UNITY OF THE SELF AMID THE DIVERSITY OF THE NOT-SELF.

There is but One self, and all the separate selves are अशा: amshah, parts or reflections of the One, are the One.

यथा प्रकाशयत्येक: कृत्स्नं लोकमिमं रवि: ।
क्षेत्र क्षेत्री तथा कृत्स्नं प्रकाशयति भारत ।।[268]

"As one sun illuminates this whole world, so the Lord of the Field illuminates the whole Field, O Bharata!"

एको देव: सर्वभूतेषु गूढ: सर्वव्यापी सर्वभूतांतरात्मा।।[269]

"One God is hidden in all beings, all-pervading, the inmost self of all."

One sun is shining, and it shines into every separate place, every separate enclosure. There may be a thousand gardens, separated from each other by high walls, but the one sun shines into all, and the light and heat in each are from the one sun, are parts of himself. So the Jivatmas in all creatures, separated from each other by the walls of prakriti, the walls of their bodies, are rays from the one Sun, sparks from the one Fire, portions of the one Atma, the one self. We cannot fully realise this, be conscious of it and live in it always, until we have become perfectly pure; but we can recognise it as a Fact, as the one all-important Fact, and in proportion as we try to make our conduct accord with this Fact, we shall become moral. We shall see, as we study morality, that all its precepts are founded on this recognition of the unity of the self. If there is only one self, any act by which I

---

[268] *Bhagavad-Gita.* xiii. 33.
[269] *Shvetashratarop.* vi. 11.

injure my neighbour *must* injure me. A man will not deliberately cut his hand, or his foot, or his face, because all these are parts of his own body, and though a cut on his hand does not directly make his foot ache, *he f*eels the pain from any part of his body. The foot, being ignorant and limited, is not conscious at once of the wound made in the hand, but the man is conscious of it, and will not let the foot carry his body, into a place where the hand will be injured. Of course the foot ultimately suffers from the general fever of the whole body caused by a severe injury to any part of it, as ignorance of the unity of the body does not alter the fact of unity. And so the man who believes that the self is one, in him and in all others, also necessarily believes that in injuring any part he is injuring himself, though, being limited and ignorant, he may not then feel it; and he learns to look on all as parts of one body, and on his innermost self as the One who uses that one body, and lives and moves in all,

If we could realise this, feel it always, there would be no need of any Science of Conduct, for we should always act for the highest good of all; but as we do not realise it, and feel it very seldom, we need rules of conduct, which are all based on this principle, to prevent us from injuring others and ourselves, and to help us to do good to others and ourselves.

The great Rishis, knowing the supreme fact that the self of all beings is one, based on this all their precepts, and on this rock they built the morality they taught. The authoritative declarations of the shruti on general morality are final because based on this fact, and they can be defended by reason, and shown to be of binding and universal obligation.

All the laws of nature are expressions of the Divine Nature, and, as one of the aspects of that Nature is Chit, the Reason can grasp and verify them. They are Supremely rational, nay Reason itself, and Reason in man is fitly concerned with their study. Now "the Reason" must not be confused with the process of reasoning—the passing from one link of an argument to another by logical sequence. This process is only one of the functions of the Reason, and is called the ratiocianative faculty, and belongs to the concrete Reason, the lower mind. "The Reason" is Chit, and includes all mental processes, concrete and abstract, the perception in the higher as well as in the lower worlds, direct clear vision of truths as of objects. As knowledge is the rightful source of authority, and as the knowledge of the Rishis was the product of their Reason, working in assonance with the Divine Reason, the shruti, given to the Hindus through the Rishis, are authoritative. Their authority is thus based on Reason, on the Divine Wisdom primarily, and on the illuminated human Reason secondarily. The Rishis, as we saw in the Introduction, have modified the shruti to meet the needs of special ages, for precepts useful at one time are not useful at another. It is further possible by the use of the Reason to distinguish between precepts of universal and those of local and temporary obligation.

The system of morality inculcated in the Sanatana Dharma may therefore be said to be authoritative; for being founded on the recognition of the Unity of the self, and drawing its precepts and its sanctions from that Supreme Fact, it is capable of appealing to and being verified by the Reason, and a perfect harmony can be established between the commands of the shruti and the dictates of the Reason.

This harmony has prevented the arising in India of independent ethical schools, such as have arisen in the West, the doctrines of which become familiar to students in their studies in Western Moral Philosophy.

The Scriptures of other nations, which have not stated clearly the Unity of the self, have necessarily been unable to state clearly the highest sanction for morality, and have directed reliance mainly to a Divine authority, the source of which is not universally seen as identical in nature with the Spirit (Jivatma) in man. Hence a certain divorce between Authority and Reason, injurious to both, and this divorce has led to the growth of two ethical schools, that stand in opposition to authoritative, *i.e.*, scriptural morality, and also in opposition to each other.

One of these schools, the intuitional, finds its basis for morality in intuition, in the dictates of the conscience, but fails to escape from the difficulties involved in the variations of conscience with racial and national traditions, social customs, and individual development.

The second, the utilitarian, has its ethical basis in "the greatest good of the greatest number," but fails to justify the exclusion of the minority from its canon, and to supply a sanction of sufficiently binding force. Besides. what constitutes "the greatest good of the greatest number" is always a debatable point; hence the "canon" is useless as a practical guide

The student can study these systems in the works of their exponents, and he will do well to under stand that the reconciliation of these schools lies in the recognition of the Unity of the self, and the consequent completion of the partial truths on which these are based. He will then see that this principle affords to the teachings of the scriptural school their proper support in Reason; that this supplies the intuitionalist with the explanation of the variations of conscience,[270] which is the voice of the Jivatma, and depends on the stage of evolution reached and the experiences assimilated ; that this shows to the utilitarian that there is no ultimate good for any which is not also good for all, that there is no question of majority and minority, but of unity, and that the sanction of morality lies in this very unity of interests, this identity of nature.

We have, then, as the basis of morality in the Sanâtana Dharma, the recognition of the Unity of the self, and therefore the establishment of mutually helpful relations between all separated selves. Every moral precept finds its sanction in this Unity, and we shall presently see that the Universal Love, which is the expression of the Unity, is the root of all virtues, as its opposite is the root of all vices.

Universal Brotherhood has its basis in the Unity; men are divided by their upadhis, both dense and subtle, but they are all rooted in the one self. Only this teaching, when generally realised, can put an end to wars, and serve as a foundation for peace. This alone can eradicate racial and national hatreds, put an end to mutual contempt and suspicion, and draw all men into one human family, in which there are elders and youngers, indeed, but no aliens.

Nor, indeed, can the Brotherhood based on the Unity of the self be limited to the human family. It must include all things within its circle, for all, without exception, are rooted in the self. In the 10th Adhyaya of the *Bhagavad-Gita* Shri Krishna declares:

---

[270]There is no exact Sanskrit equivalent for the word "conscięnce."

अहमात्मा गुडाकेश सर्वभूताशयस्थित: ।
अहमादिश्च मध्यं च भूतानामंत एव च ॥[271]

"I am the self, O Gudakesha, seated in the heart of all beings; I am the beginning, the middle, and also the end of beings."

He then names Himself as many objects, as sun and moon, as mountain and tree, as horse and cow, as bird and serpent, and many others, and sums up in one all-embracing declaration:

यच्चापि सर्वभूतानां बीजं तदहमर्जुन ।
न तदस्ति विना यत्स्यान्मया भूतं चराचरम् ॥[272]

"Whatsoever is the seed of all beings that am I, O Arjuna!, nor is there aught, moving or unmoving, that may exist bereft of Me."

Over and over again He insists on the all-importance of this recognition of the Unity of the self and of the presence of the self in each and all,

समं सर्वेषु भूतेषु तिष्ठतं परमेश्वरम् ।
विनश्यत्स्वविनश्यंतं य: पश्यति स पश्यति ॥
समं पश्यन्हि सर्वत्र समवस्थितमीश्वरम् ।
न हिनस्त्यात्मना ऽऽत्मानं ततो याति परां गतिम् ॥
यदा भूतपृथग्भावमेकस्थमनुपश्यति ।
तत एव च विस्तारं ब्रह्म संपद्यते तदा ॥[273]

"Seated equally in all beings, the Supreme Ishvara, indestructible within the destructible-he who thus seeth, he seeth.

"Seeing, indeed, everywhere the same. Ishvara equally dwelling, he doth not destroy the self by the self, and thus reacheth the Supreme goal.

"When he seeth the diversified existence of beings as rooted in One, and proceeding from It, then he reacheth Brahman."

All human relations exist because of this Unity, as Yajnavalkya explained to his wife Maitreyi when she prayed of him the secret of immortality:

न वा अरे पत्यु: कामाय पति: प्रियो भवत्यात्मनस्तु कामाय पति: प्रियो भवति ।[274]

---

[271]*Bhagavad-Gita.* x. 20.
[272]*Ibid.* 39.
[273]*Bhagavad-Gita.* xiii. 27, 28, 30.
[274]*Brihadaranyakop.* IV. iv. 5.

"Behold! not indeed for the love of the husband is the husband dear: for the love of the self is the husband dear."

And so with wife, sons, property, friends, worlds and even the Devas themselves. All are dear because the One-self is in all.

न वा अरे सर्वस्य कामाय सर्व प्रियं भवति
आत्मनस्तु कामाय सर्व प्रियं भवति ।

"Behold! not for the love of the all the all is dear, but for the love of the Sell verily the all is dear."

घृतात्परं मण्डमिवातिसूक्ष्म ज्ञात्वा शिवं सर्वभूतेषु गूढं।
विश्वस्यै कं परिवेष्टितारं ज्ञात्वा देवं मुच्यते सर्वपशि: ॥

"Having knosn the Auspicious, the exceedingly subtle, hidden in all beings, like cream in butter, having known the Supreme God, the one Pervader of the universe, he is freed from bonds."

But it is useless to multiply texts, when the shruti at every step proclaim the truth. In this and in this alone is the sure Basis of Morality, for this Unity of the self is the real cause and expla nation of Love; One self, embodied in many forms, is ever seeking to draw the forms together in order to again realise Its own unity. This is why the recognition of the Unity of the self by the Reason, which is Wisdom, shows itself in a world of separate forms as Love. So also the many-ness of the not-self is the cause and explanation of Hate, each separate form setting itself up against others. The full significance of this will be seen by the student on inaturer study ; but he should grasp the fact—which will become clearer as we proceed that all virtue, all that is good, is the immediate result of the pure Love which springs from recognising the Unity of the self, and that all vice, all that is evil, similarly arises from disregard of this truth, and from the feeling that the self is not one, but many, as the bodies are many.

CHAPTER III

RIGHT AND WRONG

The student will remember the description of the Triloki in Part I. At the beginning of a new Triloki, life-evolution begins. This evolution takes place in all the three worlds, but we may confine ourselves to our Earth. First the life forms appear. The Puranas speak in veiled words as to how sheath after sheath encloses the life; under the influence of the five forms of avidya (avidya, asmita, raga, dvesha and abhinivesha) we have the process of manifestation, till we find all the forms of creation manifested on our Earth. During this process, the idea of multiplying go. vernis all beings. This idea breaks through the in nate inertia, the remnant of pralayic tendency with which all beings start. This idea becomes refined and is then called Pravritti, or Inclination, the desire for objects; the world is then on the Pravritti Marga, the Path of "going forth."

Beings become materialised, and as they become consciously separate their self-seeking tendencies become very strong. Every such being forms a world in himself, and tries to exclude others. Men live for enjoyment, and they care for the present only. The idea of separateness develops intellect, which works from the standpoint of individuality: This element is necessary in man in order to bring out his individual faculties, and to cultivate them in such a way as will make the intellectual development fairly complete.

But the idea of separateness becomes after a while a drawback to further progress. Man has gradually to transcend it. He has to recognise the Unity of all selves, and, in practice, to do every thing that helps to strengthen the recognition of that Unity, and at last makes that recognition a part of his life. This may be called the process of spiritual evolution, and man is then on the Nivritti Marga, the Path of Return.

Lastly, Pralaya comes and the end of the Brahmanda.

During all but the latest stages of the Pravritti Marga that which favours separateness is RIGHT, and that which goes against it is WRONG.

Then follows a transition stage, preparing man to enter on the Nivritti Marga; during that, and on the Nivritti Marga, that which favours the tendency towards Unity is RIGHT, and that which goes against it is WRONG.

When the time of Pralaya comes, all that helps it will be RIGHT, all that opposes it WRONG.

Speaking generally, that which is suitable to the stage of evolution which the world has reached, that which helps it onwards, is RIGHT; that which obstructs and hinders evolution is WRONG. For the will of Ishvara points steadfastly to the highest good, and guides His universe towards good. To work with this will is to be in harmony with the great movement of the world-system, and thus to be carried on with the stream of evolution ; while to go against it is like beating against an overwhelming current, which dashes us against the rocks, bruises and wounds us. To do right is to be at peace with ourselves and with God, and is therefore happiness, to do wrong is to be at war with ourselves and with God, and is therefore misery. Hence bad people tend to be come, after a time, discontented, irritable, unsatisfied, however outwardly favourable may be their circumstances; while the good are inwardly at peace and contented, even when their outer circumstances are very unfavourable. Here again the essential fact is the same, for the will of Ishvara, being guided by the highest wisdom and love, ever necessarily and constantly points to the highest good—the more perfect realisation of the Unity of the self amid the endless diversity of forms.

Let us look further into this matter, as the question is all.important.

For this purpose we have to refer back again to the nature of evolution described before. This evolution of the jiva gives rise to that variety of relations and situations between jiva and jiva, out of which the actions arise to which the epithets "right" and "wrong" become applicable; and therefore the nature of "right" and "wrong" depends upon the nature of the scheme of evolution to which the jivas concerned belong, and cannot be described independently of that scheme.

We have gathered from the first part of this work what evolution means. Generally speaking, a world-system has a lile in the same way as a single human being; and as a single human being grows in physical life for the first half of his lifetime and decreases in respect thereof during the second half, so too a world-system, a Brahmanda, grows more and more material during the first half of its life, the Purvardha or Prathama Parardha of the kalpa, and more and more spiritual during the second half or Dvitiya Parardha thereof. This process from birth to death, from death to a higher birth, from that to a deeper death and thence again to a still higher birth—repeated endlessly—is the general plan of life and evolution. In our own world-system, the process takes the shape of a gradual descent of Spirit into the dense matter of the mineral kingdom and a reascent therefrom through the Arvaksrotas or the vegetable kingdom, the Tiryaksrotas or the animal kingdom, the Urdhvasrotas or men, and higher forms, into the realised union of Mukti Coming into still minuter detail we find that amongst men the process reappears as the descent of the primeval and simple-minded childlike human races, governed and guided by divine beings, through growth of inaterialism and the sense of separateness, and consequent selfishness and exclusivness in the appropriation of the stores of nature and the gifts of Providence, into the condition of ever-warring tribes. Then a slow reascent therefrom, through despotic and military government, to constitutional monarchy and organised society, to reach at last those distant and happy times of universal brotherhood when unselfishness and altruism shall reign Supreme, and men will see their common unity far more than their separateness from each other. Finally, in the individual Jiva, we see that evolution, or the life-process, appears as the gather ing of experience and information in the first years after birth, then the utilisation of that expelierce for the founding of a family, then the instruction of the new generation and the helping of them to take up the life of the householder themselves, and ultimately retirement from life into Sannyasa and the peace of renunciation and of a happy death.

Such being the general order of evolution, that course of conduct which helps it on is Right; all else is Wrong. If we have to go to a certain place, then all appliances that make the journey easier and help us to move forward in that direction are good; all obstacles that inake it more difficult and retard our progress are evil. If we had a different goal, if we were desirous of going to a place in the exactly opposite direction, then thie first-mentioned appliances, which would be taking us away from our new goal, would become evil. So long then as we are on the line of our present evolution, the actions that help us forward on it are good and right, and the opposite ones evil and wrong. And in order to find out what is right conduct and what is wrong in any particular situation, we must judge it according to its conduciveness or otherwise to the particular end in view, and judge the particular end again with reference to its congruity with the general goal of human evolution. Without such reference, it is impossible to say what is right and what is wrong. With such reference, on the other hand, we may map out easily the details of our path in life and through evolution and then we shall have at every step a standard of right and wrong by which to guide our actions,

These details have been supplied to us, out of their knowledge and compassion, by the ancient Sages and Seers. They have left to us a complete outline of the scheme of evolution of our world system, and have also left to us general rules for so dealing with our own life and the lives of others, not only of the human but also of the lower kingdoms, that the advance of all jivas through the various stages of evolution, mineral, vegetable, animal, human, celestial, &c., shall be made as easy as possible. These general facts and rules are outlined in the various parts of this work.

For instance, the rules of the four Ashramas are dictated by the facts and laws of individual evolution; and the rules of the four Castes by the facts and laws of human evolution at large, in the middle stage of law-governed state and social organisation and division of labour.

The conditions of the four Castes and the four Ashramas exhaust all possible situations in the whole life of the present-day humanity, and the Sanâtana Dharma therefore provides general rules for all such situations, grouping them into general classes.

The casual observer might think that because there are no expressly recognised Castes and Ashramas amongst many nations of modern humanity, therefore general conditions are radically different for different nations ; but this is not so. Though not expressly recognised, the divisions themselves are to be found everywhere, under other names and forms it may be, but still in all the races of the present day; and that they are not expressly recognised is in some respects productive of inconvenience and waste of time and trouble, economically speaking, to those nations, even as overrecognition and exaggeration are productive of inconvenience and mischief here in India.

The natural conditions of the present evolution unavoidably force upon humanity the relations of teacher and student, ruler and ruled, producer and consumer, master and servant, parent and son, husband and wife, brother and sister, worker and pensioner, employer and employed, soldier and civilian, agriculturist and tradesman, layman and priest, householder and recluse. The Sanatana Dharma, instead of leaving these relations to vague and groping experiments, rationally orders and systematises them, and teaches generally the duties and virtues proper to each relation and situation, with the injunction that the duties and virtues of two different relations and situations should never be mixed up together indiscriminately, for thus great danger and confusion result:

स्वधर्मे निधनं श्रेय: परधर्मो भयावह:।[275]

"Better to die in (the performance of) one's own duty; the duty of another is full of danger."

If a king, in the exercise of his office, come to behave as a merchant, and instead of exercising the king's virtues exhibit those of the tradesman; if a judge, in the decision of a case, instead of being guided by the virtue of justice, show active physical fighting as a soldier, or compassion as a priest; if a priest, in his ministrations, behave as an executioner; if one who should be a Brahmachari or a Grihastha in the ordinary course, should without good special reason, become a Vanaprastha or a Sannyasi, or vice-versa; if one who is fitted by nature to be a soldier should become a merchant, or one fitted for study only should take up the work of agriculture then the whole economy of the state and the nation would be more or less disturbed.

What is right then in one situation is not right in another; and the most general definition that can be given of right and wrong is, that right conduct is that which helps on a known scheme of evolution, to

---

[275] *Bhagavad-Gita.* iii. 35.

its recognised goal, and wrong conduct is the opposite.

For an instance of how the epithets right and wrong may be applied to the very same action looked at from different points of view, take this case. Two men come together: one confines the other in a closed house by force, takes away all liberty of movement from him, and also all moveable property he may have about him, and places it in the possession of others who help and obey him. This act taken by itself, without any reference to previous facts, is wrong; it hinders the life and evolution of the man confined and that of his family and dependants; in fact it amounts to robbery with wrongful confinement of an aggravated character. But suppose that the man confined had forcibly deprived a third person of some property, and the man who ordered his confinement was a judge, and the closed house a public jail, then the same act becomes the rightful imprisonment of a thief, and the removal of property from his person a necessary act of prison-discipline, all of which is perfectly right and even necessary, for thereby the evolution of society and of the thief himself is generally helped. But yet again, if the imprisoned man had forcibly deprived the other of property not belonging to that other but to himself, property which that other had stolen, then the action of the judge becomes wrong again, and his order reversible on appeal to a higher judge.

It is the same on a larger scale in the larger life of the world. The Puranas say that in the begining of the world, when the immediate object was to multiply the human population and engage it in the life of the household, Daksha Prajapati created certain classes of children, the Haryashvas, &c. The Rishi Narada, whose duty it is to bring about certain adjustments of good and evil forces and generally to promote the life of renunciation in our world, commenced his work too soon, and persuaded the Haryashvas to avoid the life of the household and take up the life of the recluse. His action, because of its inopportuneness, was found to be wrong, and he was punished by a curse under which he himself had to be born in the animal and human kingdoms and lead the life of the household with other jivas. So, again, in the earliest days of the race, the worship of Brahma, the embodiment of Rajas and action, the cause of Sarga, creation, was enjoined. Later on, the worship of Vishnu, the embodiment of Sattva, Knowledge and Love, the cause of Sthiti, maintenance, becomes appropriate. In the last days of a cycle, the worship of Shiva, the embodiment of Tamas, Vairagya or self-Sacrifice and Renunciation, the cause of the Pralaya, the dissolution of the material world, finds place.

Thus we see that right and wrong are always relative to the surrounding circumstances. If it were necessary to define them generally, without such reference, then the nearest approach to accuracy is to be found in the Samskrit verse which is on the lips of all Samskrit-knowing Indians:

अष्टादशपुराणेषु व्यासस्य वचनद्वयम् ।
परोपकार: पुण्याय पापाय परपीडनम् ॥

"Vyasa has said but two things in the whole of the eighteen Puranas:—Doing good to an other is Punya, (right); causing injury to another is Papa (wrong)"

As a general rule, when one jiva helps another, makes him happy, then, whether he wish it consciously or not, that happiness comes back to him by the law of action and reaction; this is expressed by the rule that Punya brings happiness, Exactly similar is the case as regards misery and Papa.

The three processes of creation, preservation and dissolution which have just been described are based upon the three fundamental attributes of the matter side of Nature, or prakriti-Sattva, Rajas and Tamas. To begin with, we have pralayic inertia due to Tamas influencing the matter, or praksitic, side of jivas. Then we have kamic and manasic activity, developing the Emotions and the Intellect. This is due to the prevalence of Rajas, acting on the prakritic basis of jivas. Lastly we have a tendency to free ourselves from distraction, from desires for objects, from selfish pursuits, and to attain calm, peace and bliss, whatever be the outer surroundings at any time. This spiritual evolution is brought about by the prevalence of Sattva in us. Then, on the eve of Pralaya, Tamas overtakes us once again.

Every man has in him a predominance of Sattva, or Rajas, or Tamas, and his development depends upon the relative proportions of each of these attributes. When a man is predominantly tamasic, he is indolent, inactive, dull and ignorant.

He requres at first a rajasic development. Anything that draws him out, attracts curiosity, and makes him active, is good and right for him. The constant rebuffs and touches of joy that he gets in his active life, the accumulation of painful and pleasurable experiences, develop his intellect.

Under rajasic predominance, a man is eager in material pursuits, his intellect soars high and spreads wide, he goes backwards and forwards, his cravings ever increasing, and his efforts to sa tisfy them take him through different intellectual channels. Action becomes the rule of his nature, self, the personal self, becomes the centre of all his actions, like (Raga) and dislike (Dvesha) are the motive powers which drive him in his actions.

When Sattva asserts itself, man begins to realise the littleness of efforts directed towards the personal self, the transitoriness of worldly aspirations, the unrest and disquietude attending all actions. He takes a calm and broad view of all things. He discriminates between the real and the unreal, the lasting and the fleeting, the bliss eternal and the pleasures of the moment. He loves peace, calm, and quietude.

Every man has thus his own evolutionary stage, which is generally indicated by the circumstances attending his birth, but more, precisely by the attributes which characterise him. Though particular rules may be laid down for the particular stages of development of a man, such as the Varna and Ashrama rules of old, yet for the average civilised man in general, some rules of conduct may also be laid down, and these form the general rules of Ethics.

We have now to see how on the basis above sketched a Science of Conduct is built up, a Science which cannot be overrated as to its importance.

For this Science of Conduct is, in truth, considering its relations to human happiness, the most important study in many ways that can engage human attention; and it is one which, to the youth, is all-important in its bearing on his own future. For character is that which tells most in hinman life, and on it chiefly depend both inner happiness and outer success. We have already seen that virtue and happiness are bound up together, and, in the life of the world, character is that on which lasting success depends. A man of a brilliant intellect may carry all before him, for a time, but if he be found to be a man of bad character, his fellows cease to trust him and he falls into discredit. In every walk of life, character is the thing most sought after and most trusted, and a man of good character is respected and admired everywhere.

The time of youth is the time for improving character, the time when the germs of vices can most easily be eradicated, and the germs of virtues can most easily be cultivated.

Each comes into the world with a character made by his past, and he must work upon this character, his self-created friend or foe. He can work on it at the greatest advantage if he under stands clearly what he should aim at, and by what means his aim can be reached. He needs to understand the roots of virtues and vices, to learn how to distinguish one from the other, to learn how to cultivate virtues and how to eradicate vices, as a gardener cultivates flowers and eradicates weeds. For each man has a garden in himself, and should learn to be a skilful gardener.

CHAPTER IV

THE STANDARD OF ETHICS

We have already seen that the measure used in Ethics at the present stage of evolution, by which the rightness or wrongness of an action is decided, is the tendency of the action to promote or to hinder Union.

The whole tendency of evolution at the present stage is towards the assertion of the Unity of all selves, is to seek the one Life amidst the diverse forms of life, and thus to follow the path that leads to Union, i.e., the path of Truth.

The standard of Ethics is in other words to *unite* and not to *divide.* We can unite by the establishment of harmonious relations between all the Jivatmas.

It may now be seen why it is said in the first chapter that the object of morality is to bring about happiness by establishing harmonious relations.

The "establishment of harmonious relations," which is said above to be the work of Ethic, is now seen to be the leading of the different parts of the great human body to work in harmony with each other. It is no mere figure of speech that all races of men, all nations, make up one great Man; it is a fact. "purusha," the Inner Man, the self, is indeed Purushottama, the Lord, Ishvara Himself. But there is also the purusha which is His body, and this is Humanity as a whole, and each separate being is a cell in that yast body. All the troubles which make us unhappy, the wars between nations and the quarrels between individuals, the poverty and starvation, the competition and the crushing of the weak, and the countless evils round us, are all diseases of this great body, due to the parts of it getting out of order, and working separately and competitively without a common object, instead of working together as a unity for the good of the whole.

The moral tendencies of man were classified by Shri Krishna under two broad divisions—Divine qualities (Daivi Sampat) and Infernal qualities (Asuri Sampat).

Under Daivi Sampat, Shri Krishna placed the virtues that go towards bringing about harmonious feelings amongst all beings, towards accentuating a feeling of unity and friendliness, towards securing peace and calm, in fact towards carrying out the law of evolution in its entirety.

अभयं सत्वसंशुद्धिर्ज्ञानयोगव्यवस्थिति: ।
दानं दमश्च यज्ञश्च स्वाध्यायस्तप आर्जवम् ॥
अहिंसा सत्यमक्रोधस्त्याग: शांतिरपैशुनम् ।
दया भूतेष्वलोलुप्त्वं मार्दवं हीरचापलम् ॥
तेज: क्षमा धृति: शौचमद्रोहो नातिमानिता।
भवंति संपदं दैवीमभिजातस्य भारत ॥[276]

"Fearlessness, sattvic purity, steadfast pursuit of wisdom, charity, control of the senses, sacrifice, study, austerity, uprightness,

"Harmlessness, truthfulness, absence of anger, resignation, peace of mind, avoidance of calumny, pity for all beings, absence of greed, gentleness, modesty, absence of restlessness,

"Energy, forgiveness, endurance, purity, freedom from hatred and from pride—these are his who is born to the divine qualities, O Bharata." Under Asuri Sampat He placed all the opposite vices—all that tends to divide the Jivatmas, and to accentuate the feeling of Egotism, of the separated self. He described as asuric those qualities which have their root in and grow out of the delusion of separateness.

दंभो दर्पोऽभिमानश्च क्रोध: पारुष्यमेव च ।
प्रज्ञानं चाभिजातस्य पार्थ संपदमासुरीम् ॥[277]

"Hypocrisy, arrogance and conceit, wrath and also harshness and unwisdom, are his, O Partha, who is born to the asuric qualities."

आत्मसंभाविता: स्तब्धा धनमानमदान्विता: ।
यजन्ते नाम यज्ञैस्ते दंभेनाविधिपूर्वकम् ॥
अहंकारं बलं दर्पं काम क्रोधं च संश्रिता:।
मामात्मपरदेहेषु प्रद्विषतोऽभ्यसूयका: ॥
त्रिविधं नरकस्येदं द्वारं नाशनमात्मन: ।
काम: क्रोधस्तथा लोभस्तस्मादेतत्त्रयं त्यजेत् ॥[278]

---

[276]*Bhagavad-Gita.* xv. 1–3.
[277]*Ibid.* xvi. 4.
[278]*Ibid.* 17, 18, 21.

"Self-important, obstinate, filled with the pride and intoxication of wealth, they perform lip-sacrifices for ostentation, contrary to scriptural ordinance.

"Given over to egotism, violence, insolence, lust and wrath, these malicious ones ever hate Me in the bodies of others and in their own.

"Triple is the gate of this hell, destructive of the self-lust, wrath and greed; therefore let a man renounce these three."

The whole of Chapter XVI of the *Bhagavad-Gita* should be carefully pondered by the student in this connection.

CHAPTER V

VIRTUES AND THEIR FOUNDATION

The establishment of harmonious relations means mutual sacrifice of the personal selves. It means that all beings should realise that they form component parts of one Being, and that they must all subordinate themselves to the life of that One Being. Just as there are innumerable cells in the body, but each cell-life subordinates itself to the one life that pervades the whole body, so the life of every being is to be subordinated to the life of the fshvara of the Universe. Different cells have different functions to perform, but each function is a part of the general function of the whole body. As each cell has its fixed place in the body, so each being has a definite place in the Universe, There is one general life-current that pervades all beings, and the life of each individual has to con form to the One Life, the life of the One self, Ishvara. This is the limitation under which we all work, and this limitation is the law of our very being; all beings are mutually linked to one another; and the links impose mutual relations; and mutual sacrifices. All beings are dependent on one another, and they are all dependent on the one great Life. This law of interdependence, of mutual sacrifice, is known as Yajna, and has already been explained in Parts I and II.

Whatever actions we do, we ought to do them for the sake of Yajna. Thus only can we follow the Great Law. If a man lives for self, and makes an independent centre in himself, overlooking the one great centre of the Universe, he creates bonds for himself and suffers therefrom.

यज्ञार्थात्कर्मणोऽन्यत्र लोकोऽयं कर्मबंधन: ।
तदर्थं कर्म कौंतेय मुक्तसंग: समाचर ॥[279]

"The world is bound by action, other than action done for the sake of sacrifice; with such object, free from attachment, O son of Kunti, perform thou action."

We have seen that the different classes of beings linked together

---
[279] *Bhagavad-Gita*. iii. 9.

in this universe are five:—the Devas, the Pitṛis, the Ṛishis, men and animals, and that sacrifices to these classes are a duty, which every man performing actions is bound to discharge. For when sacrifice is imposed by law, there is an obligation to perform it, and hence the performance becomes a duty.

In its exact ethical sense duty means an action which is due, which ought to be done, which is oved; it is an obligation to be discharged. Nature is ever restoring disturbed equilibrium, and the universal law of Karma, of action and re-action, is the full statement of this fact. She is always balancing her accounts. Duties are the debts a man owes to his fellows, paid to discharge the obligations under which he lies for benefits received.

While five duties are mentioned for the purposes of the five Daily Sacrifices, three of these are called *the debts* in a special and larger sense, as permeating the man's whole life. They are the ऋषि-ऋणम्, Rishi-Rinam, the debt to the Rishis; the पितृ-ऋणम्, Pitri-Rinam, the debt to the Ancestors; देव-ऋणम्, Deva-Rinam, the debt to the Devas.

अधीत्य विधिवद्वेदान् पुत्रांश्चोत्पाद्य धर्मतः ।
इष्ट्वा च शक्तितो यज्ञैर्मनो मोक्षे निवेशयेत् ॥[280]

"Having studied the Vedas according to the rules, having begotten sons according to righteousness, having offered sacrifice according to his power, let him turn his mind to moksha."

The three twice-born Castes were directed to pay these debts by passing through the three Ashramas, Brahmacharya, Garhasthya and Vanaprastha, each of which, it will be seen, answers to one of the above three duties. The debt to the Rishis was paid by अध्ययनम्, adhyayanam (including अध्यापनम्) studying the Vedas, serving the teacher in the Brahmacharya-Ashrama and by teaching others; the debt to the ancestors was paid by rearing a family and discharging the duties of Garhasthya, including दानं, danam, charitable gifts; the debt to the Devas was paid by यजनं, yajanam, sacrifice, chiefly in Vanaprastha. Sannyasa, the fourth Ashrama, sums up the three others on the highest level. For the youngest caste, the Shudra, only शुश्रूषा, shushrusha; service, was prescribed as

---
[280]*Manusmriti*, vi, 36.

summing up all duties in a single word. Looked at truly, service of the world includes all duties for the highest Sannyasi, for he has nothing left to gain for himself. Thus the duty of the youngest becomes also the duty of the eldest, but in the latter case on a much higher level.

We may illustrate the idea of duty by the relation of father and son. The father received in his childhood protection and care from his own parents, and thus incurred a debt; he pays this as parental duty to his son, to whom he, in turn, has given a physical body, which requires from him the fostering care bestowed on his own in his infancy and childhood. The son, having received his body from the father, has the duty of serving him with that body, and is also incurring a debt during his helpless years to be paid in time to his own children.

Now the quality which dictates the fulfilment of a duty is called a Virtue; that which prompts the non-fulfilment, or violation of it, is called a Vice. Happiness in any relation depends on the parties to the relation fulfilling their duties to each other; that is, on their practicing the virtues which are the fulfilment of the duties of the relation. Unhappiness in any relation results if one or both the parties do not fulfil their duties to each other ; that is, if they practise the vices which are the non fulfilment of the duties of the relation. A father and son are happy with each other if the father shows the virtues of teriderness, protection, care for the well-being of the son, and the son shows the virtues of obedience, reverence and serviceableness. A father and son are unhappy if the father shows the vices of harshness, oppression, neglect, and the son shows the vices of disobedience, disrespect and careless disregard. If father and son love each other, the virtues of that relation will be practised; if they hate each other, the vices of that relation will appear. Virtues grow out of love regularised and controlled by the righteous intelligence, that sees more the unity of the self than the diversity of the not-self; vices grow out of hate streng. thened and intensified by the unenlightened intelligence, that sees more the separateness of the bodies than the oneness of the self.

Speaking of virtues and vices, of right and wrong, of good conduct and bad conduct, we must not forget, that in whatever way they may find expressions in human conduct, they are all based on Truth, which embodies the Law itself. Sacrifice and duty follow the Law; the Law itself is an expression of Truth. In fact Ishvara Himself is Truth. The Devas adoring the Divine Lord, when He appeared as Shri Krishna, broke forth:

सत्यव्रतं सत्यपरं त्रिसत्यं सत्यस्य योनि निहितं च सत्ये।
सत्यस्य सत्यमृतसत्यनेत्रं सत्यात्मकं त्वां शरणं प्रपन्ना:।।[281]

"O True of promise, True of purpose, triply True, the Fount of Truth and dwelling in the True, the Truth of Truth, the Eye of Right and Truth, Spirit of Truth, refuge we seek in Thee."

Thus Virtues have been called forms of Truth. Bhishma describes them as follows:

सत्यं च समता चैव दमश्चैव न संशय: ।
अमात्सर्यं क्षमा चैव ह्रीस्तितिक्षाऽनसूयता ।।
त्यागो ध्यानमथार्यत्वं धृतिश्च सततं दया ।
अहिंसा चैव राजेंद्र सत्याकारास्त्रयोदश ।।[282]

"Truthfulness, equability, self-control, absence of self-display, forgiveness, modesty, endurance, absence of envy, charity, a noble well-wishing towards others, self-possession, compassion, and harmlessness-surely these are the thirteen forms of Truth."

Truth is that which is. As Bhishma says:

..........सत्यं ब्रह्म सनातनं।
..........सर्वे सत्ये प्रतिष्ठितं।।[283]

"Truth is the eternal Brahman............ Everything rests on Truth." All the laws of nature are expressions of Truth, *i.e.*, they are the methods, the expressions of the nature of That which is, of the Truth, Reality, Being, the self or purusha manifesting amidst the limitations of the Not-Self, Untruth, Non-Being, or Mulapraktiti. They work there fore with undeviating accuracy, with absolute justice and precision. To be true is to be in accord with these laws, and to have nature's constructive energies on our side and working with us. It is to be working with

---

[281] *Vishnu-Bhagarata*, X. ii, 26.
[282] *Mahabharata*, Shanti Parva, clxii. 8, 9.
[283] *Ibid.* 5.

Ishvara. The intellect has the power of discerning what is from what is not, the power of discrimination, of seeing the Real and the Unreal. Recognising the Real as stable and permanent, it seeks to grasp it and thus cultivates the virtues which are the forms of truth.

Untruth is that which IS NOT.

All vices are forms of Untruth, even as all virtues are forms of Truth. Hence the overwhelming im portance of Truth, which is thus the foundation and essential constituent of all virtues, rather than a separate virtue to be taken by itself,

Truthfulness was in ancient days, the leading characteristic of the Âryan, and is constantly alluded to as a constituent in the heroic character, Thus, when about to revive the dead child of Abhimanyu, Shri Krishna says:

न ब्रवीम्युत्तरे मिथ्या सत्यमेतद्द्रविष्यति ।
एष संजीवयाम्येनं पश्यतां सर्वदेहिनां ॥
नोक्तपूर्व मया मिथ्या स्वैरेष्वपि कदाचन ।
न च युद्धात्परावृत्तस्तथा संजीवतामयं ॥
... ...
यथाहं नाभिजानामि विजयेन कदाचन ।
विरोधन्तेन सत्येन मृतो जीवत्वयं शिशु: ॥
यथा सत्यं च धर्मश्च मयि नित्यं प्रतिष्ठितौ ।
तथा मृत: शिशुरयं जीवतामभिमन्युज: ॥[284]

"O Uttara! I speak not falsely, and this shall truly come about. Even now do I revive this child; let all beings behold it.

"As I have never uttered an untruth, even in play, as I have never turned back from battle, so may this infant live.

... ...

"As I have never known dispute with Arjuna, so by that truth may this dead babe revive.

"As truth and Dharma ever dwell in Me, so may the dead child of Abhimanyu live."

Other heroes repeatedly make the same statement: "My lips have never uttered an untruth." Shri Rama goes into exile for fourteen years in

---

[284] *Mahabharata*, Ashvamedha Parva. lxix. 18, 19, 21, 22.

order that his father's promise may remain unbroken, Yudhishthira refuses to struggle for his kingdom before due time, because he has promised to remain in exile.

The effect of these continually repeated precepts and examples was to work into the Âryan character a profound love of truth, and this has repeatedly been noticed as a predominating feature of Hindu character.

It must never be forgotten that no character can be virtuous which has not truth for its basis, and that no character can be base when truth is preserved unsullied. It is the root of all true manli ness, the glory of the hero, the crown of the virtuous, the preserver of the family, the protection of the State. Falsehood undermines alike the home and the nation, poisons the springs of virtue, degrades and pollutes the character. The liar is always weak and always despicable; scorn and contempt follow him. For the building up of charac ter, truth is the only sure foundation.

Here, again, we come back to our basis of morality, and see why Truth is so all-important. For if it be carefully traced back, every untruth uttered will be found to be ultimately connected with the desire for a separate and exclusive existence, and hence to arise from repulsion, separateness, hate, while every truth uttered is ultimately connected with the desire for the common and united life of the one self, the Real, whence all love proceeds.

CHAPTER VI

BLISS AND EMOTIONS

The life of Ishvara permeates all beings and expresses itself as conciousness and bliss, through the bodily limitation of these beings. The body becomes more and more complex, the organs become developed, so that the imprisoned life may assert itself more and more. It is the force of life that directs the development of all being. It is that force that breaks through the tamasic inertia of the mineral form, and makes the mineral matter more and more plastic and capable of receiving im pressions from the outside. It is that force which eventually makes a centre of self in all beings, and developes faculties that digest the outside impressions and work them out into tendencies that form the character of man. Ideas of virtues and vices thus arise, ideas of right and wrong, of good and bad.

The life force works itself out by *impulse*s seeking bliss, and by th*e direction* of the guiding intelli gence. We need not, in this treatise, go further back than the human stage of development. The impulses of man lead him indiscriminately to various objects in pursuit of pleasure. But the rebuffs of pain inake him stop and think. Over and over this happens in life. Over and over again the impulses propel; over and over again intelligence checks. The impulses are thus restrained, directed and refined. Bliss and intelligence act and react on each other and constantly press man onward. One becomes known as Emotion, the other as Intellect. A man may progress continually: he may no longer require a brain, he may no longer require the help of propelling emotions, he may no longer require some particular forms of intelligence and bliss; but intelligence and bliss themselves form part of his life; they are aspects of the Ishvaric life, which he assimilates and calls his own, and they are inseparable from him.

Emotions lead a man outwards and make him identify himself with the things he sees around him. But intellect forms a centre of I-ness, the centre of a small circle of personality, forces all experiences to that centre, and judges all things from the standpoint of that centre. Intellect forms the barrier of selfishness, which separates man from man, till at last by wider and wider knowledge, by knowledge embracing the whole universe, the barrier is swept away, all mankind, nay all beings, form one field, one circle; but the centre is then removed, and becomes the great centre of the Universe, the centre of Ishvaric existence; man rises above the Ahamkara tattva, the tattva that causes the limited sense of I-ness. He plunges into Mahat, or the great tattva, and becomes the possessor of universal knowledge.

The emotions of a man, bound down to the personal self, find expression through the indriyas. The indriyas rush out and bring back their experiences to the intellect of man. The experiences that cause harmonious vibrations are recorded by the intellect as pleasurable, and those that produce opposite vibrations are recorded as painful. The register is made in the memory of man, and intellect proceeds to discriminate between what is pleasurable and what is painful in the long run. Emotions thus become trained. Likes and dislikes become the natural expressions of the emotions, under the guidance of intellect which has developed Discrimination.

The senses become thus indissolubly wedded to the mind, the emotions to the intellect, the indriyas to Mahat, and man becomes normally Emotional Intellectual, or kama-manasic. This is essentially necessary at this stage of his progress.

Thus man likes in the beginning whatever is sweet, and dislikes whatever is bitter. But experience tells him that too much of a sweet thing is as bad as a bitter thing. Temperance in time becomes a normal emotion in a developed man.

What is sweet in the beginning becomes some times bitter in the end; what is apparently sweet is sometimes really bitter.

यत्तदने विषमिव परिणामेऽमृतोपमम् ।
तत्सुखं सात्त्विकम् प्रोक्तमात्मबुद्धिप्रसादजम् ॥
विषयेद्रियसंयोगाद्यत्तदग्रेऽमृतोपमम् ।
परिणाम विषमिव तत्सुखं राजसं स्मृतम् ॥[285]

---
[285]*Bhagavad-Gita.* xviii. 37, 38.

"That which at first is as venom, but in the end is as nectar; that pleasure is said to be sattvic, born of the blissful knowledge of the self.

"That which from the union of the senses with their objects at first is as nectar, but in the end is like venom, that pleasure is accounted rajasic."

As these experiences are repeated, man learns prudence, and prudence becomes a normal emotion in man.

To rush out to do a thing on the first impulse sometimes brings on disastrous results. To lose temper brings more disharmonious than harmonious experiences. Forbearance, Toleration, become thus normal emotions in man.

Emotions, rightly directed by the intelligence, are virtues. In the culture of emotions lies the formation of a man's character, his ethical development. Emotional culture is the highest culture of man, and the training of likes and dislikes is his best evolution. The man of cultured emotions is propelled by them to do what he thinks right; he becomes patriotic, he becomes philanthropic, he becomes compassionate, he becomes friendly to all beings. His emotions become predominantly those of Love, and he takes an ever wider and wider range in the manifestation of that Love. And when the barrier of personality is swept away, when the ahamkaric mind becomes manas, or the reflection of the Universal Mind, the emotions also break through the barrier of indriyas and ascend to buddhi, and reflect the life of Ishvara within. Verily then the Trinity of Atma, buddhi and manas becomes a Unity, and the man a jivanmukta.

We now understand why Ethical Science is particularly concerned with the emotions, and hence with the bliss aspect of Ishvara.

There are many ways of showing why happiness should follow right conduct, and unhappiness wrong conduct, but they are all modifications of the one essential reason, that, as there is but One self in all, to hurt or help another is virtually to hurt or help oneself.

It is written in the shruti:

विज्ञानमानन्दं ब्रह्म।[286]

"Brahman is knowledge and bliss.

---

[286]*Brihadaranyakop.* V. ix, 28.

Over and over again the "bliss of Brahman" is spoken of, and bliss is said to be His nature. In fact the threefold nature of Ishvara, of the Saguna Brahman, is expressed in the epithet, Sat-Chit-Ananda. Bliss is thus the very nature of the Jivatma, since his nature is that of Brahman; he, too, is bliss. But we learn further that the Saguna Brahman is ratat spotless, and Ti, pure.[287] Therefore only the pure, the good, is of His nature, and is compatible with His bliss. So then must the essence of the Jivatma be purity, and it is written of it:

तं विद्याच्छुक्रममृतम्[288]

"Let him know it, pure and immortal."

Thus purity and bliss are of the nature of the Jivatma and are inseparable, for unity is purity, and the feeling of unity is the feeling of bliss.

Each Jivatma being of the nature of the one self it is ever, when embodied in a separate forin, seeking union with the Selt in other forms. This search for unity, for the bliss of union, is instinctive, and results, when the union is found, in perfect happiness. In this everyone is alike. Men differ in most things, but in their longing for happiness they are all alike. Every man, woman, boy and girl wants to be happy. They seek happiness in many different ways, but they all seek happiness. The Jivatma, blinded by his body, chooses the wrong things very often, but the motive of his choice is always the same, the desire to be happy. It is his nature to be happy, and he is always trying to express that nature. Through the whole of his long pilgrimage he is searching for happiness. This is his root-motive, the object at which he invariably aims. If he does a painful thing, it is in order to gain a greater happiness. If he endures toil and discomfort, it is because the result of the toil and discomfort will be happiness. Happiness is his end; everything else is only means to that end. A life of austerity and continued self-denial and suffering is embraced in the belief that it will lead to Supreme bliss. The whole of evolution may be described in the words; "A search for happiness." Continually disappointed, with unwearying perseverance

---

[287] *Mundakop.* II. ii, 9. The statement is repeated over and over again.
[288] *Kathop.* II. vi, 7.

man returns again and again to the search, until at last he recognises that purity, wisdom, bliss, are one and indivisible. Then he goes to Peace.

For purity, wisdom and bliss, Sat, Chit and Ananda, are the very nature of Ishvara, His own self.

Thus Ethics leads us to the highest religion, to the realisation of the highest truths, and when Ethics reaches its goal, the barrier between Ethics and Religion vanishes away, Ethics becomes Religion and Religion Ethics. The goal of both is Ishvara and Ishvaric life. This is why the Hindu ethical system is a branch of the Hindu Religion, and why one cannot be separated from the other.

CHAPTER VII

"SELF-REGARDING" VIRTUES

We have already seen that Ethics has as its object the establishment of harmonious relations. These relations are concerned with the surroundings of a man—his home, city, nation, etc.—and also with his own body. Now the body of a man, according to the scriptural teachings, is, as we have seen, a complex one, consisting of several sheaths, or koshas. It is enough to remember here that we have the physical sheath, in which Prana functions, the sheath of the indriyas or senses (the sensuous or kamic sheath), the mental sheath and the buddhic sheath. Ethics concerns itself at present with the physical, the kamic, and the mental sheaths. For when the buddhic sheath is reached, man becomes divine, and the present limit of ethical teachings is crossed.

Ethical teachings have therefore reference to the lower sheaths of a man's body, and to the different classes of beings, who form his surroundings. The different classes of beings, as we have already seen, are the Devas, the pitris, the Rishis, men in general, and the lower animals, *i.e.*, beings both higher and lower than man, as well as the whole of mankind.

We have thus, in the first place, duties which we owe to the sheaths of our own body, and in the next place, duties that we owe to Devas, pitris, Rishis, mankind and the lower animals.

When the body becomes entirely harmonious with the self within, it becomes a true and subdued vehicle of the life of Atma, which is an aspect of the vara.

When the surrounding universe becomes harmonious with the self within, the life of Ishvara flows out to the universe from the centre of the self Man then becomes fully an expression of the Law, the voice of Ishvara, the sacred word Pranava. Towards that goal we should all strive, and to that goal ethics must lead us.

Now let us turn to our body, or bodies, if the term be preferred.

First, the *Sthula Sharira.* The physical body must be kept clean and healthy. Cleanliness and health mean harmony and order. Man is better able to do work with a clean and healthy body, He remains cheerful and bright. The diseased man cannot give attention to work. He is uneasy in mind. The disharmony and disorder of one sheath also react on the other sheaths of the man.

The body should be kept up by means of sattvic food. For the food retains its essential magnetic properties after its conversion into blood, and produces corresponding effects on the indriyas and the mind. The *Bhagavad-Gita* says:

आयु: सत्त्वबलारोग्यसुखप्रीतिविवर्धना:।
रस्या:स्निग्धा:स्थिरा हृद्या आहारा:सात्त्विकप्रिया:॥
कटुम्ललवणात्युष्णतीक्ष्णरूक्षविदाहिन: ।
आहारा राजसस्येष्टा दु:खशोकामयप्रदा: ॥
यातयाम गतरसं पूति पर्युषितं च यत् ॥
उच्छिष्टमपि चामेध्यं भोजनं तामसप्रियम् ॥[289]

"The foods dear to the Sattvic, increasing life, energy, strength, health, joy and cheerfulness, are those that are full of juice, oleaginous, non-volatile and heart-strengthening.

"Those dear to the Rajasic, causing pain, depression and sickness, are the bitter, acid, saline, over-hot, pungent, dry and burning.

"Stale and flat, putrid and corrupt, leavings and unclean (things), are the food loved by the Tamasic."

We have already seen that the higher evolution is brought about by the predominance of Sattva, and that Sattva means harmony.

Secondly, the *Sukshina Sharira*. The indriyas through the heredity of our past existence, are largely guided by animal appetites, which are distinctly rajasic. We should therefore subdue our indriyas. We may see, hear, smell, taste and touch, but we should not ascribe our likes and dislikes to the object of the senses. We must *sense* as a matter of course, but the sensing must not be vitiated by personal likes and dislikes, which form a barrier between ourselves and the external world and make harmonious relations impossible. Every man makes a world to himself, by means of his likes and dislikes. Thus many worlds are

---

[289]*Loc cit.* xvii. 8, 9, 113.

formed, each different from the other, and all different from the world as it is, the world of Ishvara. Men are jaundiced by the tint and taint of their personalities and, blinded by the distractions of Rajas, they do not see the Law, the word of Ishvara.

Therefore our mind should not be guided by the indriyas, but the mind should be guided by its own discriminative faculty, and should then subdue the senses.

The indriyas are divided into organs of perception and organs of action (the latter belonging to the Sthula Sharira). There is no harm done by the perception of objects, if the perception be not followed by likes and dislikes. Raga and Dvesha drive us helplessly along, using the karmendriyas for their own satisfaction.

इन्द्रियस्थेन्द्रियस्याथै रागद्वेषा व्यवस्थितौ ।
तयोर्न वशमागच्छेत्ती ह्यस्य परिपंथिनौ ।।[290]

"*Affection and aversion for the objects of sense abide in the senses; let none come under the dominion of these two; they are the obstructors of his way.*"

Affection and aversion, Raga and Dvesha, form the desire-nature of man. This, emotional in its origin, has to be controlled. The emotional nature has to be purified. Raga is to expand into universal love. Dvesha is to be eliminated entirely in personal relations, in relations between man and man, between one being and another being and is to be retained only as an abstract dislike for anything that goes against the law, against the will of Ishvara. But this abstract dislike is not at all to interfere with the universal love of all beings. It is only to make a man strong in his purity, in his rejection of all that is evil. He should dislike evil ways, but not evil men.

The mind, when wedded to the indriyas, be comes rajasic. When wedded to buddhi, it becomes sattvic. The mind of an average man is normally rajasic at the present day. He should make efforts to change it to sattvic.

We have already said that the mind should give up personal likes and dislikes, Raga and Dvesha. Raga and Dvesha form the impurities

---

[290]*Bhagavad-Gita.* iii, 34.

of the mind, and when they are given up the mind becomes purified.

There is another dosha, or fault, of the mind, It gets distracted. It applies itself to a number of outside objects. It runs away from this matter to that matter, and it can with very great difficulty be tied down to one. The mind is compared to a chariot, which is constantly being drawn away in ten different directions by ten horses, which are the ten indriyas. This Vikshepa, or distraction of the mind, has to be checked. The mind has to be concentrated, to be made one-pointed.

When the impurities and distraction of the mind are removed, it becomes sattvic. Then it reflects the self within, and causes harmony and bliss. This is harmony with the Universe, or harmony with the Divine Law as manifested in the Universe.

The first step towards removing distraction is to deal with abstractions more than with concrete objects; we must generalise truths, and come at last to the highest Truth, the one Reality, Ishvara, and grasp Him firmly. Then all the universe appears as His manifestation, all works as His action, all laws as His law. Varieties disappear. Diversities fade away. Harmony prevails.

The training of the mind is man's most important duty, and next to this follows the control of speech and actions. At the same time he must not neglect his physical body. All the vehicles forming his body must be controlled and made harmonious with each other.

The tenfold law, as laid down by Manu, gives some of the characteristics needed :

धृति: क्षमा दमोऽस्तेयं शौचमिन्द्रियनिग्रह: ।
धीर्विद्या सत्यमक्रोधो दशकं धर्मलक्षणम् ॥[291]

"Endurance, patience, self-control, integrity, purity, restraint of the senses, wisdom, learning, truth, absence of anger, are the ten signs of virtue."

In briefer form:

अहिंसा सत्यमस्तेयं शौचमिन्द्रियनिग्रह:।
एतं सामासिकं धर्मं चार्तुवरार्थेऽब्रवीन्मनु: ॥[292]

---

[291] *Manusmriti*, vi. 92.
[292] *Ibid.* 63.

"Harmlessness, truth, integrity, purity, control of the senses, saith Manu, is the summarised law for the four castes."

In the *Bhagavad-Gita* an exhaustive list of these general characteristics is given :

अभयं सत्त्वसंशुद्धिर्ज्ञानयोगव्यवस्थिति: ।
दानं दमश्च यज्ञश्च स्वाध्यायस्तप आर्जवम् ॥
अहिंसा सत्यमक्रोधस्त्याग: शान्तिरपैशुनम् ।
दया भूतेष्वलोलुप्त मार्दवं हीरचापलम् ॥
तेज: क्षमा धृति: शौचमद्रोहो नातिमानिता।
भवंति संपदं दैवीमभिजातस्य भारत ॥[293]

"Fearlessness, clean-living, steadfastness in the Yoga of wisdom, almsgiving, self-restraint, sacrifice, study of the Shastras, austerity, straightforwardness,

"Harmlessness, truth, absence of wrath, renunciation, peacefulness, absence of crookedness, compassion to living beings, uncovetousness, mildness, modesty, steadfastness,

"Energy, patience, fortitude, purity, absence of envy and pride—these are his who is born with the divine qualities, O Bharata."

Some of these virtues would fall into one or other of the three classes already spoken of, but for the most part they belong to the Jivatma as his general expression of the love-emotion, and as the balance of his own nature, the due control of his energies.

The essential importance of Truth has already been dwelt upon. As a general virtue it appears as *Truthfulness, Honesty, Integrity, Uprightness*. Its utter indispensability is concentrated by the wisdom and experience of ages into short sayings, such as: "Honesty is the best policy," "सत्यमेव जयते नानृतं" "Truth alone prevails, not falsehood."

The virtue of *self-control*, or *self-restraint*, mentioned in each of the above quotations, is the general reining-in of all the energies of the mind, desire-nature, and physical body, the holding of them all in due submission, so that each is allowed or refused exercise at the will of the man. It implies that the man is conscious of the difference between himself and his lower upadhis, and no more indentifies himself

---

[293] *Bhagavad-Gita.* xvi. 1–3.

with his lower nature than a rider, identifies himself with the horse on which he is sitting. The contrast between an uncontrolled man and a self-controlled man is very much like the contrast between a bad rider on an unbroken horse, and a good rider on a well-broken horse. In the first case, the horse rushes about, carrying his helpless rider, plunges violently, and gives his uider a bad fall; in the other case, the man sits easily, guiding the docile steed in any direction, galloping or standing still, leaping or walking every motion of the rider obeyed by the horse.

So necessary is self-control, that the teachers of morality are continually recurring to it, and enforcing it. Manu dwells on its necessity, and explains that action has three roots, and that control of each generator of action must be gained.

कर्म मनोवाग्देहसंभवम्।[294]

"Action is born of mind, speech and body."
Each of these, mind, speech, and body, must be brought under complete control, and then success is sure.

वाग्दण्डो ऽथ मनोदण्ड: कायदण्डस्तथैव च ।
यस्यैते निहिता बुद्धौ त्रिदण्डीति स उच्यते ॥
त्रिदण्डमेतन्निक्षिप्य सर्वभूतेषु मानव: ।
कामक्रोधौ तु संयम्य तत: सिद्धिं निगच्छति ॥[295]

"He is called the holder of the Tri-danda in whose reason these are fixed-control of speech, control of mind, control of body."

"The man who lays this triple rule (over himself) amidst all creatures, he verily dominates desire and wrath, and goes to perfection." Of these three, control of the mind is the most important, as speech and action alike depend on the mind. Manu says again :

मनो विद्यात्प्रवर्तकम्।[296]

"Let the mind be known as the instigator."

Once let the mind be brought under control, and all else follows, but here lies the great difficulty, owing to the extreme restlessness of the

---

[294]*Manusmriti.* xii. 3.
[295]*Ibid.* 10, 11.
[296]*Ibid.* 4.

mind. Arjuna placed this difficulty before Shri Krishna 5,000 years ago:

चंचलं हि मनः कृष्ण प्रमाथि बलवद् दृढम् ।
तस्याहं निग्रहं मन्ये वायोरिव सुदुष्करम् ॥[297]

"Verily the mind is restless, O Krishna, impetuous, strong, difficult to bend; I deem it very hard to curb, like the wind."

And no answer can be given to this, save the answer given by the Divine Teacher:

असंशयं महाबाहो मनो दुर्निग्रहं चलम्।
अभ्यासेन तु कौंतेय वैराग्येण च गृह्यते ॥[298]

"Without doubt, O mighty-armed, the mind is hard to curb and restless; yet verily, O son of Kunti, it may be curbed by constant practice and dispassion."

Only long-continued effort and perseverance can bring under control this restless vigorous mind, and yet without this control man can never be happy.

यतो यतो निश्चरति मनश्चंलमस्थिरम्।
ततस्ततो नियम्यैतदात्मन्येव वशं नयेत् ॥[299]

"As often as the restless and unstable mind goeth forth, so often reining it in, let him place it under the control of the self."

If this be done, then happiness is secured, so much so that Shri Krishna makes happiness part of the successful austerity of the mind :

मनःप्रसाद सौम्यत्वं मौनमात्मविनिग्रह।
भावसंशुद्धिरित्येतत्तपो मानसमुच्यते ॥[300]

"Mental happiness, equanimity, silence, self control, purity of nature—this is called the austerity of the mind."

But the most disturbing part of man's nature is his desires, ever-craving, never satisfied. In fact the more they are gratified, the fiercer they grow.

---

[297] *Bhagavad-Gita*, vi, 31.
[298] *Ibid.* 35.
[299] *Bhagavad-Gita.* Vi, 26.
[300] *Ibid,* xvii. 16.

न जातु काम: कामानामुपभोगेन शाम्यति ।
हविषा कृष्णवर्त्मेव भूय एवाभिवर्धते ।।[301]

"Desire is verily never quenched by the enjoy ment of objects of desire; it only increases further as fire with butter."

To bring the senses under control the mind must be used, else will a man ever be restless and uneasy.

He must learn to use his mind to control his senses, for through the senses come his chief temptations.

And every sense must be brought under control; for one uncontrolled sense may play havoc with the mind :

इन्द्रियाणां हि चरतां यन्मनोऽनुविधीयते ।
तदस्य हरति प्रज्ञां वायुनीवमिवांभसि ।।[302]

"That one of the roving senses which the mind yieldeth to, that hurries away the understanding, as a gale (hurries away) a ship on the waters."

Manu also lays stress on the danger of allowing even one sense to slip away from control, using a very graphic symbol:

इन्द्रियाणां तु सर्वेषां यद्येकं क्षरतीन्द्रियम् ।
ततो ऽस्य क्षरति प्रज्ञा दृते: पादादिवोदकम् ।।[303]

"If one sense of all the senses leaks, then under standing leaks through it, as water from the leg of the water-skin."

One open passage is enough to allow all the water to pour out from the water-skin of the water carrier; and so one uncontrolled sense is opening enough for man's understanding to flow away from him.

The mind, then, is to be brought under control, and is to be used to control the senses. In the *Kathopanishat,* the mind is therefore compared to the reins with which a driver pulls in, guides and controls his horses, the horses being compared to the senses, which run away with the body and the Jivatma, who dwells in the body;

---

[301] *Manusmriti.* ii. 91.
[302] *Bhagavad-Gita.* ii. 67.
[303] *Manusmriti.* ii. 99.

आत्मानं रथिनं विद्धि शरीरं रथमेव तु ।
बुद्धिं तु सारथिं विद्धि मनः प्रग्रहमेव च ॥
इन्द्रियाणि हयानाहुर्विषयांस्तेषु गोचरान् ।
आत्मेन्द्रियमनोयुक्तं भोक्तेत्या मनीषिणः ॥
यस्त्वविज्ञानवान् भवत्ययुक्तेन मनसा सदा ।
तस्येन्द्रियाण्यवश्यानि दुष्टाश्वा इव सारथेः ॥
यस्तु विज्ञानवान् भवति युक्तेन मनसा सदा ।
तस्येन्द्रियाणि वश्यानि सदश्वा इव सारथेः ॥
... ...
विज्ञानसारथिर्यस्तु मनःप्रग्रहवान्नरः ।
सो ऽध्वनः पारमाप्नोति तद्विष्णोः परमं पदम् ॥[304]

"Know the self as the occupant of the car, the body verily as the car. Know indeed the reason as the charioteer, the mind as the reins.

"The senses are said to be the horses, the objects of the senses the field for them. The Sell, joined to the senses and the mind, is the enjoyer—so say the wise.

"He who is unwise, with the mind ever unapplied, of him the senses are uncontrolled, like the bad horses of the charioteer.

"He who is wise, with the mind ever applied, of him the senses are controlled, like the good horses of the charioteer.

"The man whose charioteer is wise, whose mind-reins are used, he only travels to the end of the road, to the highest abode of Vishnu."
Manu uses the same imagery:

इन्द्रियाणां विचरतां विषयेष्वपहारिषु ।
संयमे यत्नमातिष्ठेद्विद्वान्यन्तेव वाजिनाम् ॥[305]

"The wise man should make effort to control the senses running amid the alluring objects of sense, as the driver the horses."
Recounting the five organs of sense and the five organs of action, Manu declares that the control of the mind includes the control of these:

एकादशं मनो ज्ञेयं स्वगुणेनोभयात्मकम् ।
यस्मिञ्जिते जितावेतौ भवतः पञ्चको गणौ ॥[306]

---

[304] *Kathop.* iii, 3–6, 2.
[305] *Manusmriti*, ii, 88.
[306] *Ibid.* 92.

"Mind is to be known as the eleventh, belonging by its nature to both; in conquering this, the two sets of five become conquered." The control of speech consists in making it respectful to superiors, courteous to equals, gentle to inferiors, and we shall return to this in studying the special virtues. For the moment we may leave it with the general description of right speech:

अनुद्वेगकर वाक्यं सत्यं प्रियहितं च यत् ।
स्वाध्यायाभ्यसनं चैव वाङ्मयं तप उच्येत ।।[307]

"Speech causing no annoyance, truthful, pleasant and beneficial, and the repetition of the Vedas, this is called the austerity of speech," And Manu remarks:

वाच्यर्था नियताः सर्वे वाङ्मूला वाग्विनिःसृताः।
तां तु यः स्तेनयेद्वाच स सर्वस्तेयकृन्नरः ।।[308]

"All things are governed by speech: speech is the root, from speech they originate; that man verily who is dishonest in speech, he is dishonest in all."

Thus important is speech said to be.

The control of the body is similarly summed up by Shri Krishna:

देवद्विजगुरुप्राज्ञपूजनं शौचमार्जवम् ।।
ब्रह्मचर्यमहिंसा च शारीरं तप उच्यते ।।[309]

"Worship of the Devas, the twice-born, the gurus and the wise, purity, straightforwardness, chastity, and harmlessness, are called the austerity of the body."

Control such as this produces a balancing of the mind, calmness, quiet and contentment.

The secret of self-control has been said above (see *ante* p. 322) to be Abhyasa and Vairagya, "constant practice and dispassion." The second word is especially significant, and the whole statement should be studied in the light of the shlokas quoted from the *Kathopanishat*. Buddhi, the Pure Reason, is there said to be the charioteer, in whose

---

[307] *Bhagavad-Gita.* xvii, 15.
[308] *Manusmriti.* iv, 256.
[309] *Bhagavad-Gita.* xvii, 14.

one hand are grasped the many-branching reins of manas. Buddhi is, as has been said, the faculty which recognises and realises the Unity of the self, as manas is that which cognises the many-ness of sense-objects. The owner of the car, the Jivatma, should make sure that buddhi drives his car, and then the reins and the horses will be well managed.

Now the student who wishes that buddhi should thus drive his car, should constantly dwell on the fact of the Unity of the self.

शनैः शनैरुपरमेदबुद्ध्या धृतिगृहीतया।
आत्मसंस्थं मनः कृत्वा न किंचिदपि चिंतयेत् ॥
यतो यतो निश्चरति मनश्चलमस्थिरम् ।
ततस्ततो नियम्यैतदात्मन्येव वशं नयेत् ॥[310]

"Little by little let him gain tranquillity by means of buddhi controlled by steadiness; having made manas abide in the self, let him not think of anything.

"As often as the wavering and unsteady manas goeth forth, so often, reining it in, let him bring it under the control of the self."

This is the Abhyasa that he needs. This Abhyasa will naturally strengthen Vairagya, the absence of desire for personal and selfish ends. Whenever he sees a desire for such personal and selfish ends rising up within himself, he should at once call up before his mental view the injury that he is likely to inflict on others by its indulgence, the evil consequences to himself in increasing selfishness, and the whole series of disturbances which will flow from his selfishness to the common life of the society to which he belongs. By picturing to himself the consequences of selfishness in his own life and in those of others, and by studying the illustrations of them given in the *Puranas,* he will gradually strengthen his power of self-control, and will establish himself in that constant mood of righteousness and performance of duty so unceasingly inculcated in the sacred books.

For that *Righteousness*, and righteousness only, should be followed is reiterated again and again:

अधार्मिको नरो यो हि यस्य चाप्यनृतं धनम् ।
हिंसारतश्च यो नित्यं नेहासौ सुखमेधते ॥

---
[310]*Bhagavad-Gita.* vi. 25, 26.

न सीदन्नपि धर्मेण मनोऽधर्मे निवेशयेत् ।
अधार्मिकाणां पापानामाशु पश्यन्विपर्ययम् ॥
नाधर्मश्चरितो लोके सद्यः फलति गौरिव ।
शनैरावर्तमानस्तु कर्तुर्मूलानि कृन्तति ॥[311]

"The man who is unrighteous, or he who (gains) wealth by falsehood, or he who ever delights in injuring, never obtains happiness in this world.

"Although suffering by righteousness, let him not turn his mind to unrighteousness; he will behold the speedy overthrow of the unrighteous, of the sinners."

"Unrighteousness, practised in this world, does not bear fruit at once like a cow; slowly re-acting, it cuts off the very roots of the doer." In a sense, righteousness is truth; its special significance may be said to be the desire to do what is right, the desire to give every one his due, the desire always to find out the truth and act according to it rather than according to anything else.

To do righteousness is to gain a companion that never fails a man, and when all else deserts him this faithful companion will remain, will cling to him through death, and clothe him with glory in the world beyond the grave. Manu writes here: on as follows:

धर्म शनैः संचिनुयाद्वल्मीकमिव पुत्तिकाः ।
परलोकसहायार्थं सर्वभूतान्यपीडयन् ॥
नामुत्र हि सहायार्थं पिता माता च तिष्ठतः ।
न पुत्रदारा न शातिर्धर्मस्तिष्ठति केवलः ॥
एकः प्रजायते जन्तुरेक एव प्रलीयते ।
एकोऽनुभुङ्क्ते सुकृतमेक एव च दुष्कृतम् ॥
मृतम् शरीरमुत्सृज्य काष्ठलोष्टसमं क्षितौ ।
विमुखा वान्धवा यान्ति धर्मस्तमनुगच्छति ॥
तस्माद्धर्म सहायार्थं नित्यं संचिनुयाच्छनैः ।
धर्मेण हि सहायेन तमस्तरति दुस्तरम् ॥
धर्मप्रधान पुरुषं तपसा हतकिल्विषम् ।
परलोकं नयत्याशु भास्वंतं स्वशरीरिणम् ॥[312]

---

[311] *Manusmriti*. iv. 170–172
[312] *Manusmriti*. iv. 238–243.

"Giving no pain to any creatures, let him slowly build up righteousness like white ants their hill, that it be to him a companion in the world beyond.

"Nor father, nor mother, nor son, nor wife, nor kinsfolk remain to accompany him to the next world; righteousness alone remaineth.

"Alone each being is born; alone verily he dies; alone he enjoys good deeds; alone also the evil.

"Leaving the dead body on the ground like a log or a clod of Earth, the relatives depart, with averted faces; righteousness alone followeth him.

"Therefore, to gain an unfailing friend let him ever gather righteousness; with righteousness as companion he will cross over the darkness, difficult to cross.

"It rapidly leadeth the man who is devoted to righteousness and has destroyed his sins by austerity, to the world beyond, radiant and clad in a celestial body."

This insistence on righteousness as the only way to happiness in this world or in any other is characteristic of the Sanatana Dharma, whose very heart is duty, as justice is its key-note and unalterable law its life-breath. A man obtains everything that he has duly earned, neither more nor less; every debt must be paid; every cause must be followed by its effect.

The virtue *of Content* springs from a full recognition of this fact, and it is itself the root of happiness, a virtue which every student should endeavour to work into his character:

संतोष परमास्थाय सुखार्थी संयतो भवेत् ।
संतोषमूलं हि सुखं दुःखमूलं विपर्यय: ॥[313]

"Let one who desires happiness be controlled and take refuge in perfect content; content is verily the root of happiness, the opposite is the root of sorrow."

The contented man is happy under the most unfavourable circumstances, the root of his happiness being in himself; whereas the discontented man finds food for his discontent, however favour able his circumstances may be. There are always some who are superior in

---

[313] *Manusmriti.* iv. 12.

position to, more wealthy, more fortunate than ourselves, and hence reasons for discontent may ever be found by the unwise. To be satisfied with what we have because we have our due is true wisdom, and all dissatisfaction is folly.

We have spoken of virtues as bringing about harmonious relations between Jivatmas, but it must not be thought that this excludes the above virtues which at the first glance seem chiefly to concern their possessor, and to aid his own general evolution. For when carefully considered, it will be found that these so-called personal virtues react upon the happiness of others, though in a way not immediately apparent. Life, evolution, virtue and vice, duty-all these things would be impossible with only a single Jivatma in existence. The idea of a community is inseparable from the ideas of these. A so-called duty to self, or a personal virtue, is also ultimately a duty to another, a giving of some help or a saving of some inconvenience to others. For instance if we are unclean, we inevitably make our neighbours uncomfortable when we come into contact with them. When a man says to another: "You owe it to yourself to do so and so," he really and instinctively means: "You owe this to the evolution of humanity generally as connected, by the unity of the self, with the evolution of your individual self." For the evolution of one jiva is inseparable from that of other jivas, and helping or hindering our own progress is also directly or indirectly helping or hindering the progress of others. An unclean or slovenly man injures himself primarily and his fellows secondarily, by lowering the general ideal and influencing their lives indirectly if not actively.

The duties to Devas, Pitris, Rishis, men and animals were mentioned in Parts I and II, and we need only add, ere turning to our duties to human beings, that our general attitude should be that of *Harmlessness*.

अहिंसा परमो धर्म:

"Harmlessness is the highest duty," taught Bhishma.
Manu also says:

यस्मादण्वपि भूतानां द्विजान्नोत्पद्यते भयम् ।
तस्य देहाद्विमुक्तस्य भयं नास्ति कुतश्चन ॥[314]

---

[314] *Mahabharata*. Anushasana Parva, cxiv.

"For the twice-born man from whom no fear arises to any living creatures, for him, freed from the body, there will be no fear from any." Ishvara is just, and the harmless man is harmed by none. The Yogi can wander without danger among wild animals, because his heart is full of love and he is a source of danger to none. Once again says Bhishma : "The slayer is slain," but the man who slays none will himself be slain of none. For the harmless man, full of love to all creatures, sees the self in each and regards each as part of his own body, and such a man is the "friend of all creatures," and is safe wherever he goes.

We have seen that by sacrifice only we can establish harmonious relations amongst all beings, and the establishment of harmonious relations, as we have seen, is the very essence of our evolution. Man cannot be selfish. The world is not for one man alone. He may think in his own way and act in his own way. But if he does not conform himself to the Lord, the word of Ishvara, the sacred Pranava, woe falls on him and misery becomes his lot. Through the repeated teachings of misery his obstinate selfishness is removed, and he be comes harmonised with the whole universe.

Let the student bear this principle in mind firmly and steadfastly, and he will easily understand what is said in the next chapter.

CHAPTER VIII

VIRTUES AND VICES IN HUMAN RELATIONS THOSE IN RELATION TO SUPERIORS

We may study the virtues and vices as the out growths from love and hate. Love prompts us to make sacrifices, to limit, to restrict ourselves, to subordinate ourselves to the cominon well-being. This love emanates from the self within, is an aspect of Bliss, and makes our duty a work of love, our sacrifice a pleasure.

Emotions in their early rushings forth transgress the law, for the law is not know. But when the law is known and realised, when Chit and Ananda combine, when the emotion proceeds from a dis criminating self-centre, when still later, the self centre becomes a universal centre, every emotion becomes a virtue, every emotion becomes a voice of the divine.

As love underlies every virtue, so hate underlies every vice. For union is law, separation is against the law; harmony is evolution, disharmony is the opposite of evolution.

If love prompts our mutual relations, we naturally and readily make sacrifices to render those relations harmonious and blissful.

Now in considering virtues and vices in human relations, we may classify them as those called out in relation to Superiors, in relation to Equals, and in relation to Inferiors.

The natural superiors of a man are: God; the Sovereign; Parents; Teachers; the Aged.[315]

There may be what may be called "accidenta superiors"—persons who are on a level with a man's parents and teachers, and persons above him in intelligence and morality, towards whom he would exercise modified forms of the virtues now to be considered. But such adaptations are readily made, and need not change our classification.

The love-emotion directed to God will show itself as the virtue of *Reverence,* carried to its highest degree. This will primarily express itself in worship, and secondarily in treating with res pect all ideas

---

[315] There is no order of superiority intended here; the Shastras give different orders.

about God, all things connected with His worship, sacred places and sacred objects Reverence being due to a sense of His infinite superiority, attracting love by virtue of His supreme wisdom and compassion, it will naturally be accompanied by *Humility,* the willing recognition of comparative littleness, unassociated with pain and coupled with the readiness to submit to guidance; by *Faith* in and therefore Sub*mission,* to His wisdom; and by *Devotion* and *Gratitude* responding to His compassion, leading to complete *self. Sacrifice* in His service. The steady cultivation of these virtues, the fruits of love directed to God, comprise our duty to Him: Reverence, Humility, Faith, Submission, Devotion, Gratitude, Self-Sacrifice.

There are many examples of great devotees in the Hindu books, men who showed out these virtues, to the fullest extent, and have set examples of love to God which should be studied in order that they may be imitated. Bhishma's noble hymn to Shri Krishna, uttered as he lay wounded on the battle-field, and which drew Shri Krishna to his side, should be carefully read and thought over.[316]

Prahlada, triumphant by devotion over all attacks, prayed: "In all the thousand births through which I may be doomed to pass, may my faith in Thee, Achyuta, never know decay. May passion, as fixed as that which the worldly-minded feel for sensual pleasures, ever animate my heart, always devoted unto Thee."[317]

Of such devotees Shri Krishna says:

महात्मानस्तु मां पार्थ दैवीं प्रकृतिमाश्रिताः।
भजन्त्यनन्यमनसो ज्ञात्वा भूतादिमव्ययम् ॥
सततं कीर्तयन्तो मां यतन्तश्च दृढव्रताः।
नमस्यन्तश्च मां भक्त्या नित्ययुक्ता उपासते ॥
ज्ञानयज्ञेन चाप्यन्ये यजन्तो मामुपासते।
एकत्वेन पृथक्त्वेन बहुधा विश्वतोमुखम् ॥[318]

"Verily the Mahatmas, O Partha, sheltered in My divine prakriti, worship with unwavering mind having known Me, the imperishable source of beings.

---

[316]*Mahabharata.* Shanti Parva, xlvii.
[317]*Vishnu Purana.* I, xx.
[318]*Bhagavad-Gita.* x. 13–15.

"Always glorifying Me, strenuous, firm in vows, bowing unto Me, they worship Me with devotion, ever harmonised.

"Others also, sacrificing with the sacrifice of wisdom, worship Me as the One and the Manifold everywhere present."

And Again:

अहं सर्वस्य प्रभवो मत्त: सर्वं प्रवर्तते।
इति मत्वा भजते मां बुधा भावसमन्विता:॥
मच्चित्ता मद्गतप्राणा बोधयंत: परस्परम् ।
कथयंतश्च मां नित्यं तुष्यंति च रमंति च ॥
तेषां सततयुक्तानां भजतां प्रीतिपूर्वकम् ।
ददामि बुद्धियोगं तं यन मामुपयांति ते॥[319]

"I am the Generator of all; all evolves from Me; understanding thus, the wise adore Me in rapt devotion,

"Mindful of Me, their life hidden in me, illumining each other, ever conversing about Me, they are content and joyful.

"To these, ever harmonious, worshipping in love, I give the buddhi-Yoga by which they come unto Me."

The cultivation of devotion is by meditating on the Object of devotion, by worshipping Him, by reading about Him, and by listening to, talking to and associating with those who are superior in devotion. In this way devotion increases.

ये तु सर्वाणि कर्माणि मयि संन्यस्य मत्परा: ।
अनन्येनैव योगेन मां ध्यायत उपासते॥
तेषामहं समुद्धर्ता मृत्युमंसारमागरात् ।
भवामि न चिरात्तार्थ मय्यावशितचेतसाम् ॥[320]

"Those verily who, renouncing all actions in Me, and intent on Me, worship meditating on me with whole hearted Yoga,

"These I speedily lift up from the ocean of death and existence, O Partha, their minds being fixed on Me."

Submission to the divine Will grows easily out of devotion, for we always readily desire to yield where we recognise and love the suprior. Wisdom and, compassion invite submission, for the wisdom will choose

---
[319]*Bhagavad-Gita.* x. 8–10.
[320]*Bhagavad-Gita.* xii. 6–7.

the best, and the compassion the least painful, path for us. Where wisdom and compassion are perfect, as in God, complete submission is the natural answer; and when all the events of life are seen as under His guidance, they can be accepted cheerfully and contentedly. The attitude of man in this respect to God should be that of a loving child to a wise and tender Father, carried to a far higher degree,

पिताहमस्य जगतो माता धाता पितामह: ।
....भर्ता......निवास: शरणं सुहृत्।।[321]

"I am the Father of this universe, the Mother, the Supporter, the Grandsire, the Husband, Home, Shelter, Lover."

Towards such a One gratitude springs up, ever increasing with increasing knowledge; and self-surrender, sell-sacrifice, is but the culmination of reverence. By daily offering of all our acts to God, the spirit of self-sacrifice is cultivated, and as it becomes perfect the lower self is conquered and the Supreme self is seen.

यत्करोषि यदश्नासि यज्जुहोषि ददासि यत् ।
यत्तपस्यसि कौतेय तत्कुरुष्व मदर्पणम् ।।[322]

"Whatsoever thou doest, whatsoever thou eatest, whatsoever thou offerest, whatsoever thou givest, whatsoever thou doest of austerity, O Kaunteya, do thou that as an offering unto Me."

As these virtues are the branches of Reverence springing from love, so do corresponding branches of vices grow out of Fear, which springs from hate in the presence of a superior. A constant attempt is made to belittle the superior, to pull him down to our own level, so that we may no longer have reason to fear him. For when we are in face of a superior whom we regard as an enemy, we are naturally inclined to dread the exercise of his power, which we feel ourselves unable to resist, and we long to lessen this hostile power or to escape from its reach.

The hate-emotion directed to God shows itself in attempts to lesson the feeling of his greatness, to diminish the recognition of His powers. *Irreverence* is the commonest vice of this class, flippant careless speech

---
[321] *Bhagavad-Gita.* ix. 17–18.
[322] *Bhagavad-Gita.* ix, 27.

and manner about sacred objects and sacred places, foolish jokes and idle laughter in speaking of the religious beliefs of others. This passes on into the vice of *Profanity* in coarse natures, and both are destructive of the finer emotions and should be sedulously guarded against. This dulling of the finer emotions leads on to complete alienation from religion, for God can only be reached through these finer emotions and by the virtues we have seen to be the offspring of love; and as a man is driven further and further away by the repellent action of hate, he loses all sense of the divine Presence, and often lapses into entire ethical unbelief, which leads to evil living.

असत्यमप्रतिष्ठं ते जगदाहुरनीश्वरम् ।[323]

"The universe is without truth, without basis, without God, they say."

Reverence to the Sovereign, the head of the State, comes naturally after Reverence to God, the representative of whose power, justice, and protection he is on Earth, if he be a true King, intent on the welfare of his subjects, always subordinating and sacrificing his own personal comforts and interests to those of his people, as did the ancient divine Kings, who give us the ideal of Kingship. The virtues spoken of above should be repeated in a lesser degree, in a subject's relation to his King. The virtues of *Loyalty, Fidelity* and *Obedience* are those which make a good subject, and the necessity of these for the prosperity of a nation is strongly insisted on. Manu says that the King was made by God to protect the world, and was made of particles taken froin Indra, Vayu, Yama, Surya, Agni, Varuna, Soma and Kubera. As Indra, he is to shower benefits on his kingdom; as Vayu, to know all that goes on; as Yama, to control his subjects; as Sarya to take taxes; as Agni, to be full of briliant energy; as Varuna, to punish the wicked; as Soma, to give joy to his subjects; as Kubera, to support his people;[324] Bhishma's dis course on the duties of King and subjects is most instructive; the King is to stand as God to his people, he being their protector and the guardian of all.[325]

---

[323] *Bhagavad-Gita.* xvi, 8.
[324] *Manusmriti.* vii, 3, 4, and ix. 303–311.
[325] *Mahabharata. Shanti Parva.* lvi–xci.

The itihasa are full of statements as to the blessings enjoyed by a loyal people ruled over by a good King.

As loyalty is insisted on, so are the corresponding vices of *Disloyalty, Treason* and *Rebellion* condemned, and the miseries are described of kingdoms that are a prey to anarchy.

Closely attached to the virtue of loyalty is that of *Patriotism,* in which the country is thought of as a collective whole, a living individual, to whom service is due. The King, in fact, is the embodied Majesty of the Nation, and loyalty to him grew out of patriotism of the purest kind. Patriotism is a virtue that has its roots in several emotions; it grows out of veneration for the past of the country, admiration of its saints, heores and warriors, its great men of every kind, of its strength, power and splendour; it identifies itself with the country by sympathy, feeling its joys and sorrows, its successes and reverses, its prosperity and adversity, as its own; it loves its natural beauties, and rejoices in its artistic and mechanical triumphs. The motherland, the country as a whole, is looked up to as an ideal, as an object of reverence, to be served and worked for above and beyond all else. Though, as a whole, the country is greater than the patriot, the patriot has the power of helping his country by his service; he gladly sacrifices ease, comfort, wealth, life itself, on the altar of his country. As a tender father seeks the good of his family so the patriot seeks the good of his land, and puts its interests before his own. The virtue of *Public Spirit* is but another name for patriotism, and the public-spirited man is the man who will exert himself for a public object even more earnestly and diligently than for a private one. The very expression "public spirit" instinctively embodies the truth that has been referred to so often as the very basis of morality the Unity of all. Public spirit is the common spirit, the spirit of all the public, the spirit which is one in all the public; and the public-spirited man is he who—consciously or unconciously—realises the oneness of the Self in all the members of that public to which he belongs; who feels that the good and the evil of each are the good and the evil of all the members of that public, and who acts accordingly, endeavouring to ameliorate the conditions of life for all.

As in the case of virtues and vices towards God, so in the case of virtues and vices to the State and its Ruler, it must be borne in mind that no man can free himself from the duty of incessantly endeavouring to base his mental attitude and his outer actions on the best reason he can reach up to, nor can he free himself from responsibility for acquiesense in flagrant injustice, or for allowing himself to be carried away by any mere public opinion which he knows to be wrong, or has not taken the trouble to test, although feeling that its accuracy is doubtful. There is a false loyalty the lip-loyalty of the flatterer—which is far more dangerous and sinful than the apparent opposition of the honest counsellor, who gives unpleasent but wholesome advice, and there is a false patriotism that merely truckles to the prejudices of the ignorant,

सुलभा: पुरुषा राजन् सततं प्रियवादिन: ।
अप्रियस्य च पथ्यस्य वक्ता श्रोता च दुर्लभ: ॥[326]

"Easy to find, O King ! are the men that always speak the words that please. Difficult to find are the men, both those that hear and those that speak (gently), the words that are not pleasant but wholesome."

These virtues of patriotism and public spirit, directing the mind to ends beyond those of the personal separated self, are enlarging and ennobling to the character, and train the man to see a larger self, and so to make some progress towards the recognition of the ONE. The public-spirited patriotic man is nearer to God than the man whose interests are restricted within a narrower area, and gradually he will widen out from love of country to love of humanity. Happy is the land whose sons are patriotic; she is sure to rise high amid the nations of the Earth.

We have now to consider the duties owed to Parents and Teachers, who also stand as Superiors. These will include those that are shown to God and the King, and we may add to them the virtues of *Gentleness, Trustfulness* and *Teachableness.* Perhaps no virtues are more strongly insisted on than those that a child owes to his parents and teachers, and down to the present time none are more characteristic of the true Âryan.

---

[326]*Ramayana*, VI. xvi, 21.

यं मातापितरौ क्लेशं सहेते संभवे नृणाम् ।
न तस्य निष्कृतिः शक्या कर्तुं वर्षशतैरप ॥
तयोर्नित्यं प्रियं कुर्यादाचार्यस्य च सर्वदा ।
तेष्वेव त्रिषु तुष्टेषु तपः सर्वं समाप्यते ॥
तेषां त्रयाणां शुश्रूषा परमं तप उच्यते ।
न तैरनभ्यनुज्ञातो धर्ममन्यं समाचरेत् ॥
त एव हि त्रयो लोकास्त एव त्रय आश्रमाः ।
त एव हि त्रयो वेदास्त एवोक्तास्त्रयो ऽग्नयः ॥

...   .

विश्वप्रमाद्यन्नेतेषु त्रीलोकान्विजयेदुगृही ।
दीप्यमानः स्ववपुषा देववद्दिवि मोदते ॥

...   .

सर्वं तस्याहता धर्मा यस्यैते त्रय आहताः ।
अनादृतास्तु यस्यैते सर्वास्तस्याफलाः क्रियाः ॥
यावत्रयस्ते जीवेयुस्तावन्नान्यं समाचरेत् ।
तेष्वेव नित्यं शुश्रूषां कुर्यात्प्रियहिते रतः ॥

...   .

त्रिवेतेष्विति कृत्यं हि पुरुषस्य समाप्यते ।
एष धर्मः परः साक्षादुपधर्मो ऽन्य उच्यते ॥[327]

"The suffering which the mother and father endure in the birth of children cannot be compensated, even in a hundred years.

"Let him do always what is pleasant to these two, and also to the acharya ; in the satisfaction of these three all (the fruit of) austerity is obtained.

"The service of these three is called the highest austerity; without the permission of these let him not perform other duties.

"For verily these are the three worlds and the three Ashramas; these also are said to be the three Vedas and the three fires.

"The householder who neglects not these three will conquer the three worlds, and in a shining body he will rejoice, as a Deva, in heaven.

"All duties are honoured by him who honours these three; for him who does not honour these all rites are fruitless.

"As long as these three live, so long let him not do ought else; let

---

[327] *Manusmriti*. ii. 227–220, 232, 234, 235, 237.

him ever do service to them, intent on what is pleasant and beneficial.

"In (honouring) these three all is achieved that should be done by man; this is plainly the highest duty; all other is called a lesser duty." Teachableness and obedience to the teacher are insisted on, and many rules were given intended to impress on the student the duty he owned to his preceptor. He was to be ever serviceable and careful not to offend, regarding the guru as his father in the highest sense.

उत्पाद कब्रह्मदात्रोर्गरीयान् ब्रह्मद: पिता।
ब्रह्मजन्म हि विप्रस्य भेत्य चेह च शाश्वतम्॥[328]

"Of the progenitor and the giver of the knowledge of Brahman, the giver of the knowledge of Brahman is the more venerable father ; for the birth of the Brahman in the Brahmana is verily eternal, both here and after death."

Only to the dutiful pupil was knowledge given:

यथा खनन्खनित्रेण नरो वार्यधिगच्छति ।
तथा गुरुगतां विद्यां शुश्रूषुरधिगच्छति ॥

"As a man by digging with a spade obtains water, so he who does service obtains the wisdom enshrined in his guru."

The vices which grow out of hate in relation to parents and teachers include, as do the virtues, those named under the relation to God and the King, and we may add to them those of S*uspiciousn*ess, *Cowardice, Falsehood,* and *Insolence.* Where there is fear of one stronger than ourselves, suspicion inevitably arises, the expectation that he will use his power for our injury and not for our benefit. There is perhaps no greater poisoner of human relations than constant suspiciousness—the suspicious nature—for it casts a false appearance over everything, distorts and exaggerates actions, and supplies evil motives to the most harmless acts. A suspicious nature sees hidden malevolence every where, and is always miserable because always afraid. Cowardice engenders falsehood, the putting on of a false appearance for the sake of protection against a dreaded exercise of hostile power. When we come to study the reaction of the emo tions of one person on those of another, we

---
[328]*Manusmriti,* ii, 206, 207.

shall see that oppression on the part of the strong leads to the growth of these vices in the weak, and that these are the vices characteristic of the slave and the down-trodden.

Arrogance and superciliousness are attempts of the inferior to diminish the distance between himself and the superior, and are the reverse of the virtues of humility and teachableness. They render impossible any happy and mutually beneficial relation between parents and children, between teachers and pupils. The sweet natural ties which grow out of the love-emotion are violently disrupted by these evil growths of the hate emotion, and they destroy the peace and happiness of families, as, when carried to a higher degree, they destroy the prosperity of States and the influence of religion.

The general attitude of the inferior to the superior is summed up by Manu as being that which is shown to the teacher:

विद्यागुरुष्वेतदेव नित्या वृत्ति: स्वयोनिषु ।
प्रतिषेधत्सु चाधर्माद्धितं चोपदिशत्स्वपि।।
श्रेय:सु गुरुवद् वृत्ति नित्यमेव समाचरेत् ।

"Such also constantly his conduct among teach ers of learning, relatives, among those who hold him back from unrighteousness and give him counsel.

"Among his superiors let him ever follow the same behaviour as with his teacher."

In cultivating the virtues and weeding out the vices above mentioned, the young man should not forget one important consideration. His parents are given to him by his prarabdha karma, while this is not completely the case with his teacher, the element of present choice also entering into the latter relation for the most part. While therefore the duty of reverence and trust and submission without reserve, short of what involves the commis sion of a positive sin, is desirable towards parents, even if they are not as loving and considerate as parents ought to be, that duty is influenced by certain other considerations in the case of the teacher. The teacher is chosen either by the parents for the student in the days of youth, or by himself when he reaches years of discretion. In the first case, the authority of the teacher is the authority of the parents, delegated to him by them. If any doubt arises in the mind of the student as to whether that authority has been duly exercised, the student should at once consult his parents and abide by their decision. In the second case, should such a doubt arise, he must exercise his own judgment, as he did when first he chose the teacher, and if teacher and student duly understand their respective duties then the wisest and most useful course is for the student to say clearly and respectfully to his teacher: "Sir, there is such and such a doubt in my mind; kindly remove it;" and for the teacher to remove the doubt either by convincing the student of the rightness of the course adopted, or by altering that course, if indefensible.

The above is important to bear in mind, as the abuse of authority and the misplacing of trust are unfortunately but too common in the world. In India especially, where the spirit of devotion to teachers is strong, having come down from the time when the teacher was a true teacher, there is exceptional danger of the misplacing of faith, and consequently there is exceptional need for preserving a balance of mind and for rejecting false claims.

To the aged *Respect* is the virtue which should ever be shown by the young, and they should ever be regarded and treated as superiors.

शय्यासने ध्याचरिते श्रेयसा न समाविशेत् ।
शय्यासनस्थश्चैवैनं प्रत्युत्थायाभिवादयेत् ॥
ऊर्च प्राणा ह्युत्क्रामन्ति यून: स्थविर आयति ।
प्रत्युत्थानाभिवादाभ्यां पुनस्तान्प्रतिपद्यते ॥
अभिवादनशीलस्य नित्यं वृद्धोपसेविन: ।
चत्वारि तस्य वर्धन्त आयु: प्रज्ञा यशो बलम् ॥[329]

"He should not take the bed or the seat belonging to a superior; and he who is occupying a bed or seat should rise and salute him.

"A young man's pranas rise upwards when an old man approaches; rising, and saluting, he again recovers them.

"He who ever salutes and shows reverence to the aged, obtains an increase of four things: life, intelligence, fame and strength."

And so again:

---

[329] *Manusmriti.* ii. 119–121.

अभिवादयेद् वृद्धांश्च दद्याच्चैवासने स्वकम् ।
कृताञ्जलिरुपासीत गच्छत: पृष्ठतोऽन्वियात् ॥[330]

"Let him salute the aged, let him give them his own seat, let him sit by them with folded hands, let him walk behind when they leave." This reverence to the aged is one of the most gracious virtues of youth and manhood, and one who shows it wins love and approval from all. It is naturally accompanied with *Modesty*, a virtue which is a lesser degree of humility. That obeisance to the aged is even physically beneficial to the young man is hinted in the second of the shlokas above quoted. By one of the laws of nature there is always a tendency towards equilibrium; as heat radiates from the warmer to the cooler, so strength and vitality go out from the stronger to the weaker. It has been proved by ordinary medical Science that invalids draw vitality from the vigorous, the feeble draw life from the healthier and stronger, and a large portion of the cures effected by magnetism are due to this fact. In accordance with this law, the pranas of the young move out towards the old and the feeble ; but when the young man rises and makes obeisance, he at once creates in the mind of the elder the mood of benevolence and of giving instead of taking, and this mood sends back those pranas to the younger man.

Good manners to a superior involve respect, modesty, truthfulness, readiness to render service, an absence of fear, suspicion and conceit. A youth, who shows those virtues will always meet with favour, and will enjoy many opportunities of im provement in the cornpany of his elders and superiors. Such a youth is always welcome, and his elders will take pleasure in helping and guiding him, and giving him the benefit of their experience.

The vices which shew themselves in relation to the aged include those noted in connection with the other classes of superiors, and *Disrespect* and *Conceit* may be added. The latter vice is peculiarly likely to arise, because the strength and vigour of the youthful body give it a physical superiority over the body of the aged, more obvious than the inferiority in experience and ripeness of judgment. *Impatience*

---

[330]*Manusmriti.* iv, 154.

is another vice that shows itself in this connection, the swift activity of youth being apt to chafe against the slowness of the aged.

No virtues need cultivation more in modern life than those dealt with in this chapter, for in the rush and hurry of the present day, and the self assertiveness that flourishes in a competitive civilisation, these are the virtues most likely to disappear.

Religious virtues have decayed with the growth of misunderstood scientific facts, and reverence and faith towards God have been depreciated as weakness and credulity. But religious virtues are the foundation-stones of a strong and manly character, and are found in history in heroes and not in base and degenerate men.

Still more, perhaps, is visible the decay of a high-minded loyalty to the Monarch, and a patriotic fidelity to the State. This, as the student will learn from the careful study of history, is due to internal organic reasons, mainly the failure in duty to each other first of Rulers and then of the Ruled, after the divine dynasties of Kings were with drawn, in order that humanity might be left to learn by painful experience how to stand on its own feet, with many falls and struggles, like an infant. The spread of general though superficial. knowledge, the growth, through bitter conflicts, of democratic institutions, and the passing of authority into the hands of a majority—in the absence of the wise and experienced, or because of their inability to take up their duties—have hidden the true rights and duties of the Sovereign from careless eyes and minds. The one-sided exaggeration of the instruments of administration—cabinets, councils, parliaments, republican senates and congresses—has veiled the Governor, the King himself. In the course of these experiments of humanity, there have arisen, in consequence of the mistakes due to inexperience and selfishness, increasing poverty and distress, the strife of labour and capital, the growing disorganisation of society. The remedy for these lies in restoring right feeling between King and Ministers and Sabha and people, in restoring right feeling between all the limbs and organs of the State, and in each and all performing. their respective duties of protecting and ruling, advising, administering, and helping with loyalty, fidelity and obedience; in restoring, in fact, the ancient system on a higher level, with fuller know ledge, according to the law of cyclic growth. Perhaps it may be for Âryan youths, trained up in the ancient virtues, to restore to modern life the ideal of the true citizen, and to set again the example of the true gentleman, pious to his God and loyal to his King and Country.

That this may be so, it will be well to begin with the cultivation of these virtues in the family, where the Father and the Mother represent the superiors. The decay of reverence, obedience, respect and serviceableness to them is only too patent in modern Indian life. Here every youth can at once begin to copy the old ideals, and to restore in his own home the ideal of the perfect son. Eager attention to their wants, prompt and cheerful obedience to their wishes, frank confidence in their good-will, trustful reliance on their deliberate judgment—these virtues will lay the foundation of the strong, dutiful, orderly character that will make a good citizen and a patriot.

In his relations to his teachers also, the student should strive to practise the appropriate virtues; and different as are the modern conditions between teacher and pupil from the ancient ones, yet the appropriate virtues might be cultivated, and the relation would then gradually again take on the affectionate intimacy of the older time.

To the aged also, the Indian youth should show unvarying respect, consideration and readiness to serve, utilising his physical advantages to supply their weaknesses, looking on aged men as his fathers, on aged women as his mothers, and showing ever to them the loving duty of a son.

Let, then, the young man study these virtues, and build them into his own character by repeated effort, earnest, deliberate and well-reasoned thought, and with reliance on the Divine self. Then shall his own life be useful and honorable, and his motherland the better for his work.

CHAPTER IX

VIRTUES AND VICES IN RELATION TO EQUALS

We have now to consider how love and hate work out in the relations that arise between equals in the family and in society, binding them together or driving them apart accordingly as love or hate prevails. The relations between husband and wife, brothers and sisters, and between relatives of the same generation, those between friends, acquaintances and members of a society of similar age and standing, give rise to emotions which are rendered permanent as virtues and vices, constantly active in the family and in the community.

The virtues belonging to the family among those of the same generation are those which gradually lead the Jivatma to recognise his unity with others, and so prepare him for the recognition of the One self in all. He finds himself surrounded by a small band of Jivatmas whose conditions, interests, hopes and fears are much the same as his own, with whom he enjoys and suffers, rises and falls, is prosperous and unsuccessful, from whom his own interests can not be disjoined. As he practises the family virtues and sees the happiness ensured by the practice, or as he falls into the family vices and sees the sorrow and discomfort arising from them, he gradually learns that to bring about general happiness he must treat all men as his brothers, as members of one family, and that the miseries that afflict humanity all have their root in the neglect of the practice of brotherliness.

Affection, or love between equals, is the form of the love-emotion here to be cultivated. It will show itself in *Kindness* of thought, speech and action. Kindness of thought is at the root of kindness of speech and of action, and one who guards himself against all harshness of thought will not err in speech or in act. We have already seen what great stress Manu lays on control of speech, and sweetness, gentleness, of speech should be cultivated in all family relations as well as in those of the outer world:

यस्य वाङ्मनसी शुद्धे सम्यग्गुप्ते च सर्वदा ।
स वै सर्वमवाप्नोति वेदान्तोपगतं फलम् ॥
नारुन्तुदः स्यादार्तो ऽपि न परद्रोहकर्मधीः ।
ययास्योद्विजते वाचा नालोक्यां तामुदीरयेत् ॥[331]

"He whose speech and mind are pure and ever carefully guarded, he obtains all the fruit that is obtained by means of the Vedanta.

"Let him not, even though distressed, cut another to the quick (by his speech), nor meditate acts of hostility to others; let him never utter the malignant word that disturbs (the mind of the hearer)."

This injunction, addressed primarily to superiors in their intercourse with inferiors, covers all human intercourse, and is, perhaps, nowhere more needed than in family relations, where close knowledge of the weakness of each is apt to barb the tongue to cutting speech. Again the right family relations are well sketched in the following:

न पाणिपादचपलो न नेत्रचपलो ऽनृजुः ।
न स्याद्वाक्चपलश्चैव न परद्रोहकर्मधीः ॥

... ...

ऋत्विक्पुरोहिताचार्यैर्मातुलातिथिसंश्रितैः ।
बालवृद्धातुरैर्वैद्यैर्ज्ञातिसंवन्धिवान्धवैः ॥
मातापितृभ्यां यामीभिर्भ्रात्रा पुत्रेण भार्यया ।
दुहित्रा दासवर्गेण विवादं न समाचरेत् ॥[332]

"Let him not be aimlessly restless with his hands and feet, nor with his eyes, nor crooked (in his conduct), nor aimlessly restless with his tongue, nor meditate acts of hostility to others.

"With the Ritvik, Purohita, Acharya, maternal uncle, guest, dependent, children, the aged, sick, physician, kinsfolk, connexions by marriage, relatives,"

"Mother, father, female relative, brother, son, wife, daughter, servant-folk, let him not enter into altercation."

And, after recounting the different worlds with which the persons above-named are connected, as representing in the organisation of human society the position of the worlds in the organisation of the Brahmanda,

---
[331] *Manusmriti*. ii. 160, 161.
[332] *Manusmriti*, vi. 177, 179, 180.

so that if a man be at peace with them he is at peace with these worlds, Manu concludes:

भ्राता ज्येष्ठः समः पित्रा भार्या पुत्रः स्वका तनुः।
छाया स्वा दासवर्गश्च दुहिता कृपणं परम् ।
तस्मादेतैरधिक्षिप्तः सहेतासंज्वरः सदा।।[333]

"The elder brother is the same as the father, the wife and the son are one's own body.

"The servant-folk are one's shadow, the daughter is most deserving of compassion; therefore, though slighted by these, let a man bear it ever undisturbed."

The right relation between husband and wife, between father and sons, and between brothers, is beautifully shown in the *Ramayana* in Shri Rama and Sita, the four divine sons and Dasharatha, and the four brothers, Shri Rama, Lakshmana, Bharata and Shatrughna. These are the models a youth should set before himself, and he should shape his conduct on these.

Of the good wife, Manu says:

प्रजनार्थं महाभागाः पूजार्हा गृहदीप्तयः ।
स्त्रियः श्रियश्च गेहेषु न विशेषोऽस्ति कश्चन ॥
उत्पादनमपत्यस्य जातस्य परिपालनम् ।
प्रत्यहं लोकयात्रायाः प्रत्यक्षं स्त्रीनिबन्धनम् ॥
अपत्यं धर्मकार्याणि शुश्रूषा रतिरुत्तमा ।
दाराधीनस्तथा स्वर्गः पितृणामात्मनश्च ह ॥
पतिं या नाभिचरति मनोवाग्देहसंयता।
सा भर्तृलोकानाप्नोति सद्भिः साध्वीति चोच्यते ॥

"There is no difference whatsoever between Shri (the Devi of Prosperity and the wife in the house, who is the mother of the children, who brings good fortune, who is worthy of worship, the light of the home.

"Of the bearing of children, the protection of those born, the continuance of the world-process, woman is evidently the only source.

"Children, religious ceremonies, service, marital happiness, heaven for one's ancestors and oneself, depend on the wise.

---

[333] *Manusmriti*, iv. 184, 183.

"She who, ruling her mind, speech and body, wrongs not her husband, she obtains the (heavenly) world with her husband and is called by the virtuous a Sadhvi."

एतावानेव पुरुषो यज्जायात्मा प्रजेति ह।
विप्रा: प्राहुस्तथा चैतद्यो भर्ता सा स्मृताङ्गना।।[334]

"This is the extent of the man, his wife, himself and his children; Brahmanas thus declare that the husband and wife are known as the same."

This view of a family as a unit, as really one life, is the view which alone gives a sure foundation for the family virtues, and the indissolubility of the marriage tie among Âryans grows out of this idea. Father, mother and children are *one,* and each should love the other as himself; what pleases one should please all: what saddens one should sadden all. All the virtues can be practised in the family, which is a little world in itself; the parents represent the superiors, the children among each other the equals, the children to the parents the inferiors. A youth who cultivates the virtues in his home will be ready to show them out in the wider field of the world, and will be equipped for the duties of a good citizen. He can practise there all that he will require in his manhood, and develop all the qualities which will make him a faithful friend, an honourable, courteous and upright gentleman, a brave and unselfish patriot.

Tender affection between brothers and sisters lies at the root of family prosperity, and we may see in the story of the Pandavas how this consoled them in adversity and raised them finally to the height of prosperity.

Courtesy and *Consideration for the feelings of others* are enjoined as general principles of conduct, and noble bearing and manners have ever been held to be characteristic of the true Âryan. Thus speech must be true, but also pleasing:

सत्यं ब्रूयात्प्रियं ब्रूयान्न ब्रूयात्सत्यमप्रियम् ।
प्रियं च नानृतं ब्रूयादेष धर्म: सनातन:।।[335]

---

[334] *Manusmriti,* ix, 45.
[335] *Manusmriti.* ii. 138.

"Let him speak the true, let him speak the pleasing, let him not speak an unpleasing truth, nor speak a pleasing falsehood; this is the ancient law."

Of course, there are occasions when it is the plain and positive duty of the person concerned to tell the truth even though it be unpleasant, as when a person in authority rebukes or corrects a subordinate. But even in such cases he should speak gently, and such instances of special duty do not justify uncalled-for and rude language or sharpness, which only mar the due effect of the rebuke and prevent its entering into the heart of the reproved.

Good manners are very apt to be undervalued in modern times, partly because of the hurry and rush of modern civilisation, and partly from ignorance. But this undervaluing is a mistake. Good manners spring from a good heart and a gentle nature, and show kindness and refinement of character. They imply self-control and a sense of self-respect and dignity, and many difficult social situations, which cause quarrels among ill-mannered people, are passed through without any trouble or ruffle by the nobly inannered. Soft words, courteous gestures, pleasant siniles, dignified bearing, make social intercourse refreshing and a source of enjoyment, and the young Hindu should sedulously cultivate the noble manners of the elder generation, and thus sweeten the tone of modern society. Even gold becomes more beautiful by being refined and a noble and strong character is beautified by courtly bearing.

Hospitality is a virtue on which great stress is laid, and the guest must ever be honoured as a Deva.

संप्राप्ताय त्वतिथये प्रदद्यादासनोदके।
अन्नं चैव यथाशक्ति सत्कृत्या विधिपूर्वकम् ॥
तृणानि भूमिरुदकं वाक्चतुर्थी च सूनृता ।
एतान्यपि सतां गेहे नोच्छिद्यन्ते कदा चन॥
अप्रणोद्यो ऽतिथि: सायं सूर्योढो गृहमेधिना।
काले प्राप्तस्त्वकाले वा नास्यानशनन्गृहे वसेत्॥[336]

"Let him offer to the guest who has come a seat, water and food, hospitably according to his power, in accordance with rule.

---

[336]*Manusmriti.* iii. 99, 101, 105.

"Grass (for seat), room, water, and, fourthly, a kind word-these are never wanting in the houses of the good.

"The guest sent in the evening by the (setting) sun must not be sent away by the householder; whether arrived at a convenient or inconvenient time, he must not remain in the house unentertained."
That there was as much travel, with its beneficent results, in ancient India as there is now, when the means of locomotion were not so easy and rapid as they are today, was due solely to the general prevalence of this virtue, and the regarding of hospitality as an essential part of religion. The continuous pilgrimages from shrine to shrine and from city to city—with all their educative effects in broadening men's minds and experience, and in promoting affection and good-will between different and distant communities, by bringing them into familiar intercourse with each other—were only made possible by the generous provision of houses of rest, and of food and clothing, on an immense scale, by the voluntary hospitality and charity of the well-to-do.

Uprightness, Fair Dealing, Trust, Honour, S*traightforwardness, Urbanity, Fidelity, Fortitude, Endurance, Co-operation*—these are virtues which are necessary for happy and prosperous social life. Where these are found, the life of a community or of a nation is peaceful and contented, and men who show out these virtues in their characters make good citizens and lead happy lives.

Readiness to forgive injuries is a virtue necessary for peaceful living, for all, at times, do some wrong to another, moved by passion, or envy, or some other evil emotion. Readiness to forgive such wrong is a sign of a noble disposition, and *Magnanimity* includes this readiness, as well as the large heartedness which makes allowance for the weaknesses of others, and takes a generous view of their motives and actions.

Toleration is an allied virtue that may be practised towards equals or towards inferiors—the recognition that the self expresses itself in many ways, and that none should seek to force on another his own views or his own methods. Tolerance has always been a characteristic of Hinduism, whichi has never sought to convert men from their own faith; nor to impose on those within its own pale any special form of intellectual belief. The variety of philosophic views embraced within its circle, as shown in the six darshanas, testifies to the tolerance and wide-mindedness which have ever marked it. This tolerance is based on the belief in the One self, and the reverent acceptance of the infinite variety of Its intellectual manifestations. Hence Hinduism has ever been permeated by the large-hearted toleration which is the very spirit of Ishvara; all are His; all paths by which men seek God lead to Him; as men walking from opposite quarters reach the same city, though walking in opposite directions, so men from all quarters, seek ing God, meet in Him at last. It is foolish and childish, then, to quarrel about the ways.

ये यथा मां प्रपद्यन्ते तांस्तथैव भजाम्यहम्।
मम वानुवर्तन्ते मनुष्या: पार्थ सर्वश:॥[337]

"However men approach Me even so do I accept them, for the path men take from every side is Mine, O Partha."

Even when want of sufficient growth and knowledge keeps men away from the higher and attached to the lower manifestations of Deity, even then it is the One Ishvara who inspires their faith in the lower forms suited to their undeveloped intelligence, and it is He who gives the perishable fruit on which their desires are fixed.

कामैस्तेस्तैर्हृतज्ञाना: प्रपद्यन्ते ऽन्यदेवता: ।
तं तं नियममास्थाय प्रकृत्या नियता: स्वया ॥
यो यो यां यां तनुं भक्त: श्रद्धयार्चितुमिच्छति ।
तस्य तस्याचलां श्रद्धां तामेव विदधाम्यहम् ॥
स तया श्रद्धया युक्तस्तस्याराधनमीहते ।
लभते च तत: कामान्मयैव विहितान्हितान् ॥
अन्तवत्तु फलं तेषां तद्भवत्यल्पमेधसाम् ।[338]

"They whose wisdom hath been rent away by desires go forth to other Devas resorting to various external observances, compelled by their own natures.

"Any devotee who seeketh to worship with faith any such aspect, I verily bestow the unswerving faith of that man.

"He, endowed with that faith, seeketh the worship of such a one and from him he obtaineth his desires, I verily decreeing the benefits.

---

[337] *Bhagavad-Gita.* iv, 11.
[338] *Bhagavad-Gita.* vii. 20–23.

"Finite indeed the fruit; that belongeth to those who are of small intelligence."

ये ऽप्यन्यदेवताभक्ता यजंते श्रद्धयान्विता: ।
तेऽपि मामेव कौंतेय यजन्त्यविधिपूर्वकम्।।
अहं हि सर्वयज्ञानां भोक्ता च प्रभुरेव च ।
न तु मामभिजानन्ति तत्त्वेनातश्च्यवन्ति ते।।[339]

"Even the devotees of other Devas who worship, full of faith, they also worship Me, O son of Kunti, though contrary to the ancient rule.

"I verily am the enjoyer of all sacrifices, and also the Lord, but they know Me not in essence, and hence they slip."
Such is the noble and liberal teaching of Hinduism, and it should shape the thoughts of every true Âryan, so that he may never fall into the error of trying to belittle or injure any of the religions of the world. Let him be tolerant even to the in tolerant, and thus set a good example.

This tolerance of the religious beliefs, views, and *bona fide* opinions of others should not be misunderstood to mean toleration of and acquiescence in the active infliction of wrong by the wicked on the righteous and the innocent. A good man, while forgiving as far as possble wrong done to himself, should endeavour to set right—by gentle means at first, and, if these do not succeed, then by stern ones in accordance with the law of the land—all wrong inflicted on others. Such is the duty that Shri Krishna expressly laid upon Arjuna, with the whole weight of the wisdom embodied in the *Bhagavad-Gita.* Nor should any action be mistaken for intolerance which is only of the nature of conselling or education, even though it be the education of public opinion, or constitutional and sober endeavour to wean men from injurious ways, or a thoughtful discussion with the express object of eliciting truth. What is condemned is only the bigoted pride which imagines itself to be in sole possession of Truth, and would visit with punishment the slightest deviation from the course laid down by itself.

The vices which grow out of the hate-emotion when it prevails among equals correspond on the side of evil to the virtues we have been studying on the side of good. "It may almost shock the student

---
[339]*Bhagavad-Gita.* ix. 23–24.

to see very common faults of character class d as the fruits of the hate-emotion, and yet if he thinks a little he will see that they have the marks of that emotion, as they drive men apart from each other, separating them and setting them in antagonism to each other, and that is clearly the result of the repellent force, which is Hate and not Love.

The opposite of Kindness is *Harshness*, which shows itself but too often in the family as *Moroseness, Sullenness, Irritability,* and *Peevishness*—very common failings, and the destroyers of family affection and peace. These faults bring dark shadows into the family circle, in strong contrast to the light spread by the kind and sunny temper, and are but forms of *Anger*, one of the root manifestations of the hate-emotion. Manu classes anger and harshness among the sins which are to be specially avoided:

नास्तिक्यं वेदनिन्दां च देवतानां च कुत्सनम् ।
द्वेषं स्तम्भं च मानं च क्रोधतैक्ष्ण्ये च वर्जयेत् ॥[340]

"Let him avoid unbelief, censure of the Vedas, and slighting of the Devas, hatred, obstinacy, pride, anger, and harshness."

And this is natural, for these are sins which are especially productive of misery, and probably most of the daily troubles of life which cause harassment and worry are due to anger in one form or another. It is classed by Shri Krishna[341] with lust and greed as forming part of the triple gate of hell and as one of the asuric characteristics.[342] The mind confused by anger is easily hurried into other sins, and it is one of the chief roots of crime. *Impatience* is one of its smaller manifestations, and the student who is intent on improving his character should be on his watch against even this comparatively minor form of his great enemy. The steady effort to be patient with, kind to, all, will gradually eradicate from his character the fault of Anger.

Harsh Fault-Finding, Backbiting, Slander and Abuse are the opposites of Magnanimity. They proceed from the same source as Irreverence, etc. The way to correct these faults is always to examine whether the defect for which we wish to condemn another is not present

---

[340] *Manusmriti.* iv, 153.
[341] *Bhagavad-Gita.* xvi. 21.
[342] *Ibid.* 4.

in ourselves. As Vidura says to Dhritarashtra:

राजन् सर्षपमात्राणि परछिद्राणि पश्यसि ।
प्रात्मनो विल्वमात्राणि पश्यन्नपि न पश्यसि ॥

"Thou seest the holes of another, though small as the mustard-grain, O King!; thine own, that are large as the Bel-fruit, even seeing thou ignorest!"

Rudeness, Churlishness of bearing, a rough manner, are the faults which are the opposites of courtesy and consideration. They are exceedingly com mon in modern days, and are spreading in modern India. They are signs of a coarse and vulgar nature which—uncertain of its own power and of the respect of others—tries to assert itself by loudness and to force itself on the attention of others, and it is thus always a mark of weakness. The gentle courteous bearing of a man conscious of his own strength and position contrasts with the rough rude manner of a weak man, unfit for the position he is in and trying to cover his unfitness by self-assertion.

Crookedness, Unfairness, Deceit, Infidelity, Quarrelsomeness, Fickleness, Instability, are other common faults which appear in the relations between equals, and cause many troubles alike in family and social life. They all help to disintegrate families and nations, and men who have these vices are bad citizens, and sooner or later fall into well-deserved contempt and distrust.

Vindictiveness and *Revengefulness* are the opposite of the readiness to forgive, which we have seen is a part of magnanimity, and they perpetuate troubles, keeping them alive when they might die by forgetfulness. The wish to return an injury suffered by inflicting an injury in return is a sign of complete ignorance of the working of the law. 'A man who suffers an injury should think that he has inflicted an injury on another in the past, and that his own fault comes back to him in the injury now inflicted on himself. Thus he closes the account. But if he revenges himself now, he will in the future again suffer the equivalent of the revenge he takes on his enemy. For that enemy will not be likely to think that he has been justly punished, and will nurse revenge again, and so the chain of claim and counterclaim will continue endlessly. The only way to get rid of an enemy is to forgive him; revengefulness stores up trouble for the future, which will inevitably come to the revengeful person, and the injuries we suffer now are only our own revenge coming home to ourselves. No one can wound us unless our own past places a weapon in his hands, Letza student remember this when some one injures him; let him pay his debt like an honest man; and have done with it.

Intolerance is a vice which has caused immense destruction in the world, especially in modern times. Endless wars have been caused by men of one religion wishing to impose their faith on men of another creed, and torrents of human blood have been shed in the name of God. Persecutions stain the page of history with blood and tears, and we may see a striking example of national ruin caused by religious persecution in the case of Spain, once the greatest of Western Powers, whose decay dates from the days when she slew by thousands the Jews and the Moors, and finally expelled the survivors be cause their faiths differed from her own.

Sectarianism, when it is bitter and quarrelsome, is a form of intolerance, and in modern India this subtle enemy of religion is undermining the ancient noble toleration of Hinduism. Sectarian bigotry divides Hindu from Hindu, and blinds them, by magnifying unessential differences, to the essential unity in which they are rooted. As men lose the spirit of religion and cling chiefly to its forms, caring only for the external ceremony and not even understanding its meaning and the objects it is intended to bring about, they become more and more bigoted and intolerant, and split up into more and more numerous parties. Thus religion, which should bind men together, is changed by intolerant bigotry into a disintegrating force.

The remarks which apply to religious intolerance in India apply with even greater force to social convention in India as well as elsewhere. In India they have a special application because of the inseparable interblending of social customs with religious, so that the paltriest and most trifling customs, having their origin in some temporary need on some special occasion, rapidly assume a deeply religious and permanent importance.

The true Âryan must avoid intolerance and bigotry as he would avoid poison, and should remember that it is utterly alien from the spirit of his ancestral religion. He must look on all Hindu sects as members of his own family, and refuse to quarrel with or to antagonise any. And he must look outside the pale of Hinduism, and see in the other religions that surround him rays of the same Spiritual Sun in which he himself is basking, and thus spread peace over India, and make possible for her a united national existence. Let his religious watchword be "Include," not "Exclude," since the self is One.

CHAPTER X

VIRTUES AND VICES TOWARDS INFERIORS

To complete the outline of the virtues and vices evolved in human relations, we must consider those which arise in a man's relation to his inferiors, accordingly as he is ruled by the love-emotion or by the hate-emotion. The virtues in this case will come under the general name of *Benevolence,* the will to do good to those who are weaker than ourselves; the vices will come under the general name *of Pride*, the sentiment which causes a man to look down on others, and to do them injury, according to the activity of the hate-emotion in him Love showing itself to an inferior inevitably takes the form of Benevolence, and its commonest form is that of *Compassion* and *Pity.* Weakness, ignorance, folly, arouse in the man ruled by the love-emotion the desire to help the person who is at such disadvantage, by bestowing on him strength, knowledge, wisdom. Compassion at once springs up in him, as by *Sympathy* he feels the weakness, ignorance, and folly as though they were his own, and thus becomes anxious to remove them, to raise the sufferer above them. From these virtues springs *Beneficenc*e, the active carrying out of the will to do good, the performance of actions expressive of the good-will felt.

In the conduct of parents to their children we see these virtues brightly shown forth. The weakness of the child, its dependence and helplessness, awaken the tenderness of the parent, and he be comes filled with compassion and pity for the little creature that is so unable to protect and support itself. These virtues express themselves in softness of language, caressing gestures, encouraging looks and smiles, so that the child may lose the feeling of its own littleness and feebleness, and may in effect share and direct the strength and skill of its elders, and thus supply its own deficiencies. Compassion and pity seek, as does all love, to lessen the distance between itself and its object, to raise its object towards itself. It allays the apprehension which might arise in the inferior, in presence of strength greater than his own, by gracious aspect of *Kindlines*s, expressing in every way that there is no reason for fear. Where it sees timidity and shrinking in the weak, it increases the outward manifestations of *Gentleness, Softness* and *Sweetness*, becoming the more gentle as the object of compassion is the more fearful and hesitating.

The stronger, the older, those who are in any way superior, should always remember to practise these gentle virtues towards the weaker, the yonnger, the inferior in any way, and should especially bear in mind that their exercise is *the more* needed when the inferior shows any of the manifestations of fear, of the idea that the superior is a hostile power, likely to inflict injury on him. Power is so constantly used to oppress and to injure, that the first feeling of the inferior in the presence of his superior is apt to be one of fear, and it is necessary to remove this by a manifestation of love.

Compassion and Pity readily give rise to *Protection* of the weak, whenever they are threatened by those stronger than themselves, and in protecting them *Heroism* appears, the cheerful risking of oneself for the sake of a weaker, The Hero is the man who risks his life for the good of another who is in need of help, without grudging the cost. The name is most often given to the warrior who gives his life for his King and his country, or to the martyr who dies for his faith; but it is deserved equally by many an unknown man and woman, who in ordinary human circumstances sacrifices life or health for others—the physician or nurse, 'who dies, worn out by strenuous exertions in aid of the plague-stricken; the mother, who rescues a child from death by ceaseless tendance, careless of her life and health, caring only to supply everything that the babe needs; the bread-winner, who be comes exhausted by excessive toil, sacrificing leisure, strength, health, that the weaker ones dependent on him may not feel the pinch of starvation. The heroic virtues—*Courage, Valour, Enduranc*e, etc.—have for the most part their root in Compassion and in a sense of duty to the weak, a sympathy with them in their sufferings and a desire to remove these sufferings; they are most readily evoked in presence of the inferior in need of help. In fact, when they appear in the relations to superi ors and equals, it is always in connexion with the *need* of these persons, and the man showing the heroic virtues has something to give of which they are in want. It may be a King who, though occupying the position of a superior to his soldiers in dividually, needs their help for the protection of his crown; or a brother who, normally equal, has a deficiency which his brother can supply at the moment, and so on. It still remains that the Hero is always the giver, and leaves in his debt those for whom he pours out his life or his possessions. Compassion, Protection, Heroism, are virtues that especially befit Kings and Rulers.

Liberality is a virtue, again, which is called out by the presence of inferiors, and the readiness to give, the virtue of *Charity,* is one which has been placed by Hinduism in the very first rank gift, has always been an essential part of every sacrifice, and the feeding and supporting of true and learned Brahmanas has been no less essential. By these rules men were trained to sacrifice part of their wealth for the benefit of others, and thus were led onwards to a true understanding and acceptance of the great Law of Sacrifice.

Manu says:

श्रद्धयेष्टं च पूर्तं च नित्यं कुर्यादतन्द्रित: ।
श्रद्धाकृते ह्यक्षये ते भवत: स्वागतैर्धनै: ॥
दानधर्म निषेवेत नित्यमैष्टिकपौर्तिकम् ।
परितुष्टेन भावेन पात्रमासाद्य शक्तित:॥
यत्किंचिदपि दातव्यं याचितेनानसूयया ।
उत्पत्स्यते हि तत्पात्रं यत्तारयति सर्वत: ॥[343]

"Let him diligently offer sacrifices and oblations with faith; these, if performed with faith and with rightly earned vealth, become unperishing.

"Let him always observe the duty of charity, connected with sacrifices and oblations, with a contented mind, having sought with diligence a worthy recipient.

"Something verily ought to be given ungrudgingly by him who has been asked, for a worthy recipient will surely arise who will save him from all (sins)."

The way in which charity should be done is very clearly laid down by Shri Krishna, who divides gifts, according to their nature, into sattvic, rajasic and tamasic.

---

[343] *Manusmriti.* iv, 226–228.

दातव्यमिति यद्दानं दीयते ऽनुपकारिणे ।
देशे काले च पात्रे च तद्दानं सात्त्विकं स्मृतम् ॥
यस्तु प्रत्युपकारार्थं फलमुद्दिश्य वा पुनः ।
दीयते च परिक्लिष्टं तहानं राजसं स्मृतम् ॥
अदेशकाले यद्दानमपात्रेभ्यश्च दीयते ।
असत्कृतमवज्ञानं तत्तामसमुदाहृतम् ॥[344]

"That gift given to one who does nothing in return, saying, 'It ought to be given,' at right place and time and to a worthy recipient, that gift is accounted sattvic.

"That verily which is given for the sake of receiving in return, or again with a view to fruit, or grudgingly, that gift is accounted rajasic.

"That gift which is given at unfit place and time and to unworthy recipients, disrespectfully and contemptuously, that is declared tamasic." That charity should be done with courtesy and gentle kindliness is a rule on which much stress is laid. We often read in the Itihāsa directions to show careful respect in the making of gifts; charity should ever be gracious, for even a trace of contempt or disrespect makes it, as above said, tamasic,

The idea of showing to weakness the same courtesy that is extended to rank and superiority a tender deference and consideration, comes out strongly in the following shloka:

चक्रिणो दशमीस्थस्य रोगिणो भारिणः स्त्रियाः।
स्नातकस्य च राज्ञश्च पन्था देयो वरस्य च॥[345]

"Way should be made for a man in a carriage, for one who is above ninety years old, for a sick person, for one who carries a burden, for a woman, a Snataka, a king and a bridegroom."

Similarly we find, when directions are being laid down as to the giving of food to people in the due order of their position, preference over all is given to the weak;

सुवासिनीः कुमारीश्च रोगिणो गर्भिणीस्तथा।
अतिथिभ्यो ऽय एवैतान् भोजयेद्विचारयन् ॥[346]

---

[344]*Bhagavad-Gita.* xvii, 20–22.
[345]*Manusmriti,* ii. 13.
[346]*Ibid.* iii. 114.

"Let him, without making distinctions, feed newly-married women, young maidens, the sick, and pregnant women, even before his guests."

Another virtue which should be cultivated in relation to inferiors is what may, for lack of a better term, be called *Appreciativeness*, the full recognition of all that is best in them. This recognition, generously expressed, has a most encouraging effect; and stimulates them to put out all their energies. The sense of weakness, of littleness, of inferiority, tends to paralyse, and many a man fails simply by lack of confidence in his own powers. A word of hearty appreciation gives the encouragement needed, and acts like sunshine on a flower, causing the whole nature to expand and glow.

Patience is also most necessary in all dealings with inferiors; lesser ability generally implies less quickness of understanding, less power to grasp or to perforin, and the superior needs to practise patience in order not to confuse and bewilder the inferior. With children and servants this virtue has special opportunity for exercise, and its existence in the elders is peculiarly helpful and peace making in the family. Strength should be used to help and support weakness, not to crush and terrify it, and "patience sweet that naught can ruffle" is a sign of a truly great and strong nature. Appreciativeness and Patience are specially needed in parents and teachers.

The vices that spring out of the hate-emotion to inferiors are of the nature of *Pride,* the sense of superiority in the separated self, looking down on those below it, and desiring to still further lower them, in order to make its own superiority more marked. The character of a man filled with pride is graphically described by Shri Krishna:

इदमद्य मया लब्धमिमं प्राप्स्ये मनोरथम् ।
इदमस्तीदमपि मे भविष्यति पुनर्धनम् ॥
असौ मया हत: शत्रुर्हनिष्ये चापरानपि ।
ईश्वरोऽहमहम् भोगी सिद्धो ऽहं बलवान्सुखी ॥
पाठ्यो ऽभिजनवानस्मि कोऽन्यो ऽस्ति सदृशो मया।
यक्ष्ये दास्यामि मोदिष्ये ...   ...॥[347]

---

[347] *Bhagavad-Gita.* xvi. 13–16.

"This to-day by me hath been obtained, that purpose I shall gain; this wealth is mine already, and this also shall be mine in future.

"This enemy hath been slain by me, and these others I shall also slay. I am Ishvara, I am the enjoyer, I am perfect, powerful, happy.

"I am wealthy and well-born; what other is there that is like unto me? I will sacrifice, I will give, I will rejoice."

Such a man, looking down on his inferiors, seeking only his own gain and his own advantage, will see in them only persons to be used for his own purpose. To them he will show the vices of *Scorn, Contempt, Arrogance, Disdain,* expressing in words and actions his sense of the distance between himself and them. His own bearing will be marked by *Aggressiveness, self-assertion, Overbearingness,* implanting dislike and hatred in those with whom he comes into contact, unless they are thoroughly dominated by the love-emotion. If his inferiors possess anything which he desires, and he is able to deprive them of it without danger to himself, he may fall into robbery and murder; and he will use his superiority to oppress and enslave. The characters of many such men may be studied in history tyrants, oppressors, causing widespread destruction and misery, and thus sowing in the breasts of the oppressed the seeds of evil passions which sprang up into a crop of revolt, bloodshed and anarchy. Manu sternly condemns the Kings that fail in the duty of protection:

अदंड्यान्दंडयन् राजा दंड्याश्चैवाप्यदंडयन् ।
अयशो महदाप्नोति नरकं चैव गच्छति ॥[348]

"The king that punishes the innocent and punishes not the criminal, he goeth into infamy and hell."

In smaller fashion these evils are reproduced in the family and in society, where the superiors show out the fruits of hate instead of love. The tyrannical father or master implants and fosters in his children and servants the vices of the oppressed, and creates the evils which he later endeavours in vain to destroy.

Hauteur, Haughtiness, Reserve, are subtler forms of this same emotion, and work much mischief when they appear between those

---
[348] *Manusmriti.* viii. 128.

between whom cordiality, affection and openness alone should prevail. They should be very carefully guarded against by the student, when he comes to deal with those who are younger than he, or those towards whom nature or circumstances place him in the position of superior to inferior. He should ever remember that the duty of the superior is to bring the inferior up to his own level so far as is possible, and not to keep him inferior and constantly remind him of any distance that there may be between them. If he make the mistake of following the latter course, the probable, nay the certain, result will be that he will drive the inferior either into a slavish cringing and timidity and nervousness, on the one hand, or rebellion, pride and contempt, on the other. But if he behave otherwise, and treat his inferior as his equal, then the probability; almost the certainty, is that the inferior will readily see his superiority, and treat him with due respect and reverence. It is they who selflessly help others to rise that are honoured, not they who desire aggrandisement for themselves.

Let the student then remember in all his relations with his inferiors to cultivate sympathy and compassion and active beneficence. If in the family he shows these virtues to the younger and to the servants, in his later life in society and in the nation these virtues will still mark his character, and he will become a true philanthropist, a benefactor of his community and of his country.

CHAPTER XI

THE REACTION OF VIRTUES AND VICES ON EACH OTHER

In order that a youth may understand how to improve his own character and meet the difficulties and temptations which surround him, it is impor tant that he should know how the virtues and vices of people react' on each other. By understanding this, he will know how to be on his watch against evil reactions, and how to promote the good both in himself and in others.

The general law is that an emotion—and the virtue or the vice that is its permanent mood—when exhibited by one person to another, provokes in that other a similar emotion, virtue or vice. An exhibition of love calls out love in response; an exhibition of hate is answered by hate. Anger produces anger; irritation causes irritation; gentleness brings out gentleness; patience is responded to by patience. If the student will observe himself and his neighbours, he will soon discover for himself the reality of this law, and will see how the moods of people are affected by the moods they meet with in others. One ill-tempered man will set a whole company jangling; one sweet tempered man will keep everybody at peace.

This is the general law, working among average people who are equals, in whom the love-emotion and the hate-emotion are both present and are about equally balanced. When the people are not equals, but one is inferior to the other, the emotion, virtue or vice shown by one will also produce in the other one similar in kind, but *corresponding* to the one first shown, not *identical* with it. Thus an exhibition of love to an inferior will produce in him love, but the nature of the love will be governed by this inferiority, and will be reverence, trust, serviceableness, and so on. Benevolence will be answered by gratitude, and pity by confidence. An exhibition of hate to an inferior will produce in him hate, but the nature of the hate, again, will be governed by his inferiority, and will be fear, deceit, treacherous revenge, and so on. Oppression will be met with sullenness, and cruelty with silent vindictiveness. The good will produce good, and the evil, evil, according to the general law; but the particular nature of the good or evil shown will be governed by the relative positions of the individuals concerned.

When we come to study exceptional people, another law comes in. If an exceptionally good man is observed, one in whom the love-emotion is dominant, then it will be seen that he does not answer anger with anger, but that when anyone shows the vice of anger to him, he meets it with *the opposite virtue,* kindness; if a man shows him the vice of pride, he meets it with the opposite virtue, humility; if a man shows him the vice of irritation, he meets: it with the opposite virtue, patience, and so on. The result is that the vice is checked, and very often the person who showed it is: led, by the exhibition of the opposite virtue, to himself imitate that instead.

In the case of an exceptionally bad man, one who is dominated by the hate-emotion, there is but too often an exhibition of vice in answer to an exhibition of virtue. A man showing humility to such a one is met by pride; gentleness provokes insult; patience stimulates oppression.

We have thus two laws:

1. Among ordinary persons, emotions, virtues and vices provoke their own likenesses, or correspondences.
2. In persons who are definitely dominated by love or hate, emotions, virtues and vices provoke the appropriate subdivision of their own dominant emotion.

Let us consider instances.

Two ordinary men, equals, meet, and one, in a bad temper, speaks angrily; the other flares up in reply, answering angrily; the first retorts, yet more angrily; and so it goes on, each getting more and more angry, until there is a furious quarrel. How often have friends been parted by a quarrel beginning in the ill-temper of one.

Two other men meet, and one, in a bad temper, speaks angrily; the other answers softly; with a pleasant smile and friendly gesture; the anger of the first, finding no fuel, dies down, and the soft words and smile awaken an answering smile, the anger is gone, and the two walk off arm-in-arm.

A man in whom the hate-emotion predominates, superior to another, treats the latter with insolence and threat, trying to force him to yield to his will. The inferior meets this exhibition of evil emotion with fear, distrust and sullen submission, and in his heart springs up the desire for revenge, which he nourishes until an opportunity occurs to injure the superior. The latter, seeing the fear and sullen submission, shows yet more insolence and scorn, the sight of the fear increasing the original contempt for the inferiority of the other. This again leads to increased fear and distrust and more slavish submission, with growing longing for revenge, and thus the vicious cycle is repeated over and over again.

A superior man, in whom the love-emotion predominates, comes into contact with an inferior, in whom the very sight of his superiority arouses fear and distrust. The exhibition of these vices moves him to pity and compassion, and he answers the fear and distrust by increased kindness of manner and softness of language. The inferior thus met is soothed and encouraged, and his fear diminishes to slight timidity of approach; this in its turn disappears, and is replaced by trust and confidence in the good-will of the superior. Thus in his heart the love-emotion is aroused, and the seeds of virtue are implanted instead of those of vice, and the relation established is one which conduces to the happiness of each of the persons concerned.

The Itihasa and Puranas have many instances of this interplay of emotions, of the effects of the exhibition of virtues and vices reacting on each other. Bhima's scornful laughter over the blunders of Duryodhana awakens hatred and the desire for revenge in the bosom of the latter, and the hatred grows into one of the causes of the destructive war between the Pandavas and the Kurns. Kaushalya's angry reproaches as to the treatment of Rama are met by Dasharatha with gentle humility, and she is quickly moved to repentance and shows loving humility in return. Arjuna's fear at the sight: of the Virat-rupa is allayed by Shri Krishna's gentle words and re-assumption of His ordinary form. These stories are told for our instruction, that we may learn how we should meet and couquer evil, not by imitating it, but by exhibiting the opposite emotion. A fire is easily put out at the beginning, but when it has fuel thrown into it, it grows and increases, and at last destroys all with which it comes into contact.

The student will now understand the scientific nature of the command addressed to their followers by all the great Teachers, never to return evil with evil, but always with good. We can understand now why and how it has ever been said: Do unto others as you would they should do unto you.

यदन्यर्विहितं नेच्छेदात्मन: कर्म पूरूष: ।
न तत्परेषु कुर्वीत जाननप्रियमात्मन:।
यद्यदात्मनि चेच्छत तत्परस्यापि चिन्तयेत् ।।[349]

This is the summary of the Science of Conduct, because the "others" are in very truth "you" yourself. Says Manu :

क्रुध्यन्तं न प्रतिक्रुध्येदाक्रुष्ट: कुशलं वदत् ।[350]

"Let him not be angry again with the angry man; being harshly addressed, let him speak softly."

The *Sama-Veda* says:

सेतूंस्तर दुस्तरान् अक्रोधेन क्रोधं सत्येनानृतं।[351]

"Cross the passes difficult to cross; (conquer) wrath with peace; untruth with truth."

Says the Buddha :

"Hatred ceases not by hatred at any time: hatred ceases by love."

And again :

"To the man that causelessly injures me, I will return the protection of my ungrudging love; the more evil comes from him, the more good shall flow from me."

And again :

"He who bears ill-will to those who bear ill-will can never become pure; but he who feels no ill-will pacifies those who hate... Overcome anger by not being angered; overcome evil by good; overcome avarice by liberality; overcome falsehood by truth."

---

[349] *Mahabharata.* Shanti Parva, lxxxvi.
[350] *Manusmriti.* vi. 48.
[351] *Aranya-gana. Arka-parra,* 2nd *Prapathak.a*

Says Lao-tze :

"To those who are good, I am good; and to those who are not good, I am also good; and thus all get to be good. To those who are sincere, I am sincere; and to those who are not sincere, I am also sincere; and thus all get to be sincere.'

· Says Jesus-Christ :

"Love your enemies, bless them that curse you, do good to them that hate you, and pray for them which despitefully use you and persecute you."

Evil is only perpetuated when it is returned, the wrong emotion growing ever stronger as it is fed with fuel of its own nature; but as water poured on fire is love poured on hate. Happinesss can only be gained as the fires of hatred are quenched, and this can only be done by love, generously and freely outpoured.

This is the general law, and, in the strictest sense, this the last method of finally changing an evil nature into a good one. But, in dealing with limited times and spaces, it becomes the duty of those occupying special positions or offices in the community, or finding themselves in special situations created by the exceptionally evil, to apply the law of justice and punishment rather than that of charity. The Sovereign and the judge, representing the aspect of nature embodied in the law of equilibrium, find it their special duty to punish the evil doer and suppress the disturbances caused by crime, restoring the equilibrium of society. Apart from this special modification, the general law holds good.

Further, understanding the nature of virtues and vices, and their relations to and re-actions upon each other, the student will now be in a position to cultivate deliberately the love-emotion in his own nature, with the virtues which are its permanent moods, and he will learn also to awaken and stimulate these in others by exhibiting them in his own conduct.

In his superiors he will awaken benevolence, compassion, tenderness, by showing to them reverence, service, dutifulness and obedience; and if he meets a superior who shows any harshness or pride, he will check in himself the feeling of fear which springs up, and by showing a frank humility and a confidence in his good-will, he will awaken the love-emotion, and will thus turn the harshness into kindness and the pride into compassion.

In his equals he will ever seek to arouse affection by showing it himself, to win them to kindness by showing kindness, to courtesy by showing courtesy, to uprightness by showing uprightness. When they show any of the vices of the hate-emotion to him, he will restrain the similar emotion that leaps up in himself in answer, and will deliberately show the opposite virtue that belongs to the love-emotion, and will oppose kindness to unkindness, courtesy to rudeness, uprightness to deceit. Thus, he will not only avoid increasing the mischief caused by others; but in those others themselves, unless they be exceptionally evil, he will arouse right emotion and help them to improve.

In his inferiors he will try to plant the seeds of trust and confidence, encouraging them by his gentleness and patience, and eradicating all suspicion and fear. When he finds an inferior showing these vices, he will not allow himself to give way to scorn and contempt, but will increase his own gentleness and patience, and gradually lead the weaker into the love-relation with himself that will make their relations mutually pleasant.

If these principles ruled human relations in the family, the community, the nation, how changed would be the aspect of the world. How quickly would discord change to peace, storm to calm, misery to happiness. To use knowledge to guide action, so that right action may spring from right knowledge, should be the aim of every student of the Science of Ethics. Only thus can character be builded, and India's sons become worthy of their motherland. The student of to-day is the citizen of to-morrow. May right instruction lead him to noble life.

"I am giving you complete union of hearts and minds, in which ill-feeling finds no place. Even as the cow is pleased with the new-born calf, so let one be pleased with another. Let the son follow his father and be of one mind with his mother. Let the wife remain in peace with the husband and speak sweet words to him. Let not the brother bear malice towards brother or sister. Let all become harmonious with each other, and let all treat each other well."

PEACE TO ALL BEINGS.

INDEX

5 Ideal Types of Action, 47
5 Ideal Types of Sense Organs, 47

Abhimanyu, 186
abhinivesha, 170
Abhyasa, 202, 203
Absolute, The, 6, 76
Achamana, 134
Âchâra (Conduct), 8
Acharya, 109, 223
Achyuta, 209
Action, 74, 153, 177, 198
Adhvaryuh (conductor), 4
Adhyatma, 35, 37
Adi Bhuta, 46
Adi-tattva, 46, 91
Adityas, 50
Advaita, 19
Agami Karma, 74, 75
age, 2, 9, 10, 109, 111, 112, 148, 149, 150, 152, 222
Agha-marshana, 134
Agni, 9, 48, 50, 91, 112
Agnihotra, 5, 127, 128
Agrayana, 127
agriculturist, 5, 174
Ahamkara, 47, 158, 189
Ahavaniya fire, 116, 128
Ahnika-Sutravali, 104, 128
Aitareya Aranyaka, Brahmana, 5
Ananda (see Sat), 31, 131, 191, 192, 208
Ancestors, 183
andajah, 58
Angas, The Six, 9, 12
Anger, 230, 241
Angirasas, 4
animal kingdom, 50, 59, 81, 172
aniruddha, 15
antelope skin, 109
Anupadaka, 91
anus, 47
Apah Tattva, 91
Apana, 92
Apsaras, 50
archetypes, 52

Archika, 4
Arghya-pradana, 134
Arjuna, 30, 131, 168, 186, 199, 229, 243
Artha, 63, 128
Arvaksrotas, or Vegetable Kingdom, 172
Âryan, 1, 2, 4, 5, 6, 7, 10, 11, 21, 22, 55, 66, 78, 81, 106, 111, 113, 114, 123, 125, 142, 152, 158, 186, 187, 215, 221, 225, 229, 233
Âryavarta, 11
Asat, 30
ascetics, 53, 54, 96
Ashramas, Brahmachari (Student), 137
Ashramas, Grihastha (House-holder), 137
Ashramas, Sannyasi (Ascetic), 137
Ashramas, The Four, 137
Ashramas, Vanaprastha (Forest-dweller), 137
Ashramas, Yatih (controlled) see Sannyasi, 137
Ashtaka ceremony, 117
Ashvamedha, 186
Astrology, 12
Asuras, 50, 55
Atalam, 89
Atharvana, 42
Atharvaveda, 3, 4, 5, 12
Atma, 11, 15, 20, 21, 27, 28, 30, 37, 43, 44, 46, 51, 52, 60, 87, 88, 92, 93, 97, 99, 164, 190, 193
Atri, 54
avahana, 115
Avatara, 11
Avataras of Vishnu, 10
Avataras Shri Krishna, 11
avidya, 14, 18, 19, 20, 21, 34, 37, 43, 55, 60, 170
avyakta, 19, 46

Backbiting, 230
Bali offering, 117, 126
bandhah, 14
bath, 111, 120, 128
benevolence, 219, 245
Bhagavad-Gita, 11, 18, 20, 28, 30, 31, 32, 35, 40, 49, 57, 62, 63, 65, 70, 79, 80, 88, 132, 146, 153, 162, 164, 167, 168, 174, 180,

181, 182, 189, 194, 195, 197, 199, 200, 202, 203, 209, 210, 211, 212, 228, 229, 230, 237, 238
Bhagavan (Vishnu), 54
Bhagavati, 36
bhakti, 65, 67, 131
Bharata, 20, 164, 180, 197, 224
Bhashya, 2, 4, 16, 58, 108
Bhashya Vatsyayana, 58
Bhima, 243
Bhishma, 11, 72, 85, 185, 206, 207, 209, 212
Bhrigu, 7, 45, 54
Bhurloka, Bhuloka, 88, 90, 91, 94, 95, 98, 114, 118
Bhutadi, 47
bhutani, 89
Bhuvarloka, 90, 91, 92, 94, 96, 97, 98, 100, 118
Brahmacharya, 26, 141, 145, 183
Brahmaloka, 84, 90, 96, 98, 99, 113
Brahmanas, 3, 110, 116, 117, 125, 143, 153, 154, 155, 156, 225, 236
Brahmanda, 42, 43, 44, 46, 89, 90, 91, 97, 100, 170, 172, 223
Brahma, Night of, 89
Brahman, Nirguna, 25
Brahman, Saguna, 19, 30, 36, 39, 40, 43, 55, 131, 191
Brahman-wheel, 56
Brahman world, 64
Brahmapura, 99
Brahma-Sûtras, 17
Brahmaveda, 4
Brahmavidya or Uma, 3, 43
bride, 112
Brihaspati, 110
Buddha, 163, 244
buddhi, 16, 21, 35, 46, 47, 61, 62, 63, 110, 145, 162, 190, 195, 203, 210

cannibals, 55
castes, 8, 109, 148, 149, 150, 152, 153, 154, 157, 158, 197
Charana-Vyuha, 3
charity, 143, 149, 151, 180, 185, 227, 236, 237, 245
Chetana (consciousness), 53
Chhandah (metre), 13
chhaya, 54

Chit (see Sat), 31, 131, 165, 166, 191, 192, 208
Chudakarana, 116
Compassion, 234, 235, 236
Conceit, 219
Conduct, 8, 157, 161, 162, 165, 177, 244
Consciousness, Jagrat, Svapna, and Sushupti, 100
Content, 205
Co-operation, 227
courage, 149
Courtesy, 225
cow skin, 109
Creation, Day of, 78, 89

Daityas, 55, 125
Daksha, 54, 175
Dakshinagni, 117
Danavas, 55, 125
Darsha, 127
darshanas, 13
Darshanas, The Six, 3, 13, 20, 162
Dasharatha, 224, 243
day of Brahma, 78
Death, 26, 50
Deer skin, Spotted, 109
Deha, Karana, 46
Deha, Sthula, 46
Deha, Sukshma, 46
Deha, Virat, 46
Desire, 69, 70, 200
Devarajas, 50
Devas, 4, 30, 42, 47, 48, 49, 50, 52, 55, 62, 75, 76, 82, 91, 98, 114, 117, 124, 125, 128, 130, 142, 169, 183, 185, 193, 202, 206, 228, 229, 230
Deva world, 98
Devayana, 98
Devi Bhagavata, 2, 9, 34, 35, 37, 45, 61, 68, 73, 74, 76, 90, 92, 93, 94
devotees, 96, 209, 229
devotion, 19, 27, 65, 104, 130, 131, 133, 209, 210, 218
Dharana, 135, 136
Dharma, 1, 6, 7, 9, 11, 13, 21, 26, 31, 41, 63, 78, 84, 86, 106, 116, 128, 137, 145, 149, 150, 154, 166, 167, 173, 174, 186, 205
Dharma, Sanâtana, 1, 7, 21, 31, 78, 106, 137, 145, 149, 167, 173

INDEX • 249

Dharmashastras, 128
Dharma Sûtras, Apastamba, 116
Dharma Sûtras, Gautama, 84
Dharma, Vaidika, 1, 6
Dhritarashtra, 231
Dhyana, 135, 136
Dictionary, 12
disrespect, 184, 237
Droṇa, 11
Duryodhana, 243
dvaitam, 17
dvesha, 170
Dvijah, 109

Egg-Brahma (See Brahmanda), 44
Egg-Golden (See Hiranyagarbha), 44
Egg-World, 45, 89
Elements, The Five, 58, 62
endurance, 18, 180, 185
Equals, Conduct to, 222
Ethical Science what it is, 161
Ethics, Foundation of, 164
Ethics, Standard of, 179
Euclid, 12
Evolution, 58, 62
Evolution and Ethics, Huxley, 58

Fair Dealing, 227
Faith, 209
Fault-Finding, 230
Fidelity, 212, 227
Fire, Household, 128
Fire, Pillar of, 133
Fire, Region Svarga, 98
Fire, Sacrificial, 143
Five Daily Sacrifices (see Sacrifices), 116
five Devarajas, 50
five elements, 58, 62
Flowers, 134
Food, 139
Fortitude, 227

gamut, 4
ganas, 53
gandharvas, 78
Ganesha, 9, 50, 73
Gargya, 156
Garuda, 9, 43
Garutman, 48

Gautama, 14, 58, 84, 113
Gautama, the Rishi of Nyaya, 14
Gayatri, 134
Goloka, 89, 90, 91
gotra, 156
Grammar, 12
Grass, 227
Gratitude, 209
Grihya Sûtras, Apastamba, 107
Grihya Sûtras, Ashvalayana, 107
Grihya Sûtras, Parashara, 108
Grihya Sûtras, Shankhayana, 107
guest, 126, 223, 226, 227
gunas, 16, 32, 33, 47, 54
Guru, 134, 145

Hamsa, 9
Hari, 53, 73
Haridrumata, 156
Harmlessness, 135, 180, 197, 206
Harshness, 230
Haryashvas, 175
Haughtiness, 239
Havih, 117
hell, 181, 230, 239
heredity, 59, 194
heroes, 112, 186, 220
Hindu, 7, 23, 123, 148, 150, 158, 187, 192, 209, 226, 232, 233
Hinduism, 158, 227, 228, 229, 232, 233, 236
Hiranyagarbha, 44
Hiranyakeshin, 117
Homa, 124, 125
Horses, the Senses, 60
hospitality, 124, 143, 227
Hotâ, 4
Hotri, 5
Hrim Mantra, 46
Humility, 209
Husband, 211
Huxley, Professor, 58

Ikṣhvâku, 10
Image in worship, 133
Impatience, 220, 230
Indra, 48, 50, 73, 82, 105, 212
Indraloka, 89, 98
Indriyas, 16, 47
Irreverence, 212, 230

Isha, 6, 93
Ishta-deva, 134
Itihasas, 146

Jaimini, 17
Janaka, 66
Janaloka, 90, 91, 92, 94, 96, 100
Japa, 121, 124, 134, 139
jarayujah, 58
Jatakarma ceremony, 107
Jivatmas, division of, 100
jnana, 46, 59, 65, 67, 69, 110
Jnanendriyas, The   Five, 94
Jyotisham, 13

Kailasa, 53
Kali Yuga, 10, 11, 150
kalpa, 98, 99, 172
kalpas, 50, 52, 54, 55
Kama, 21, 62, 63, 96
Kanada, 15
kapila, 15
Karana Sharira, 93, 94, 96, 100
Kardama, 54
Karma, 11, 46, 61, 65, 68, 69, 70, 71, 72, 73, 74, 75, 76, 77, 80, 153, 154, 183
Karmendriyas, 94
Karna, 1, 11
Karnavedha Ceremony, 108
Kashyapa, 54
kaupina, 109, 110
Kavi, 156
Kingdom, Animal, 50, 59, 81, 172
Kingdom, Mineral, 58, 80, 172
Kingdom, Vegetable, 80, 81, 172
Kinnaras, 50, 125
Kosha, Anandamaya, 96
Kosha, Annamaya, 97, 107, 114, 115, 119, 120, 122
Kosha, Manomaya, 96, 97, 98, 100
Kosha, Pranamaya, 96, 97, 107, 114, 115, 119, 120, 122
Kosha, Vijnanamaya, 96, 97
Kratu, 54
Krishna, Dvaipayana, 10, 17
Krishna, Shri, 28, 35, 65, 66, 78, 79, 80, 84, 88, 131, 152, 167, 179, 180, 185, 186, 199, 202, 209, 229, 230, 236, 238, 243
Kriya, 65

Kshattriya, 108, 109, 149, 150, 151, 153, 155, 156
Kubera, 50, 212
Kula-deva, 134
Kumara Rishis, 138
Kumaras, 54, 96
Kurus, 11, 78
Kusha, or Darbha Grass, 116

Lakshmana, 224
Lakshmi, 43, 55, 63
Law, Civil, 8
Law, Hindu, 7, 123
liberality, 143, 244
liberation, 5, 8, 14, 15, 18, 37, 43, 54, 55, 56, 64, 65, 66, 67, 80, 130, 145, 146
Linga, 9
lingam, 133
lokas, 89, 91, 93, 94, 96, 99, 100
Lokas, Preta or Yama, 118
Lokas, Seven, 89, 91, 93, 94, 99, 100
Loka Svarga, 116
Loyalty, 212

Madhava or Madhva, 9, 17
Madhusudana Sarasvati, 13
magic, 55
Magnanimity, 227, 230
magnetic properties, 105, 194
Mahabharata, 1, 10, 45, 62, 64, 71, 85, 141, 155, 156, 157, 185, 186, 206, 209, 213, 244
Mahâbhâṣhya Patañjali's, 3
Mahabhashya Vyakarana, 105
Mahamaya, 35
Maharlokah, 89, 90, 91, 92, 94, 96, 100
Maharshis, 52
mahat, 16, 18
Mahat, 32, 44, 46, 47, 50, 91, 189
Mahatalam, 89
Mahat Buddhi, or Pure Reason, 16
Mahat Tattva, 91
Mahavidya, 34
Maitreyi, 168
manas, 16, 21, 35, 47, 54, 61, 62, 63, 67, 71, 84, 88, 94, 96, 132, 145, 190, 203
Mandalâni, 3
Mantra, 134
Manu, 6, 7, 29, 44, 46, 47, 48, 52, 79, 97, 100, 109, 112, 117, 124, 125, 127, 136, 138,

INDEX • 251

140, 141, 142, 146, 151, 152, 153, 154, 158, 196, 197, 198, 200, 201, 202, 204, 206, 212, 217, 222, 224, 230, 236, 239, 244
Manusmriti, 29, 31, 40, 44, 52, 106, 107, 109, 110, 112, 116, 117, 120, 121, 122, 124, 126, 127, 137, 139, 140, 141, 142, 144, 151, 154, 183, 196, 198, 200, 201, 202, 204, 205, 212, 215, 216, 218, 219, 223, 224, 225, 226, 230, 236, 237, 239, 244
margas, 65
Markandeya, 7
marriage, 106, 111, 112, 113, 116, 141, 145, 157, 223, 225
Maruts, 50
Matarishva, 48
Maya, 34, 35, 37, 38, 39, 46
meditation, 6, 18, 52, 71, 133, 134, 135, 136, 144, 145, 146
mimansa, 17
modesty, 180, 185, 197, 219
Moksha or Mukti (and see Liberation), 16, 18, 65, 66, 73, 91, 132, 172, 183
Morality, 161, 162, 163, 169
Moroseness, 230
Mudgala, 156
mukta, 66
Mulaprakriti, 31, 33, 35, 36, 39, 40, 43, 44, 55
munis, 13
Munja grass, 109
music, 4

Nachiketa, 50
Nagas, 50
Namakarana, 116
Narada, 7, 54, 90, 100, 175
Narada Smriti, 7
Naraka, 61
Narayana, 42, 43, 131
New moon Day, 116
Nilakantha, 34, 37
Nilalohita, 54
Niruktam, 13
nirvana, 28
Niyama, 135, 136
nyaya, 14, 20
Nyaya Sutras, Gautama, 58

obedience, 105, 122, 149, 163, 184, 216, 220, 221, 245

Pakayajnah, 116, 123
Panchajanas, 158
Panchikarana, 46
Pandavas, 225, 243
Panini, 13
Paramatma, 18, 19, 26, 39
Parashara, 6, 9, 108
Parashara Smriti, 108
Parjanya, 98
Parvana-shraddham, 127
Patala, 53, 90
Patanjali, 17, 135
patience, 150, 196, 197, 238, 241, 242, 246
Peevishness, 230
penances, 8, 86
Philology, 12
philosophy, 1, 3, 11, 14, 16, 18, 26
pilgrimages, 227
Pindanvaharyakam, 116
Pingala, 13, 104
Pitri-kriya, 114
Pitriloka, 98, 100, 116, 118
pitris, 91, 115, 116, 117, 125, 127, 128, 193
Pitri-yajna, 116
Pitriyana, 98
Prachetas, 54
Pradhana, 46
Pragna, 92
Prahlada, 209
Prajapati, 48, 80, 175
prajna, 93, 97
prakriti, 16, 18, 30, 32, 35, 36, 37, 47, 58, 88, 89, 91, 103, 164, 176, 209
Pralaya, 32, 36, 40, 170, 171, 176
prana, 51, 52, 53, 55, 92, 95, 97
Prana Flames, 92
Praṇava, 6
Prarabdham, Karma, 74
Prasthana Bheda, 13
Prathama Parardha, 172
Pratyahara, 135
Prayashchitta, 8
pretah, 114
Pretah Kriya, 114
pride, 151, 157, 158, 180, 181, 197, 229, 230, 238, 240, 242, 245, 246
Prithvi, 91, 94
Profanity, 212
Prosody, 12

Public Spirit, 213
puja, 134
Pulaha, 54
Pulastya, 54
Puranas, 9, 10, 45, 78, 128, 146, 170, 175, 176, 203, 243
Purohita, 223
Purusha, 16, 51
Purushottama, 179
Purvardha, 172
Pushkararuni, 156

Qualifications, the four, 18

Race, Lunar, 11
Races of Men, 179
Race, Solar, 10
Raga, 177, 195
Rajasûya, 4
Rajo-guna, 47
Rakshasa, 55, 125
Ramanuja, 17
Rama, Shri, 131, 186, 224
Ramayana, 10, 35, 37, 89, 141, 156, 214, 224
Rasa, 51
Rasatalam, 89
Ravana, 10
Real and Unreal, 14
Reason, Pure, 16, 21, 47, 63
rebirth, 5, 56, 61, 66, 85, 98, 132, 156, 157
Reserve, 239
Reverence, 208, 209, 211, 212
Ribhu, 54
Richas, 4
right and wrong, 170, 173, 174, 175, 176, 184, 188
Rigveda, 3, 4, 5, 12, 25, 29, 38, 47, 78, 82, 107, 108, 111, 112, 115, 152
Rishis, 28, 125, 138, 165, 166, 183, 193, 206
rites, 1, 8, 80, 105, 106, 121, 124, 136, 142, 146, 215
Rudeness, 231
Rudra, 52, 53, 54

sacrifice, 3, 4, 27, 49, 62, 63, 77, 78, 79, 80, 81, 82, 83, 84, 85, 86, 105, 111, 116, 117, 123, 124, 125, 126, 128, 129, 143, 144, 149, 150, 180, 182, 183, 197, 207, 208, 210, 211, 236, 239

Sadhyas, 50, 125
Samadhi, 135, 136
Samana, 92
Samavartanam, 106, 110, 111
Samavritta, 111
Samhitas, 82, 110
Samsara, 37, 38, 50, 55, 57, 60, 65, 66, 68, 153
Samskara, 46, 107, 156
Sanatkumara and others, 8, 9, 54
Sanchita Karmas, 61
Sandhya, 128
Sankhya, 14, 15, 16
Sankhya-karika, 15
Sannyasi, 110, 123, 136, 137, 138, 144, 146, 174, 184
sapindas, 122
Sapindikarana, 114, 115
Sarasvati, 13, 43, 55
Sarpas, 50
Satyakama, 28, 156
Satyaloka, 89, 90, 91, 92, 94
Savitri, 109
science, 9, 11, 26, 32, 48, 59, 96, 122, 125
Science of conduct, or Ethics, 161, 162
Seers, 173
self-Sacrifice, 176
senses, 16, 21, 30, 41, 47, 60, 62, 65, 83, 88, 132, 135, 141, 145, 154, 162, 180, 189, 190, 193, 194, 195, 196, 197, 200, 201
shadangas, 78
Shaivagana, 37
shâkhâs, 3
Shakti, 37
Shalagrama, 133
Shankara, 8, 17, 20, 29, 32, 70, 99
Shankhayana, 5, 107, 109, 112, 115
Sharira, 96, 97, 193, 194, 195
Shastras, 46, 163, 197, 208
Shatapatha Brahmana, 3, 5
Shatrughna, 224
Shaucham, 119
Sheaths, 100
Shiksha (method of study), 12
Shiriraka Bhashya, 2
Shiva Purana, 52, 53, 54
Shiva Sutras, 34
Shraddhas, 118
Shrauta, 12, 123, 127, 128

Shuka, 138
siddhis, 8, 10
Sita, 224
Six Systems, Max Muller, 13
Slander, 230
Snataka, 7, 111, 237
Soma, 4, 5, 98, 123, 212
Straightforwardness, 227
Submission, 209, 210
Suktas, 3
Sullenness, 230
Superiors, Conduct to, 208
Suryaloka, 89
Sushupti, 100
Sutalam, 89
Sutrani, Patanjali, 16, 135
Sutra (the Lord), 93
Svara, 105
Svargaloka, 100
Svayambhu, Brahma, 2
Svayambhuva Manu, 52
symbolising, 31

Taijasa, 47, 93, 96, 100
Talas, 89, 90, 100
Talatalam, 89
Tandya Mahabrahmana, 3
Tanmatra, 18, 46, 47
Tapas, 2, 29, 52, 53, 79
Tarpana, 124
tattvas, 46, 53, 91
Tattva-Samasa-Sutras, 15
the sacred thread, 109
Tika on Vishnu Bhagavata Shridhara Svami, 155
Tiryaksrotas, 50, 172
Toleration, 190, 227
transmigration, 8, 58, 59, 61, 99, 114, 145
travel, 18, 227
Trayyaruni, 156
triangle, 31, 33
Tridandi, 110
Triloki, 91, 170
Trimurti, 43, 49, 110
Triple, 110, 181
trust, 178, 217, 218, 227, 241, 243, 246
Tuladhara, 66

Udana, 92

udbhijjah, 58
Udgata, 4
Udgâtri, 5
Uma, 34, 43, 55
Upadhis, 20, 52, 93
Upanayana, 109, 138
Upanishat, 5, 25, 61, 78, 97
Upanishat, Amritabindu, 21
Upanishat, Brahmabindu, 6
Upanishat, Chhandogya, 6
Upanishat, Katha, 5
Upanishat, Kaushitaki Br, 97
Upanishat, Kena, 6
Upanishat, Mandukya, 26
Upanishat, Muktika, 5
Upanishat, Mundaka, 5, 6
Upanishat, Prashna, 5, 6
Upanishats, 3, 5, 18, 110
Upanishat, Shvetåskvatara, 5
Upanishat, Taittiriya, 134
Upasana, 135
Upasthâna, 134
uprightness, 153, 180, 246
Urbanity, 227

Vaikarika, 47
Vaikuntha, 89, 90, 91
Vairagya, 176, 202, 203
Vaisheshika, 15
Vaishvanara, 92, 93, 94, 100
Valmiki, 10
Valour, 235
Vartamana Karma, 74, 75
Varuna, 48, 50, 82, 212
Vasishtha, 54, 156
Vasishtha-Smriti, 156
Vasus, 50
Vatsyayana, 14, 58
Vayu, 50, 91, 92, 212
Vedangas, 128
Vedanta, 3, 11, 14, 17, 18, 19, 21, 37, 38, 223
Vedas, 1, 2, 3, 6, 7, 8, 9, 11, 12, 13, 17, 26, 49, 52, 85, 109, 111, 123, 125, 128, 137, 138, 154, 156, 157, 183, 202, 215, 230
Vedavit, 6
Vice, 184
Vidura, 231
Vidya, 35, 37
Vidyadharas, 50

vijnana, 15, 94
Vijnana, 15
Virat, 46, 52, 53, 93, 243
virtue, 11, 84, 86, 140, 169, 174, 178, 186, 187, 196, 197, 205, 206, 208, 209, 213, 218, 219, 226, 227, 236, 238, 241, 242, 243, 246
virtues and vices, 178, 184, 188, 208, 214, 222, 234, 241, 242, 243, 245
vishishtadvaitam, 17
Vishnu, 2, 9, 10, 18, 38, 39, 42, 43, 44, 45, 47, 50, 52, 53, 54, 55, 63, 73, 89, 90, 99, 133, 155, 156, 176, 185, 201, 209
Vishnu Bhagavata, 9, 52, 54, 90, 156
Vishnu Purana, 38, 43, 44, 47, 50, 89, 99, 209
Vishvamitra, 156
Vishvedevas, 115
Vitahavya, 156
Vitalam, 89
Vivaha, 111
Vratas, 111
Vyakaranam, 13
Vyanah, 95
Vyasa, 2, 8, 16, 17, 176
Vyavahara (Civil Law), 8
Vyavahara Mayukha, 6

wheel of life, 83, 126
wife, 8, 10, 107, 111, 113, 128, 141, 142, 143, 168, 169, 174, 205, 222, 223, 224, 225, 246
women, 5, 7, 108, 113, 140, 141, 142, 143, 221, 238
world-process, 53, 54, 55, 224
worlds visible and invisible, 50
world-systems, 36, 42, 44
Worship, 130, 134, 202

Yajna, 116, 141, 182
Yajna Paribhasha, Apastambas, 116
Yajnavalkya, 104, 106, 108, 109, 168
Yajnavalkya Smriti, 106
Yajnopavitam, 109
Yajurveda, 3, 4, 5, 12
Yakshas, 50, 125
Yama, 26, 48, 50, 135, 136, 212
Yaska, 13
Yoga, 6, 10, 16, 17, 21, 35, 58, 65, 83, 96, 99, 100, 132, 141, 162, 197, 210
Yoga-maya, 35
Yoga-siddhis, 10
Yogis, 43
Yojanas, 90
Yudhishthira, 155, 187
Yuga, 6, 7, 10, 11, 150